Marcelo Rios
The Man We Barely Knew
Scoop Malinowski

ISBN: 1461162416
ISBN-13: 9781461162414

Introduction

I wrote this book because Marcelo Rios is the most entertaining and talented tennis champion I ever saw. No disrespect to John McEnroe, Roger Federer, Jimmy Connors, Bjorn Borg, Rafael Nadal, Rod Laver, Steffi Graf, Andre Agassi, Pete Sampras, Serena Williams, Don Budge, but Rios had something they didn't.

It's hard to describe what that elusive, mysterious quality was. This book will try to solve the puzzle of the man we barely knew, Marcelo Rios...

TABLE OF CONTENTS

Chapter 1
"I'm going to kick your ass!"

No tennis player ever awed us with his beautiful talents quite like Marcelo Rios. Even his name flowed smoothly, like that of some legendary artist from centuries ago.

The great Rios started to play tennis at age 11 and turned pro in 1994 and went on to win 18 career singles titles, including five Masters Series. He produced his finest season in 1998, capturing three consecutive Masters Series titles (Rome, Indian Wells, Key Biscayne) along with four other titles. Rios even became #1 — at the age of 22 — for six weeks after conquering Andre Agassi 7-5 6-3 6-4 in a captivating performance on Key Biscayne to become the first South American to rise to the top of the ATP rankings.

But for how familiar we were with the Rios style on the court — that leaping two-handed backhand, the graceful and artful movements, those uncanny angles, the Chilean chanting from his flag-waving supporters — there was always an aura of mystery about Rios. Why did he seem so often to be joyless on the court? For what reasons was he so reluctant to do media interviews or engage with the fans or even other players? Was his reputation for being unapproachable an act of self-defense because he was actually very shy?

The enigma of Rios will continue to confound us since he retired (due to repeated leg and back injuries) in the summer of 2004 at the age of 28. His last ATP matches were in April of 2004, losses in Satellite events in Ecuador and Mexico City to Mariano Delfino and Juan Pablo Guzman. Suddenly the career of Rios was over, without any final applause or a befitting tribute.

Even the idea for this story only came by a chance comment during an unrelated interview with former Australian Open winner Thomas Johansson. The Swede just so happened to share this anecdote of Rios when I asked him for a funny tennis memory, something from tennis that made him laugh:

"All the guys have different humors, outside of the court," Johansson said. "A player that I really liked to watch was Rios. I think he was one of the best players, ever. Because I remember one year when he was gonna play Thomas Muster in Rome (in 1998). And I saw the press conference before the match. And they asked him, so how are you gonna be able to beat Muster, because he only had lost one or two matches on clay so far. And Rios said, 'The guy should be happy if he gets like a couple of games.' And Rios went out there the next day and killed him, 1 and 2. And that's for me unbelievable. I really liked to watch him. I didn't like to play him though. But I really liked to watch him."

Asked why he didn't enjoy the experience of playing Rios, Johansson replied: "He could make you feel like it was the first time you were standing on a tennis court, you know [smiling]? So I hated to play him. You could get killed by him easily, 1 and 1 or something like that, and you could have played a good match."

Johansson's high regard for Rios sparked a curiosity to investigate further insights about Rios from others in the tennis community. If a Grand Slam champion like Thomas Johansson had such respect for Rios, just what else would some of the other ATP insiders have to say?

This book required five years of research and investigation and collecting as many pieces of the puzzle as possible - and then assembling it all together. The final result is a unique, abstract chronicle portrait of one of the greatest, most aesthetic tennis players to ever grace a tennis court, Marcelo Rios...

• • •

"Be not afraid of greatness: some are born great, some achieve greatness and some have greatness thrust upon them." — Shakespeare

"There is no great genius without some touch of madness." — Seneca

• • •

I'm running down the corridor inside Arthur Ashe Stadium and heading towards me is the former top 10 player Jimmy Arias. It's early evening during the first week of the U.S. Open. He's in a hurry for international TV commentating duties, so am I to the interview room for a quick Biofile with Igor Andreev. But what the heck, I feel inspired by that anecdote from Thomas Johansson. Let me just ask Jimmy if has any kind of memory of Rios...

Jimmy Arias (ATP Player): "My one memory of Marcelo Rios is — I was retired for a number of years already — and he was ranked #2 in the world in 1998. And he lost first round of Wimbledon. And made some disparaging remarks about Wimbledon. He came to Bollettieri's because he had to practice for the rest of the summer. And I was the only one there. Everyone else that played was still at Wimbledon. So I was a decent enough player for him to practice with. So Nick called, 'Can you come? Marcelo Rios is here for a couple of weeks?' So we play the first day, the first set — and he's not trying at all [smiles]. He's just sort of lounging around. And I win the set 6-4. And, as is my way, when I play a top guy of today, I find a way to give them a little jab, just to see how they react. So we finish the set and as we're shaking hands after, I said, 'Marcelo, what would you rank me if I were playing today? Two or three in the world?' And he said, 'Man, tomorrow, I'm going to kick your ass!' And I liked his attitude. And actually, some of the top players, when I give them a hard time, they actually didn't want to play with me anymore. When I would say something like that, they would get insulted. They didn't want to play with me. Rios came at me. He said, 'No, I'm gonna kick your ass tomorrow.' And sure enough, we came back the next day, and for about three games, he was fired up. And I was playing well and was down 3-love. And he couldn't keep that intensity, because it's practice. He's just so relaxed. Eventually the set was close. But I did see for those three games what talent he had. He would hit a couple of forehands in a rally, and with that same swing — not a bigger backswing, nothing — he'd suddenly hit it 20 miles-per-hour harder. Down the line for a winner. You didn't know how that happened. You couldn't understand how the same swing produced such a different pace on the ball. So that's part of what he had that the other players couldn't figure out."

Hernan Gumy (Coach and ATP Player): "I have a personal memory about him because we were kind of close. He didn't get along with many players. But we were kind of friends in a way. And we play against each other many times. The greatness of his game — I didn't see anybody who play like him in the past 10 years. All the most difficult things he made it easy. I mean, it was so nice to watch him play. It would have been great to have him for a couple of more years. He's still young but, every time I spoke with him, he said that he was not made to travel 25 weeks a year. Or play 20 tournaments. He loved to play the big tournaments but he didn't like the whole life of a tennis player. So you have to understand that also. But I think he was a great. He was a nice guy from, I repeat, my side. And he was a helluva tennis player...The fans and the media never got to him — really close. I think you have to check the background. In Chile, when he was a kid, he had some problems with the media when he was 16. When he stepped up to complain about something about the Federation. So maybe after that he took some distance from the media around the world. With the fans also. Like I said, he was gifted to play tennis. But he was maybe not gifted to do whatever is outside to the inside of the tennis court. Because he loved to practice, sacrifice. He loved to compete. But everything else outside of the tennis — you name it, the fans, the kids — he wasn't able to do it. Because of his character, he didn't enjoy to do that. He's a guy who, I believe, he do things that he enjoy...We were close. I mean, he was a sensitive guy. Personally, he was a guy that I really liked. I know that not many players like him, but I like him."

Luis Lobo (Former Rios Coach and ATP Player): "I just have good things to talk about Marcelo. I think he was the most professional player that I've ever seen. I know the people think of him another way, but for me he was a very good professional. He was one of the best players in the world, for sure. For sure he's one of the best players in history. For me, yes. Because, about tennis, if he made a Grand Slam or #1 for more time, for sure he's one of the best guys I ever see. Very talented. If you play against him on a day when he's focused, very tough to beat him, very tough. He had so many great matches — Monte Carlo against Kuerten, Paris against Albert Costa, indoors when he make Singapore — so many good matches. (What held him back from winning a Slam?) It's a good question, I don't know. I'm not a psychologist [laughs]. He was very close to winning a Grand Slam. He lost the final (in Australian Open to Korda in '98), and then personal problems. I don't know. One part of each player — some players when they're this close to the final, they make it. And others, no, they can't do it. But I think he was injured a long time too. And the moment for him was a stress fracture in the lower back, and problems with legs... He was very nice person. Very nice. When he was in a tournament, he would be alone and no say hello to anybody. Just a few guys. He didn't believe too much in the people. And I think he was right. Because in tennis, the world is very tough to be friends."

Marat Safin (ATP Player): "He had the talent to win ten Grand Slams."

Fabrice Santoro (ATP Player): "I played Marcelo three times. You could say, on the court, he was a great, great player. And one of the greats of the game. He was to serve well and he hit the ball really, really well on both sides. He hit the backhand moving well too. I remember when he won Indian Wells and Key Biscayne in a row, he was playing one of the best tennis I've ever seen... We played three times, he beat me twice. It was always a good match. Because I like to use the spins and slice on the court and when I was playing against him, it was a very fun match, but it was a very good competition. His talents — one of the best. A lefty Agassi. (What was he missing?) Sometimes a little bit short physically. Because other guys can serve really well. He can play well forehands, backhands, moves pretty well. But five sets for two weeks — too tough for him."

Thomas Johansson (ATP Player): "Sometimes he looked like he didn't want to play. Sometimes he REALLY didn't want to play. But when he REALLY wanted to play, you didn't want to be on the other side of the net."

Wayne Ferreira (ATP Player): "He was really good because he took the ball early and he had a lot of feel on the ball. He moved pretty well and he was a good competitor. But he was so good at finding where the ball was going and taking it so early...I didn't really have a problem with him. I actually did pretty well against him. I beat him most of the times that I played against him (actually Rios won the ATP head to head series, 5-3, including the final three consecutive meetings). I just felt like I could overpower him a lot. He got a lot of balls back and he took it early but, to me, he was a little bit soft at times. He didn't hit the ball that hard. I felt like he hit the ball, I could still run down everything. I could overpower him. But he was difficult. He could get a lot of balls back, make you play a lot of balls. I had to be in great shape and I had to be really competitive and concentrate a lot to beat him. (Why did he not win a Slam?) Maybe for that reason. I think he was just a little bit soft. Guys like Pete and Andre — on a regular basis — when it got tight, tough like this, they used to overpower him."

Dave Butterfield (Teaching Pro): "I saw Rios play here at the Nasdaq one year in Miami. I saw Rios play Guga Kuerten in a practice set. It was late in the afternoon and I was the only one in the stands. And it was mesmerizing. Rios ended up winning the match. I didn't say one word the whole match. I just sat there, dazzled the whole time. He reminded me of Fred Astaire, incredible coordination. I really appreciated him. I also saw Rios play at the French Open, five-setter, against Wayne Ferreira, in 2001. I was in Paris at the French Open. Ferreira was up two sets to one. Rios came back and beat him in five. And after Ferreira lost the match, he took every racquet in his bag and smashed it against the umpire's chair. True story. My girlfriend can verify it for you. She saw it too. It was out on court 11."

Roger Federer (ATP Player): "I was a big admirer of Marcelo. I thought he was one of the best players with the best talent around. He was one of my favorite players at the time, being around 1998. Him and Pete Sampras back then were my favorite players. Happy for him that he got to be #1 in the world. Not happy that he never won a Grand Slam. But I was fortunate enough to play him a few times and practice with him a few times. I have good memories of Marcelo."

Vera Zvonareva (WTA Player): "I think Rios was a great tennis player. I watched him play in Washington. And I think he was a great player to watch for me. I think he was like an actor on the court. And I love it because he was doing his show. Everybody knows it's tough to play tennis, especially when it's 100 degrees. And he was like performing like an actor. You can always see his emotions. He wasn't just like standing there, doing his job, you could see how he feels."

Patrick McEnroe (his ESPN commentary during the first set of the 2002 NASDAQ semifinal vs. Agassi): "...I'm not even sure if he goes out there with a strategy, Cliff. He just goes out there and just swings away, angles the ball, it looks like he just sort of free-wheels it out there and relies on his talent. Agassi used to do that. Agassi would just bomb the ball and just say, I'm just gonna be a shotmaker and I'm gonna rely on that. But why Agassi has won seven Slams now and Rios has won zero is because Agassi has learned to play his opponents, to play within himself, to come out there focused, to be physically fit, to have a strategy, have a gameplan... The players are just too good these days, to think you can go out there and just free-wheel it...THAT IS SCARY RIGHT THERE! That is pure genius right there. What a one-two from Rios. Just launching himself into that backhand, taking it in mid-flight for the clean winner cross court (at 7-7 in the first-set tiebreak - which Rios won 9-7, but he retired after losing the second set 6-4.)."

"That was one of the most enjoyable sets of tennis I've seen. Rios hit some of the most amazing shots I've seen - and some of the worst shots."

Nick Bollettieri (Former Rios Coach): "I believe the player who has probably disappointed me the most was Marcelo Rios. He disappointed me because God really awarded him hands and eyes and feet that were just beyond description. He never lived up to his expectations both as a role model for the game and to really fulfill the talent that he had as a player. I believe that he was probably the person. Remember Larry Stefanki did a great job with him as well. I believe that Marcelo Rios could have been a far better player then what he is."

Fred Stolle (Hall of Famer and former ESPN Commentator): "Yes, I got to know Marcelo reasonably well. He's a nice kid but was - I don't know if you want to say had a bit of a chip on his shoulder. But tough fellow to get to know. A lot of the players will probably tell you that. Just through the television (ESPN) I was able to meet him and thought he was a great talent. And it's tough to see talent like that, through injury, get out of it. And he was a natural stroke maker, along the lines of McEnroe, one of the greatest. But again, when he reached #1 he couldn't handle it, and by his own admission, he said, I don't want to be #1, I want to be a spoiler. I want to be someone out there who's knockin' off the #1 or #2 player in the world. I don't think he really had the fire in his belly that is needed to remain at the top and be a champion...We used to run into each other at the tournaments and say hello. I was one of the people he said hello to. There was a lot of people that he didn't say hello to."

Guillermo Vilas (Hall of Famer): "I talked to him a couple of times. He didn't talk too much. He had a strong character. It's like when you are in front of a lion — you are not going give some candy to a lion, right? Everybody knew he was like that. Some people are like that. If you give him enough space, he's okay...He play well, but he could never win something very big. He had the qualities to do that, then his body gave out. But he left his image to the players — a very good way of playing and the attitude was like a rebel. He was very interesting, to add color to the game. If he wouldn't have had all those injuries, he would have been better, much better. The time he was there, he was exciting. But it's sad, because the body gave out. He was a great player, but you have to be champion of the world. He was geared to do that, but the body didn't allow him to do that. Like it happened to Muster. Muster was gearing to be #1. Suddenly he had the accident (hit by car in Miami) and three years after, he did it. Rios didn't have that second chance. You can say Rios was one of the most gifted ever. But not one of the best ever. Because you have to win something, you have to do a little bit more. He looked very nice, everything he did. But the body did not allow him to do it."

Ilie Nastase (Hall of Famer): "He's the worst prick I ever met. The players of today probably have the same opinion of him. Ask all the players what they think of him, you'll get the same thing. When somebody doesn't sign autographs for the kids, that is a prick for me. (What about his game?) I don't give a shit. I don't look at him. For me, he's an idiot. I don't know what else to tell about him. And that's the first time I say something about somebody like that. I think he was the worst thing for tennis. He did not deserve to be #1 — one or two days. To live with the other players like he did — terrible. He really was the worst. I never say anything about anybody else like this but about him I have to say this. Sorry."

Pat Cash (Wimbledon champion): "Rios is one of the most talented players I've ever seen. I thought he had a control like a McEnroe. He was definitely a wasted talent but he still got to #1 in the world. I loved watching him. He was brilliant. He hit the ball anywhere. Anywhere...I played doubles with him one week, in Scottsdale in '95 or '96. When I was making a comeback. We practiced quite a bit. And when I practiced with him, I never ran so much in my life. I played with a lot of the top guys in practice and he was just able to hit the ball anywhere. He used to run me everywhere. (How did you do in doubles with Rios?) Not very good. It wasn't his fault though [smiles]. I was making a bit of a comeback and I was pretty terrible. But he was a brilliant player and I was disappointed that he never actually fulfilled his potential. (Get along well with him?) I got on all right with him. A lot of other guys didn't like him, that's for sure. Not many guys, I think, got along with him. And he was fine to me. We always had a good time, we practiced hard and I liked his game. And I think he appreciated somebody that was nice to him, I think."

Melchior DiGiacomo (Photographer): "I think he's one of the best players I've ever seen play the game. I've been following tennis since 1971. And I thought Rios was a bit of a throwback in many ways. He reminded me of guys like Ken Rosewall — who had so many great shots. Guys like Tom Okker who was a brilliant player. Rios was that way. But I couldn't figure Rios' head. Because I never knew where he was on the court. Whereas the older players, you always knew where their head was at, their head was: To win. At all costs. But Rios, I don't know. There's a wonderful line written by Norman Mailer in a book called 'The Bullfighter.' He's talking about how a man cannot be judged by what he is, the man is best judged at his greatest moment. (Melchior actually brings the exact quote to me the next day: "The one thing that can keep the sweet nerve of life alive is the knowledge that a man cannot be judged by what he is every day, but only at his greatest moment, for that is when he shows what he was intended to be..It is a Latin approach, their allegiance is to the genius of blood. So they judge a man by what he is at his best.") And that's what Rios was to me. There are times when you look at him and you say, Nobody in the world has ever done what he has just done, in terms of the match. And then you may see him the next day or two days later and you go, What happened to that guy that was out here a couple of days ago? Is it the same guy? I don't know how you get to a kid like that. Again, he was brilliant. There were other players who were like that — Mel Purcell never had a killer shot. But you had to hit him over the head with a shovel if you wanted to beat him. But Rios' head was the thing. He had every shot in the game. There was nothing he couldn't do. (How was Rios as a photography subject to shoot?) Brilliant. Because of his athleticism. He wasn't like Adriano Panatta, who was like this stand-up, at-attention Italian. He had a beautiful game but there really wasn't anything to shoot, in terms of physical action. Rios is the kind of guy that could stop on a dime and give you five cents change. He was very exciting to shoot. Connors was not very exciting to shoot, in the sense that he played basically a baseline game, rarely came to the net. And the only time Jimmy was exciting was when he pumped up the crowd. Then he was exciting. But photographing Rios during a match was always exciting. And you had to be quick, because he was quick. When guys are running as fast as he is and lunging out making shots, that's exciting for me, because he fills the frame. He's not standing up straight. But Rios was exciting. And he'll be missed. By me. I don't know about everybody else."

Carl Munnerlyn (U.S. Open locker room manager): "Rios was very giving. When I knew him, when he was a player, he always, after each practice, he would come in and go up to one of the (U.S. Open locker room) attendants and always offer a pair of his shoes that he just practiced in. And even after the match. His match shoe, that he wore in the match. He'd always come up to us and give us his shoes. Every time, every day he was here. It was unbelievable how such a giving person he was. Not too many people knew him that way, but we, as locker room attendants, knew him that way — as a very giving, courteous person. And he always joked with us, he liked to joke with us. Because he saw us as people he could relate to. He was relaxed with us. And we brought out his lighter side, his personality, instead of serious all the time, like always getting ready for a match. One time I was standing next to the soda refrigerator and he walked by and gave my head a push. I turned around and Marcelo's walking out the door, smiling. So that's how I know him. He was friendly to me. In that sense, I know him that way. He was never not the slightest bit sarcastic to me. That's what I know of Marcelo Rios. Nice guy."

Petr Korda (ATP Player): "I beat him badly (in 1998 Australian Open final 6-2, 6-2, 6-2). It was very — actually I had the chance to see the match on video for the first time a month and a half ago. And in TV it looked completely different than it did on the court. But I remember I was really dominating and I was ready for that. I knew this was probably my last chance to win a Slam — and if I played the right game, then I could beat him. I think I really shot him down that day. I know we were hitting the balls very hard. On the TV it doesn't look like it. I was hitting balls very hard. (What kind of person was Rios?) I think that not many people knew him. Some people had problems with him, he was like a controversial, not many people did like him. But I know him, we play doubles. I don't know if it was before or after we played in Australian Open. He was a nice guy. Gifted player. And I said in Australia, he can be maybe #1. But it's most important to win the Slam. Unfortunately for him, he never achieved it. Maybe I was that reason, probably."

Andre Agassi (before the 1998 Lipton final in Miami): "If he (Rios) can Dr. Feelgood my power then he's just too good. But we'll see."

Gabriel Silberstein (ATP Player): "I don't have many interesting memories of Marcelo from childhood.

I am trying to think of something but nothing really interesting comes to mind. He was just a normal kid playing lots of hours of tennis. Nothing more and nothing less than that."

Anonymous: "I worked at transportation for the Key Biscayne tournament for many years. One year Rios had a tournament car and he didn't return it after he lost his match. We almost had to call the police and have him held at the airport to get the car back."

Bud Collins (Hall of Fame Journalist): "Very disagreeable player. Very negative memories. He was rude, impolite. He would tank matches - he did that at the U.S. Pro in Boston one year. It was so obvious I said they should have played the match in a swimming pool. One time in Longwood Cricket Club in Boston again, the kid came up with a pencil or pen with something to autograph. And Rios just took it and broke it in half. He was just a bad guy. When he became #1 he was on the balcony with the President of the country. I said maybe this will make him a better behaved guy. His attitude was Fuck you, Fuck everybody, but me."

Taylor Dent (ATP Player): "He was a little bit older than me. He was actually nice to me. I know his reputation wasn't stellar when he was on the Tour but he was always nice to me. In the locker room he would say, Hey, Taylor, how did you do? And we would try and talk, I would try and speak Spanish. He'd laugh at me and we'd have a chuckle. And I see him every so often still down at Bollettieri. And, to me, he was always just a quiet guy. But I know his reputation was somewhat different. But I never had any problems with him. I'm nice to everybody - unless I get rubbed the wrong way. I played an exhibition with him one time. I may have played him in a tournament, I don't remember. But the exhibition, we played in Thailand, we played on these synthetic courts that were so hard to play on. I ended up beating him and he was just laughing and dicking around the whole time."

Xavier Malisse (ATP Player): "I saw him a lot but I never really talked with him much. He did his thing and obviously it was working. We were at the same Academy (Bollettieri) but that was it. We practiced once or twice. All I know is he was doing a lot of drop shots [smiles]. That's all I know. And I was doing a lot of running."

Angelica Gavaldon (WTA Player): "My mom remembers him carrying my laundry bag in Sydney. I think he is a really sweet person. I really like Marcelo Rios. I know a lot of people had mixed feelings about him but I personally thought he was very shy, very honest and very misunderstood. The first time I met him was at the U.S. Open and my coach at the time, Pato Rodriguez, scheduled a practice session with him, we played baseline games and after he went up to Pato and said, 'Wow, I did not know girls could actually play tennis.' I thought it was funny. Later on in Australia we were at the same tournaments and I remember him waking up super early almost every day to practice with me at 6:30 am. I played okay that year and I think he didn't win a match, so I felt guilty that it was probably because I don't hit the ball like a guy. I remember a conversation we had. I remember he told me after he lost in Australia, 'In three months I will be top 30, then 20 and then 10.' He said it with amazing confidence. And that's how it happened."

Mike Agassi (Coach and Father of Andre Agassi): "Marcelo Rios was like Andre in that he could take the ball early and had very good timing so he could hit it up the line or play angles. In a way, he was better than Andre because you could not read Rios' shot. You could not tell where he was hitting the ball from the angle of his racquet face - for that reason it was difficult to read his shot. Because he had great timing he could hit the ball harder off the same swing. It's hard to hit hard. You have 200 fighters, for example, and you have maybe six who have a knockout punch. Why can't the other 194 do it? It's hard, that's why. Hitting hard, that is an art. It is a talent."

Manuela Davies (Photographer): "It was my first year as a professional tennis photographer. I didn't know what I was doing yet. It was in Delray Beach in 2002. Rios was in the interview room. I think I waited until after the interview. I walked up to him and asked, Can I take a picture of you? And he said, 'No.' Stone-cold looking at me. No. Then I was stumped. He left the interview room. I didn't know whether to laugh or cry."

Jaime Fillol (ATP Player): "I first met him in New York when he was a junior. And he was already playing well in Futures. We became very close. We run an ATP event in Chile. We would have to many times negotiate with him, his participation, especially when he was top 10. I think he was a very good player, he had a lot of talent. Not just with his hands, but with his mind. Very good at feeling no pressure and I think that's what made him so good. There's a lot of people that have talent but when it comes to winning, they have a hard time winning. And he was winning a lot of matches at a young age. Then I think he got hurt too much, too often, he couldn't keep it up. There was criticism over his attitude — that he wouldn't fight hard enough. But I would say that his personality was not a disciplined mentality. He was very erratic in that respect. He was not a Saxon or a Slavic, he's Chilean, he's kind of moody. And if he doesn't feel good, he just doesn't try. Not because he's lazy, because he doesn't feel good. So I think that was the criticism — which was fair — in order to be a champion and stay there as champion — you have to have the discipline too. Have the discipline, as far as to be a champion."

(I ask Fillol for his lasting image of Rios?) "Playing so well that it was so much fun to watch him play. In fact, he really could make almost anyone look like a beginner. If things were right, he would guess exactly where the ball was coming. He would anticipate. He didn't have to be strong physically to make the ball go and to have the guy run from one side to the other. I think his body didn't hold the pressure of the circuit. He was weak in his preparation, probably coming from Chile, not knowing exactly what was gonna happen if he was that good. I don't think he was prepared physically for the

Tour. (Did he ever win the Chile event?) He never won the tournament, that's why I didn't mention it [smiles]. He got to the finals four times. He would make the crowd very upset because everybody was waiting for him to win the first time. He made the finals four times and lost to guys he should have beat — Slava Dosedel, Hernan Gumy and most recently he lost in 2002 to David Sanchez (also lost to Julian Alonso of Spain). He was winning 6-1 and 40-love to go up 4-1 and lost the game. And then he couldn't play. He became nervous."

"He was very — the word is in Spanish, 'contradictorio' — he would do the unexpected. If you were waiting for him to say hello to you, he's not gonna say hello to you. If you didn't think he'd say hello to you, he'd come up and say hello to you. He treated people like that. Not that he didn't care for people, it was just like a game. He made a lot of enemies because of that, but I don't think he's a bad person. I would say he didn't have the same discipline you need to have off the court. Many times he would do things — I mean the President of Chile was practically disgraced by him. When he became #1 and the President invited him to the Palace and he came in a shirt, looking like he was going to the beach. And the President said, 'Marcelo would you like to say something to the people?' 'No, I don't want to say anything.' So he turned the President of the country off just by being different. He didn't think it was a big occasion, but he's not a bad person."

"I saw him several years ago in Santiago, at the gym where he was training. I was talking to his physical trainer. And Marcelo was there, although he is retired, he still goes to the gym every day and trains, so he's in good shape, other than the pain that he says he feels when he plays tennis."

Diego Malaga (College Player): "I saw Rios play in Peru when he was 16 or 17, I was a little kid, eight or nine. I just remember he was always grumpy. He was always banging his racquet on the ground. I thought, He's crazy. It was the COSAT junior, it's a South American tour, they play in Peru, Ecuador, Colombia. The three best players of the COSAT tour get to go on the European circuit. The match I remember was Rios was playing a guy from Colombia. He was losing so bad. The referee gave him two warnings for cursing and hitting his racquet on the ground. My mom was like, He's never going to be top ten in the world with that attitude. My mom is the kind of person that when I played and hit my racquet on the ground, she would tell me if I kept on behaving like that she would go over to the umpire and tell him to take me out of the tournament. Then later we saw Rios on TV playing against a big player in a big tournament and my mom was like, Oh my God, I can't believe it. I was also at the Los Angeles tournament in VIP seats because my uncle is a doctor in L.A. and he had the seats. Rios was defaulted from the tournament and I was so mad because I really wanted to see him play."

Cliff Drysdale (ESPN commentator and former ATP Player): "There was nobody in all of sports that I met who was more negative. He had the biggest chip on his shoulder. One time I walked up to him, knowing his reputation, he looked at me, looked at my extended hand, and walked away. He walked over to the elevator and went up to his hotel room. It was the damdest thing I ever saw."

Craig Gabriel (Journalist): "Very talented. I never thought much of Marcelo Rios. I thought he was an obnoxious, rude individual. He had a world of talent, he was a glorious tennis player to watch. But I hated to watch him because of his personality. I mean, there was just something about the guy, he rubbed everybody the wrong way. And it was very unfortunate because we get a lot of wonderful players from South America and all the ones I've had any sort of contact with or any association with, have all been fantastic people to deal with. Unfortunately, Rios was the exception. Which, as I say, is a great shame, because his personality, behavior and attitude unfortunately got in the way of his great tennis talent."

Anonymous: "In Singapore Rios was with a girl at the time and I saw him involved in a major makeout session in the elevator. It was really rude, you just don't do that sort of thing in Singapore."

Jim Courier (ATP Player): "I think of his hands most of all. Marcelo had great hands. He took the ball so early. Really, he was kind of a left-handed version of Agassi in many ways, where he saw the ball early, would take time away from an opponent. (Ever talk with Rios?) No. Marcelo didn't really talk with anyone. Because I didn't talk with him and he didn't socialize, I don't have any memories or information other than what I saw on the court."

Tim Curry (USTA Communications): "I first saw Marcelo at the Orange Bowl. The way he behaved started at an early age. Sometimes the way a player handles the juniors translates to exactly how they're going to treat their pro career. Sometimes it's just part of the transition. They reach the pinnacle of the juniors and they know they have to start over again. And Marcelo, at the Orange Bowl, kept that same attitude through his pro career. (Describe his attitude?) Sometimes he came across as bigger than the event. Bigger than where he was playing or what he was doing. Or it wasn't as important to him as the other people competing in the event. Or the people that might have been putting on everything. Or people who had history with the event. None of that seemed important to him."

Petr Pala (ATP Player): "I played him in doubles. And also as a junior, because he was one year younger. I remember he was one of the most talented players who ever played. And when he played well he was always a pleasure to watch. And I think he retired too early because he could have achieved a lot more though he did become #1. But always fun to watch. I played him a couple of times, he played with Mariano Puerta. I remember we won. It's a different game - doubles and singles. But he was a tough opponent. Because he could hit any shot from any place on the court. I played him in juniors before the French Open, there's a big junior tournament in Belgium. And he

beat me. I was surprised the way he played. Bec
thought I was going to win. Because when he walked
on the court and he warmed up [smiles] - I thought I
was going to win. Then he played shots I didn't see up
till then [smiles]."

Arnaud Di Pasquale (ATP Player): "He actually kicked
my butt. He beat me 4 and 0 (in Lyon in 1998). So he
was just amazing. I didn't know what he was doing on
the court. You never knew. Sometimes you expect the
shot, against him, never, especially on the backhand.
His backhand was amazing, so beautiful. So I played
him a second time. That doesn't count in the sense
because that was the second tournament of the
year - in Auckland (2001). He won the week before in
Doha. So he played on Sunday. He flew over, Doha to
Auckland on Monday and we played on Tuesday. So he
was totally dead. And so I think I beat him. I mean, he
saved two match points. Anyway, he was #1. No one
liked him on the Tour and as a player. The image that
he gave was a player that was cocky, arrogant, he didn't
say hello that much. But he was always nice with me. I
don't know why. I played the tournament in Santiago,
his hometown I believe. And we went out together.
We stayed together the whole night, drinks, just like,
talking and talking and talking. So I have a different
image than all the other players. I think maybe he was
shy. Maybe there was a border, something like that, that
he didn't want to pass. There was something blocking
him. He was good for tennis. You need controversial
guys. Like people that you love or you hate. That's very
good. That's what we need. You hate him or you love

him. Now we need guys like him. I think we miss him actually in tennis today."

Question: What do you remember talking with Rios that night?

Arnaud Di Pasquale: "[Laughs] I'm going to keep that a secret [laughs]."

Question: Why do you think he was friendly to you?

Arnaud Di Pasquale: "I have no idea. I don't know. We practiced a few times together. He was comfortable with me. Sometimes you feel comfortable. We practiced, he was always very nice and very friendly. We didn't go to dinner together but I told you, we spent that night. We practiced, his coach came to me many times just asking me if I wanted to hit with him. Okay, of course."

Question: Your first memory or Rios?

Arnaud Di Pasquale: "He was #1 in juniors, right? That was the first time. I think that was his declaration in the press. I think the first time he played the French Open, maybe he lost to the guy (Sampras), he said something like, I'm going to kick his ass soon. It was a provocation. But that was cool. Interesting. He was so confident. But was it really confidence?"

Question: Your lasting memory or images of Rios?

Arnaud Di Pasquale: "That was tough when he decided to retire. Because I don't think he wanted to. Just too many injuries, the back, maybe the knees, I don't remember. Maybe everything at the end. But he wasn't very healthy."

Question: Did you ever see Rios laugh?

Arnaud Di Pasquale: "Laugh? Oh yeah. At that party we had. We had a big, big laugh actually. We had a lot of fun. Lot of fun. I mean, he stumbled down the stairs, you know [smiles]? Because we did not only drink fruit juice, you know [smiles]? That was funny. Real life, you know?"

• • •

"A man of genius makes no mistakes. His errors are volitional and are the portals of discovery." — James Joyce, Ulysses

"We don't see things as they are, we see things as we are." — Anais Nin

"To be great is to be misunderstood." — Ralph Waldo Emerson

Chapter 2
The Unique Talent

"No man of woman born, coward or brave, can shun his destiny." -Homer

"Everything that deceives is said to enchant." -Plato

"It is an unhappy lot which finds no enemies." -Pubilius Syrus

I will never forget the first time seeing Rios play. It was at the U.S. Open in 1995 on one of the outer courts. Rios was playing a seeded player, the Swede Thomas Enqvist. They were in the fifth set and Enqvist was up two breaks. The Rios name had generated some buzz in the American media, so, with curiosity, I ran over to watch the conclusion of this first round encounter. My eyes and tennis sensibilities were in awe. The long hair ponytail, the sneering, mocking arrogance, a badass attitude, and a court strut like no other player. This kid was going toe-to-toe with an established, top-notch pro. While performing wondrous tennis, Rios was at the same time spitting at Enqvist's shots, blowing others out, grabbing his crotch, making all kinds of facial expressions and gestures that were more befitting of an East L.A. gang member engaged in a knife fight. Had the sport of grace ever seen anything like this before?

Rios was in trouble in the fifth set but fought back against Enqvist from two breaks down to force a fifth set tiebreak, which he ultimately would lose 9-7.

Carlos Di Palma (Tennis Fan): "I am a huge tennis fan and a recreational player that spends more than 15 hours a week on the courts. Since 1991 until 2010, I have been to all the U.S. Opens that have been played. During the first days of the tournament, sometimes I will spend more than 14 hours between the morning hours of one day and the early morning of the following one."

"I have so many memories of great matches, especially in the small courts, or hiding in the bathrooms of the Stadium in between day and night sessions, if there was a match that I didn't want to miss, and I didn't have tickets. Of course, in the early 1990's I had a lot of arguments with my ex-wife and sometimes with friends that wanted to leave because they couldn't watch tennis any longer."

"Of all my memories of this great sport, there is one match that strangely I consider one of the best I have seen. Not because it was in the final stages of the tournament, or because the best players of the time were involved but because of the amazing tennis I had the privilege of witnessing that afternoon."

"To be honest I didn't even know one of the players involved, and if it weren't for my friend Carlos Cagneux that asked me to stay in that small court, frankly I would have kept walking to another court or the Stadium. It was 1995 and I remembered that I recognized Thomas Enqvist, and because I couldn't see the board from outside, I didn't have a clue who the other guy was. My friend told me to wait in line because the weird looking guy was one of the best junior players in the world during the previous years, and he said that eventually he would become one of the best in the ATP Tour. 'His name is Marcelo Rios, and he is from Chile.'"

"Finally we got our seats on the second row during the third set, and we enjoyed fantastic tennis for the rest of the match. Each point was the result of unbelievable beautiful shot making and I didn't want the match to ever end. Marcelo Rios' performance was simply amazing and his backhand passing shots, were art pieces. Especially the jumping one with topspin. I think that with the exception of a couple of Swedes, everybody there wanted Rios to win. Since that day I became an admirer of the great player that Marcelo Rios was, and I followed his career very close. I learned to love his game and his artistry, and during all those years I really disliked his personality and manners almost as much. I truly believe that he was an underachiever because with all that 'magic' and talent he should have been at the top of the rankings for a very long time, and he just spent six weeks as #1. I guess that his personality, his mouth and some injuries got in his way. But I will always love his fantastic style and creativity, and the way he moved on the court with the grace of a dancer. I always tell my friend Carlos that he really knows and has a great eye for tennis."

Natalia Baez (Competitor At 2003 Pan American Games): "I saw Marcelo Rios play at the Pan-Am Games which were held in the Dominican Republic in Santo Domingo in 2003. All the people were happy to see Rios play and wanted to support him. But his attitude was very bad and he was rude to many people during the tournament and by the time of the final match against the Brazilian (Fernando Meligeni), all the fans were cheering for Meligeni and against Rios. [33-year-old Meligeni saved four match points and won the final match of his professional career 5-7, 7-6 (8-6), 7-6 (7-5) to win the gold medal.]

Some of Rios' quotes during the Pan American Games tennis tournament:

"I'm not at the level I have been in the past, but I will still win the title in my present condition."

"I've played finals of major tournaments and I am used to the pressure and different types of opponents. I also know how to control anxiety and remain calm."

"What happened here does not happen anywhere else in the world. There were no towels and everything was a mess. It's not right that the main court is faster than the training courts, this is bad."

• • •

Alberto Garrido Campos (Chilean Tennis Supporter): "I used to play tennis when I was a kid, in those days my whole family did. Until I was 13-years-old I played every tournament I could and I was always ranked among the top 25 of Chile. The 90's were just starting and more than mass popular or a competitive sporting activity, tennis was considered a preppy hobby just for people that enjoyed white traditional clothes and could afford it."

"Cable TV didn't exist at all and only the Grand Slam finals were televised. Of course, local tennis was almost impossible to find on TV. Hardly any Chileans not related to the family of a good player could name players other than McEnroe, Connors or Lendl from the first world of tennis. Most certainly, the only sport in Chilean's minds was football."

"The two best Chilean players from the end of the 80's and the beginning of the 90's are legends for me and probably for all the old school players. Their names are Sergio Cortes and Pedro Rebolledo, both normally around the 200 ATP ranking position and, as every Chilean player, clay specialists. And when you read a clay specialist do not imagine someone like Nadal or Coria. At that time, for me, that meant: Forget about winners, nets are for fishing, why use a top spin backhand if slicing the ball is so safe? And of course the other surfaces were reserved for the first world tennis. And when I say they are legends, I'm not being ironic, they were the best we had, the guys that won the most important Chilean tournaments, the ones representing the country, they played the best live tennis by far I had witnessed. This was the best a Chilean could do, the South American reality."

"Those beautiful days. I still remember the nice feeling of going to see the Chilean Davis Cup team facing extremely complicated matches trying not to be relegated to the American B zone. These classic duels were always against countries like Bahamas, Cuba or another country normally without a player among top 150 (sometimes top 300). Tickets for free, not many people, small courts, the same faces from the kids tournaments and our heroes playing unbearably marathonic points the whole weekend to keep the category, and as far as I remember they always did."

"The story started changing around 1991 with a lucky coincidence: A new Federation with the idea of lifting tennis up in Chile to a first level – or better at least – and a once-rejected by Bollettieri - 5-foot-4-inch tall, 15-year-old kid with the talent of Maradona – but in tennis not football."

"Suddenly there were sponsors, a new system of junior tournaments in the country, tennis on TV and the Federation supporting the risky Marcelo Rios project, where the main goal was to create an idol. The first success was in 1992 when Rios won the new Satelite Futuro set of tournaments created to develop young tennis with enough prizes and some ATP points (the only one in Chile at that time) to attract some good

South American players. At that time, Rios looked like a 14-year-old kid playing against adults, probably he didn't weigh more than 130 pounds."

"Then in 1993, Rios ended up in a top position and he was supported to travel around the world, playing the most prestigious junior tournaments, something absolutely unthinkable for a Chilean junior tennis player at that time. The result was brilliant, Rios was able to defeat players from Europe and the United States that looked like basketball players when they shake hands at the net. And at the end of the year Rios ended up being the #1 ITF Junior, winning the U.S. Open junior event, showing how great his future could be."

"During the following years we experienced the side effects of having a "rock star" tennis player…the whole country watching tennis at 3 o'clock in the morning if necessary, my friends that didn't know about tennis at all were now playing frequently, an ATP tournament with many players in the top 50 staged in Chile, Rios ranked #1, Chile playing in the World Group in the Davis Cup, two more high quality tennis players in the country (Fernando Gonzalez and Nicolas Massu) and many South American players in the top 25 recognizing Rios as the one that showed that being a #1 from the south of the continent was also possible. I would say that those were the golden years of Chilean tennis."

"Perhaps Rios wasn't the best example for kids since he was involved in many scandals, including being captured drunk many time by the press, fighting in a bar, fighting with the police and even urinating on a guy in the washroom of a disco – and the day after he missed a flight with the Davis Cup team. But the guy did something impossible those days: Being Chilean or South American, with an average body type and being #1 of the world at the same time."

"And that lesson is priceless for the ones able to see it. It's like those films where kids are recommended parental advisory, there's definitely a marvelous key learning there and I really thank him for that, although, of course, there was a lot of bad behavior to throw away to the garbage."

"Last month (late February 2010) I went to see an exhibition match of Rios called 'The Maestros of Tennis.' And at the event there were around 4,000 people, while in the same month the ATP staged a tournament in Santiago, which as almost empty – and barely shown on TV. There's no new generation of players after Rios, Massu and Gonzalez. I also had a chat with an old friend still associated with the Chilean tennis world and he told me that just a few people are participating in tournaments and the same people that were in charge of Chilean tennis at the end of the 80's are back in directing the Federation, even with the same president."

"Unfortunately it seems that the coming Federations couldn't take any advantage of the extremely positive scenery we had and that the golden days of Chilean tennis are gone with Rios and his unforgettable jumping backhand. Rios is missed."

Bob Brett (Coach): "The first time I remember seeing Rios was in Rome. It was very early in his time on the Tour. And he was just by himself out there watching the matches. I saw him the following year in Barcelona. Beating someone in qualifying love and love - and a very good player. Or it might have been the other way around (Barcelona, then Rome). And he was okay. He was happy to be by himself and just watching these matches. And you could see this is someone who does something a little different. And that is what really gets your attention. And then you see him becoming, Oh, one of the nicest movers around the court. Watching him play in Miami one year in the final. Just seeing him move like that, taking the ball and just hitting it down the line when he needed to. He was really impressive."

"I think Larry Stefanki did a great job with him. Of course he's a world class talent but I think that, honestly, Larry did a very good job. Because it's almost like taming a lion or a tiger. He had some moments where he did some things that weren't popular. And you know what? He was always, for me, he was always polite. He didn't talk to everybody, especially in the beginning of his career. He'd come in the locker room - some of the older players were, 'Oh!' He didn't say hello, he didn't say hello to us. He was just different. And they're entitled to be different. And Marcelo was like that. He was different. And a great thing for tennis. And a shame he finished early. And wasn't able to win a Grand Slam that year when, I think, he should have won the French Open. He was the favorite. I just remember, I thought he was the better player. Just maybe the occasion got to him that first one."

"And then he played Korda in the finals of the Australian Open. That particular period. Then he, all of a sudden, he's fallen off that level instead of raising a notch. And that's often the way a career goes. And he had that ball on a string and he looked absolutely brilliant. And it can be different things. It can be getting into trouble with the authorities. Just maybe something that was taken out of proportion, or was unnecessary for him to do it. Whatever. It just causes a little too much attention. Or maybe it was something that wasn't necessary for attention to be given. From his aspect. Because being at the top or maybe being average can be maybe one percent. And that's really where he lost that one percent. And that was a shame."

"I talked to him. He was someone I always said hello to. I think it's always important for older people - whether it's a coach to say hello to the younger ones, make them feel welcome. And then I, of course, knew Larry Stefanki really well and so sometimes there were practice sessions or whatever. Basically, it's having respect for his ability to play the game. And that's really what is important. And, to be honest with you, I can see in my mind now, I can see that match against Agassi in Miami. And I can remember him being in there, different places. Not that I was paying too much attention to it. But he was a very good example of the way to play tennis. And he also set up the point really well. And he also had these little combinations, he knew what to go for, when to wait. Playing. He knew how to play. As I said, it was a shame that he fell off that level. He had such a short time at his peak. And that's the difference when you see guys like Federer. Some players stay around, like the true greats, stay around a long time. But he was a great player."

"I think the last time I saw him was about 2004, Chile vs. Japan in Davis Cup. And it was just fun. Because Chile was in the relegation match with a chance to go up or stay in Zone 1. And it was a great achievement for the Japanese. But Marcelo was there. He wasn't playing but he came around, he said hello. He was just there and he talked about, he wanted to play more. He wanted to play some exhibitions. But it was just, he was there and he was real friendly. The people don't see that side. It's so important for people to realize to accept that they're very famous in their country. And maybe there's, to some degree, an invasion of privacy, that they really want to guard. And they don't have this freedom in which to be themselves. Their things are reported and they may not be the best of things. And then sometimes they're a little more cautious in what they do and what sort of relationships they have. Goran (Ivanisevic) was not too dissimilar, in some of those periods of wildness. And both fairly quiet in some areas, looking down and not looking in your eye. And that's so different in terms of style of play but not so in terms of character. And I found Goran to be a really, really nice person. And a person I have a lot of contact with. Marcelo is really - I think he comes out of himself more now, than he was when he was 19."

• • •

Rios vs. Gustavo Kuerten in Rome 1998: Match Study

Semifinal matchup. This is the first meeting between the two on the ATP Tour.

Rios quickly jumps out to a 2-love lead. Rios beat Kuerten all three times they played as juniors.

Eurosport commentator: "Surely Gustavo Kuerten remembers that and so does Rios. You almost got the feeling in the last game that Rios was beginning to toy with Kuerten a little bit."

Rios extends lead to 3-love.

"Much of the traffic has been to the Kuerten backhand side. He has a good backhand, the problem is it's coming from Rios' strength."

Kuerten misses another backhand. "No, he's missed it. Four-love Rios."

"Talking last night to Larry Stefanki after he beat Krajicek, he is absolutely thrilled with how Rios is playing, how he has regained his form so quickly after the injury layoff."

"Kuerten warmed up Rios last year before Rios won Monte Carlo, he was almost unrecognized then. Of course, he went on to win the French Open."

"This year Kuerten hasn't lost to a lefthander. He's beaten all five of them - Carlsen, Woodforde, Clavet, Arazi and Ivanisevic. He's taken them all on and sent them all home. But at the moment, no sign of sending Rios home. 18 minutes, 5-love, Marcelo Rios."

"Kuerten is just so inconsistent at the moment. We are at set point. And where Kuerten has been inconsistent, Rios has been Mr. Consistency."

Rios lashes a forehand winner up the line to seal the set at 6-love.

Second set:

"Back in Chile, the match is being shown live. Every Rios match is shown live. They just clear the networks."

Rios connects on a serve and volley. "No answer there. Rios able to vary his tactics with a solid serve and volley. 1-love."

"The man who won the French Open last year against the man expected to win it this year. I'm certainly in that category."

Kuerten hits his fifth ace. "And a huge roar as Gustavo Kuerten acknowledges the crowd and lifts his arms as if to say, Hey, I've won a game here!"

Rios' excellent serving continues. "That's a terrific facility to move the ball around on the serve. 3-2, Rios."

Rios hits a swing volley winner after a serve wide to the deuce court. "He's beginning to rival Agassi for his drive volley."

"Another linesweeper there from Rios. He leads 4-3, second set."

Rios sends a Kuerten second serve return long. "A strangely wasteful shot by Rios."

Rios puts another forehand into the net. "My word. Kuerten has to take advantage of the sudden hesitancy by Rios."

"It's almost as if Kuerten has brought Rios down to his level."

"The problem for Kuerten, he has no confidence in the backhand side. He's happy to get it in. So slow."

"Just one deuce on serve against Krajicek, none today for Kuerten."

"Hasn't played like a French Open champion today Gustavo Kuerten - 5-4, Rios."

"Rios moves ahead 6-5."

"Again he was there, he was anticipating, and it's match point."

"Sad end for Gustavo Kuerten. There's no doubt about who the best player is from South America at the moment and, frankly, I have little doubt who the best player in the world is at the moment."

• • •

An Expert Analysis of Rios (Author Unknown)

Actually, Rios had one of the most difficult, crafty serves for a short guy on Tour. Todd Martin said he served with the leverage of a guy 6-ft-5. Rios' funky lefty spin and pinpoint placement and variety managed to befuddle even Agassi on the return, certainly far more than Chang's serve ever did. Which is emblematic of Rios's entire game at his best.

A lot of players can be cute with the ball. Rios was, but it's not like others don't try to wrong foot you or go for short angles or drop shots. What made Rios so difficult to play at his best was that he had a rifling accuracy to his shots when needed, but more than that it was like he almost lulled you into sleep because his movement and strokes were so transparently silky and simple. Like a lullabye really, then BAM.

In reality, Rios did have a fairly big forehand, not Moya big but just one notch down. I've heard commentators describe Rios' forehand as a "big forehand." Have you ever heard that about Chang or Hewitt's forehand? I haven't. Rios also took the ball on the rise which effectively assimilates and often beats raw power when executed to perfection. Bottom-line, Rios was not overpowered by Agassi when he was at his best. He was also able to out-do Agassi by taking the ball on the rise better than Agassi and using Agassi's power against him and sending HIM on the yo-yo ride. As stated, when this is done well, it's quite effective, no? Furthermore, as I said Rios could lull you to sleep, then bam a screaming winner. He could hit with DECEPTIVE power, he just didn't do it all the time; and that's what made

it so effective when he did. When Rios was at his best, he made his opponents look asleep at the wheel.

I believe most of that simply has to do with his sly stroke mechanics.

Seriously, it's awfully difficult to read Rios' shots, which is what made him so difficult. I mean when you see Roddick winding up for his huge inside-out forehand you generally know the conclusion...an inside-out forehand. Someone with the hands/touch/hand-eye coordination and the economically stealth stroking technique to simply meet, greet, and then redirect Roddick's power can

trouble him, as Nalbandian has proved. It's not easy, but that's the

general plan when facing a Roddick/Courier type baseline basher; or even when Rios faced Agassi, and Agassi "tried" to bully him.

I think of Nalbandian as a slightly less talented version of Rios personally, less effective serve but far better head. They both have those economical groundstrokes that make their shots hard to read, and also enable them to handle pace more comfortably than most of today's players who have more exaggerated swings. Both Rios and Nalbandian have surprising pop on their groundies when needed, again, they just don't go for the kill shot on every shot.

They are NOT Karol Kucera, however, who merely had the economical, difficult to read groundies, "massage" groundies but with NO put-away power when the time was right...which was Kucera's limiting factor and why he at his best was just a slight notch down from Nalbandian or Rios at their best. Which is saying something, because Kucera at his best was DAMN GOOD, which speaks volumes for this style of play's effectiveness.

In general, I feel like it's too simplistic to simply say a player like

Nalbandian or Rios didn't/don't have the big weapons to win a major. There is some truth to that since, winning a major entails TWO consecutive weeks of five set matches. During that time, you have to expect a bad day. You have to survive those days to win. Sampras managed to hang around and mope around and stay alive even on bad days, because he had a HUGE serve to keep him at least

competitive, and give his opponent a chance to choke, and a chance for him to "bide time" and try to "find his game." That said, it's not like Wilander, Borg, Chang, Edberg, Connors, Rafter, Federer, and Muster weren't able to win Slams without the heaping dosage of "cheap" points guys like Becker, Sampras, Courier, Roddick, and Agassi could reel off simply with screaming winners here

or there on an as-needed basis. There are many ways to win a match, and having huge weapons a la Gonzalez and Philippoussis isn't the only way.

What prevented Rios from winning a Slam is what has kept Gonzalez and Philipoussis from winning one yet, is what took Korda and Goran so long before winning one, is what stopped Novotna, etc.

Talent is talent, and you can win with that talent in any number of playing styles. However, if you don't have the head or the heart or both a la Rios; then, you're less likely to come through when it matters most. So is the case with Rios, it still doesn't mean that he was incapable because of any failing in his game.

The truth is that when Rios reached his peak form in '98, other players were gunning for him, but Rios made them look foolish OUTSIDE of the Slams. When it mattered most, however, he choked at both the Australian (loss to Korda in final) and the French (16 62 26 46 loss to Moya in QF). You can't win Tennis Masters Series titles without some serious talent. At the same time, you can't win Grand Slams without heart and nerve. Which is the greater, more respectable talent?

There's a reason why Grand Slams are so revered. It's not just about tennis, it's about heart and nerve... in addition to talent. Rios certainly had the talent, but he didn't have the heart or the nerve. Why was Rocky more formidable than Mr. T on the big screen? You guessed it, he didn't think he was too cool to grandstand his talent before his heart and nerve. Have we ever seen Rios get down and dirty? Maybe, here or there. That's not enough, period. Now, Guga on the other hand? He had talent, but without the pretense. He was like a dog, ready to get down and dirty, to do whatever it takes. Rios, however? He was one bitch cat!

Talented, but still just one, bitchy cat. Always licking himself, always preening, always afraid to get dirty, aloof, and always acting like he had better things to do with his time. At his best, Rios was one bitchy-witchy shot from glory. He fell short, because he wasn't willing to run for the ball.

The injuries that befell Rios in what should have been his peak years? Well, no athlete deserves to go through that. But, some deserve it more than others. Rios was never willing to sacrifice his heart and soul on the court, so maybe it was for the best that he wasn't healthy enough in ensuing years. Not for us, but him. Certainly, Muster didn't deserve to have his aspirations get crushed by a drunk driver. That's right, Muster didn't. He did something about it. Why? Because he cared in more than just a half-hearted way.

As far as Safin's assessment of Rios' talent? Well, he knows better than me. I've never actually played or practiced with Rios. I can only judge from afar, but never truly know. For the record, though, I do not think of Rios' talent as the greatest talent. There is a variety of talent in this game, and numerous ways to quantify and identify them.

Even though Rios does not have a Slam cup in his trophy case, when he was playing his best, Rios produced much better - and very much more enjoyable - tennis than some Slam winners. You don't see people bringing up Rios just because they liked the bad attitude, people bring him up now years after he's retired because his tennis did give something to talk about, and that makes you remember the player.

Chapter 3
The Quiet Man Speaks

"The player owes the gallery as much as an actor owes the audience." - Bill Tilden

"Only two people in this world can do exactly what they want to do - artists and criminals." -Al Capone

"All art is but imitation of nature." -Seneca

"Be undeniably good. When people ask me how do you make it, what I always tell them and nobody ever takes note of it because it's not the answer they wanted to hear — what they want to hear is here's how you get an agent, here's how you write a script, here's how you do this — but I always say, 'Be so good they can't ignore you.' If somebody's thinking, 'How can I be really good?', people are going to come to you. It's much easier doing it that way than going to cocktail parties." - Steve Martin

• • •

The one and only time I ever spoke with Rios was at the 1999 U.S. Open. I had tried for years, unsuccessfully to do a Biofile interview with Rios for my syndicated newspaper column. He blew me off each time I asked him in the locker room, without even acknowledging my presence or making eye contact, he just sneered a 'Phht' sound and strutted off to somewhere.

A Biofile entails simple questions, such as an athlete's heroes, hobbies, favorite movies, first car, favorite meal, favorite ice cream flavor, greatest moment, funny memory, so I thought it would be possible to get Rios to do it at some point, despite his well-known reputation of not being cooperative with journalists, whether Chilean or foreign. After about five failures, I decided a different tact to get Rios to respond to my questions: attend his post-match press conference and ask the questions one at a time, with USTA and ITF officials present. Once again, Rios shot me down like a put away volley...

An Interview with Marcelo Rios after his first round win at the 1999 U.S. Open against Martin Damm 64 76 36 57 61 at Interview Room 1 (August 30, 1999).

USTA: Questions for Marcelo Rios. (There were only three or four reporters there for Rios.)

Another reporter: It was a tough match. What happened?

Marcelo Rios: He played pretty good. I slowed down my game a little bit, but like I say, I'm not hitting very good the ball. Really nice to win like that.

Me: Who were your childhood heroes?

Marcelo Rios: What is that?

Me: Who were your childhood heroes?

Marcelo Rios: I don't understand what you say.

Me: Tennis people you admired when you were growing up?

Marcelo Rios: Nobody.

Me: What are your hobbies and interests?

Marcelo Rios: Nothing.

Me: What is your greatest sports moment?

Marcelo Rios: I don't remember, man.

Me: Come on.

Marcelo Rios: What do you want me to tell you?

Me: Just answer the questions.

Marcelo Rios: Don't ask me questions like that.

Me: What's your favorite movies?

Marcelo Rios: [No response. Re-angles chair slightly to face other side of room.]

• • •

I actually witnessed Rios gently rebuff John McEnroe. In 1998 or 1999, Rios won a match at the U.S. Open and was walking down the hallway back to the locker room, escorted by two security guards. It was a pure coincidence that I saw Rios as I was on my way back to the media center from another match, and was walking about 30 yards behind him, when suddenly, between us, John McEnroe emerged out of a door on the right wall of the corridor. McEnroe walked about ten steps behind Rios and and attempted to engage Rios in a conversation. The seven-time Grand Slam champion asked Rios about Hans Gildermeister and Rios turned around slightly while not stopping his walk and said something very concise which I could not understand. And that was the extent of the discussion between McEnroe and Rios, which lasted a total of about five seconds.

"There is no excellent beauty that hath not some strangeness in the proportion." -Francis Bacon

Todd Woodbridge (ATP Player): "We didn't have many conversations. I think that was one of the things he needed to work on, away from being on the court. Within the community he wasn't as respected by the playing community, by the way he treated people. And that hurt him. Because that made people want to beat him more than if he'd have been a nice guy. And there was a real determination to go out hard against him."

"Marcelo was a sort of guy that when I was on the Tour that I'd deliberately try to get in his face in a way that, he hated responding. So you would get in front of him and say, 'Hey, Marcelo, Hello. How are you?' And he wouldn't want to speak to you but you had to make him speak to you. And that was a way for me to have a bit of fun during the day, sort of bit of an Aussie-spirited, fun thing to do. Put people in positions they don't want to be in. And that was one for him - he hated talking to people. To make him say hello and make him find some manners. And yeah, he would in the end. And in some ways he appreciated the fact that you did it. Because later on in our playing careers, and I'd been out there a while, he would say hello. And so you chipped away at him."

"I picked that up from Pat Rafter. He would do that with some of the guys who didn't like to talk sometimes. I remember he did it to Pete Sampras a few times. Kind of invade his space. Pete, sometimes, didn't want to talk. I remember Pat, sort of in his face in the trainer's room, kind of forcing Pete to talk."

(Confirmation note: Another top 10 player told me that he played 18 holes of golf with Sampras and two other ATP players. And during the entire 18 holes, Sampras did not say a single word to anyone.)

August 4, 1997
Marcelo Rios d. Jonas Bjorkman 6-3 7-5
CINCINNATI, OHIO

Question: Seemed like both you and Jonas (Bjorkman) had some problems with your first serve today. Anything with the balls?

Marcelo Rios: I think I served really good today. I think I didn't serve bad. I think I played pretty solid and when I have to serve good I served really good.

Question: As for Jonas, you were obviously aware that – he said he can't remember having a bad serving percentage. Did you notice that at all?

Marcelo Rios: He returned better than what he served. He used the return really good. He served bad a couple of times that I broke, but I don't think he served that bad.

Question: Was this a tough first draw match for you? When you say the draw wouldn't you have rather had someone that was ranked a lot lower?

Marcelo Rios: Well, I think I had one of the toughest draws. Bjorkman is a great hard court player. I knew it was going to be a tough match. But, I played really confident and not rushing too much and playing every point. I think I played pretty good for being out two weeks without playing tournaments. I felt pretty okay.

Question: Did it mean anything that he beat you the last time? Did that enter your mind at all?

Marcelo Rios: Well, yeah, we played at Lipton, but it was at night, it was really tough to play. I don't like that much playing at night. But, today was different condition. It was really hot and the balls were going really fast. Different match.

Question: How important is it to you to do well this week and also at the Open and start to gain more notoriety in America?

Marcelo Rios: Well, I think all these tournaments you play to be ready for the Open. I always you always try to do your best - I think every tournament I play, I try to do my best even if it is before the Open or not.

Question: You have not only been off for a couple of weeks, but the two tournaments that you played you were out early. Do you not have enough matches in that you would like to have at this point of the year?

Marcelo Rios: I think I played pretty good in Wimbledon. I had two clay court tournaments didn't play that good. Then I have a week off and I have been practicing in Bollettieri's, it was really good. And, I think it helped me a lot. I was looking to have some weeks off. I have been playing a lot since the beginning of the year and it helped me a lot to not to play.

Question: Do you find it tougher the higher your ranking gets - that you have more guys coming after you and know who you are as opposed to a couple of years ago when you were just getting into the top 20 and top 10?

Marcelo Rios: Well, I think when you are like 10, 20 I think that at that part of the ranking I think everybody is good and even if you play No. 10 or No. 2 it is going to be a tough match and all the players are good in that – like in that section, top 20 anybody can beat anybody.

Question: You have been up at this ranking for a little bit now. How close do you think you are maybe to joining the top leaders like Sampras and Chang up there?

Marcelo Rios: I think all the guys have a chance, the guys that are ranked 10, 11, 8 have the same chance to beating 2 or 3. I think everybody is playing really close and you play a lot of tournaments in the year you have many chances to play them and to be ranked.

Question: How popular are you in Chile now?

Marcelo Rios: There are not many sports guys, there are only soccer players. I don't think that I am that popular.

Question: Is it difficult for you to go around your hometown?

Marcelo Rios: No, it is not that difficult.

Question: Do you think that is just because they are not used to having so many stars in tennis?

Marcelo Rios: I think there is never a good player in Chile and there are not that many sportsman. There is only one soccer player, me and there is nobody playing out of the country, and that is why you are popular in your country.

Question: What made you become a tennis player and play like you do when you had no one to really follow? You just liked it?

Marcelo Rios: I think so. It was a long time ago, so I don't even remember.

Question: Did you follow tennis as a child? Did you look at Wimbledon? Did you look at the U.S. Open?

Marcelo Rios: In Chile I never followed tennis. It was a lot of soccer, no tennis, so I never followed tennis.

Question: You played soccer too?

Marcelo Rios: A little bit.

Question: When did you realize that you were really good at tennis?

Marcelo Rios: I started playing juniors and tournaments in juniors and I did pretty good and after I decide to play professional so that is when I realized I could play.

Question: Having not been following it, how did you come to realize the significance of being a top-10 player and playing in something like Wimbledon or a U.S. Open?

Marcelo Rios: When did I realize?

Question: Yes.

Marcelo Rios: I think when they play – when I be top 10, be in top 10, that is something you try to do and I think when I start playing tennis I was really good at the beginning so I always have the confidence that I can improve my ranking.

Question: Is there one Grand Slam event that you like overall the others?

Marcelo Rios: I like all the Grand Slams, but I prefer the French Open.

Q&A with Goran Ivanisevic April 10, 1998

Question: Marcelo Rios today is a first-ranked player in the world and he hadn't won any Grand Slam tournament?

Goran: That's what ATP ranking lists says, but for me Rios is not the best. The man just had a lot of things going on his behalf and from no where he climbs to

'#1 seat.' That's the way things happen - you win some matches, the card goes to your direction and it seems the whole world is yours.

Question: If not Rios, who is the #1 in the world?

Goran: Sampras! But he is a man also, so the 'ups and downs' exist in his career as well. He just had more ups then downs and he was always the best when he need to be. And that's why I will always put my money on Sampras, Agassi, or Chang. They did plenty in the past and they will do plenty more.

INDIAN WELLS NEWSWEEK CHAMPIONS CUP

March 7, 1999 Marcelo Rios

Miki Singh, ATP Tour: Marcelo Rios has joined us today. He's the defending champion here at Indian Wells. He also won Lipton the week after last year, and went up to #1. This is his second event of the year. He played in Auckland, had a back injury which forced him out of his first match of the year against Andre Pavel. He lost almost two months of the year. This is his second event. He's ready to go. First question?

Question: How is the back?

Marcelo Rios: Feeling much better. A long time ago, I didn't feel this good, since November last year. But you can't say you're a hundred percent. I'm going to try to play, start slow, just try to rally some balls, try to do my best. But always the first tournament is really tough.

Question: You're still wearing that protection on practice?

Marcelo Rios: I just took it out yesterday for the first time after three months, two months. In the beginning, it's pretty tough. You lose balance after being two months with that. But you got to go slowly. I'm trying to recover my tennis. The toughest thing is to be fit and try to move the way I move before.

Question: How long did you actually not get on a court?

Marcelo Rios: What is that?

Question: How long did you not play any tennis?

Marcelo Rios: It was like four or five weeks without playing any tennis – doing exercise, try to recover. But I really slow. I couldn't even hit some balls or move. Was really, really tough.

Question: What is the injury? What is it diagnosed as?

Miki Singh: It was diagnosed as a stress injury to the lower spine, lower lumbar.

Question: Stress from one thing that happened on a court or stress from playing too much? Do you have any idea?

Marcelo Rios: I think it's playing too much. Being on hardcourt, playing a little too much all during the year, during my career. I think I've been playing a lot maybe.

Question: This was a big month for you last year. Obviously you're coming in here with not much matchplay. Are you concerned about defending your two titles, or whatever happens, happens?

Marcelo Rios: Bad luck coming first tournament, tournament I won last year. That's the way it goes. I can't do anything. I just try to do my best, try to play good. But I'm happy I recover. I thought it was going to take longer. But I think I'm pretty good right now, really happy I can play, I can practice. Now try to do as much as I can.

Question: Many players from South America and Europe, born and bred on clay, have a difficult time on hard courts. Why does it seem to be so easy for you, to go from one to the other?

Marcelo Rios: I think I have a game for hard court. I take the ball really early. I've been playing better on hard courts than on clay, though I was born on clay. But I think it's the type of game each player have.

Question: Do you actually prefer hard courts?

Marcelo Rios: I've been playing much better on hard court. I don't mind playing on clay, but maybe right now my favorite surface is hard.

Question: I saw you practicing on clay yesterday. Was that a precaution?

Marcelo Rios: I just was serving a little bit because I didn't serve in a long time.

Question: What did the doctor say about the long-term prognosis for the back? Do you have to play less now or can you do the same schedule that you did last year?

Marcelo Rios: Well, I've not been playing that much this year, so I don't think it's going to be much difference all the way through this year. But maybe try to play maybe a little bit less or try not to fly that much. I've been flying a lot all over the world. That maybe make it tired.

Question: What are your plans for this year? Grand Slam?

Marcelo Rios: I'm just starting the year. I'll try to keep my ranking maybe Top 10. I'll try to do as much as I can.

Question: If you get the problem coming back again, what do you face then? Operation possibly?

Marcelo Rios: Well, I'm not thinking about that, so I don't know what I'm going to do.

Question: Did you change your schedule for this year as a reaction to the injury or anything?

Marcelo Rios: Well, like I say, I haven't played anything this year, so I haven't changed anything. Just going to play maybe more tournaments on clay than hard court, try to feel much better and try to feel – feel my back much powerful until I can start playing again.

Question: What have you been doing when you were not playing tennis?

Marcelo Rios: I've been practicing, like not practicing tennis. I've been doing a lot of exercise and swimming, exercise in the pool, just hanging around.

Question: Did you find yourself missing the competition?

Marcelo Rios: Well, I think for somebody that do this all his life, and you have all the day like doing something all day, playing tennis, suddenly you don't have anything to do, and you can't do anything, so maybe you miss a little bit playing. But that's the way it goes. I think maybe it help me a little bit for rest. But for sure you miss playing tournaments that you won, you miss playing tournaments that you did good, tournaments that you like. But I think it's a hard time. You've got to be tough mentally and not go down or try to think positive that you're going to come back.

Question: You probably follow the thing with IMG. Pete says he's going to stay with Jeff Schwartz. I know Jeff manages you. What is your situation with the whole thing?

Marcelo Rios: Well, yeah, he left IMG. He's still my Lawyer. He's going to work as my lawyer still. Right now I'm still with IMG. I have a contract still. But I think was really fast what happened. I've been all my career with Jeff. It's really disappointing him to leave. But I think it's maybe a good decision for him, for his self, doing his own company, trying to work as a lawyer. But I still have a contract with IMG.

Question: So you're a client of IMG and you're going to be using Jeff for legal – as your lawyer?

Marcelo Rios: Yes.

Question: Both then?

Marcelo Rios: That's it right now.

Question: How long is your contract with IMG?

Marcelo Rios: I think it's until July.

Question: So like all those hours that you're not playing tennis, did you go to the movies, read, watch TV? Besides your exercise, what did you do?

Marcelo Rios: Yeah. I was in the States. Just trying to keep my body, be on a diet, try not to eat too much, try to stay healthy. I watching some movies, going to the beach. But couldn't do that much.

Question: In Bradenton?

Marcelo Rios: Yeah, I was in Bradenton.

Question: So it hasn't helped your golf game, I would assume?

Marcelo Rios: I've been not playing golf since a long time. I think it's going to take a while for me to go back. I'm really kind of scared coming back again. Think it's going to take a while.

Question: What's your handicap?

Marcelo Rios: I was like a nine, ten.

Question: A lot of players have had problems playing here with the wind and a little bit of the altitude. You seemed to adjust really well. Did you like it? Did it bother you?

Marcelo Rios: I think this year is much different. Balls are faster, I think. Maybe it's because I'm not playing that well. I just came here. I couldn't put a ball in play. I think you get used. I've been playing here a lot of times before. I think once the tournament start going, I'm going to feel better.

Question: What are your memories of last year at this time, how well you were playing?

Marcelo Rios: I have a very good beginning of the year. I was feeling really good. Basically I was a hundred percent, playing good in this tournament, winning Lipton. But I think bad luck a little bit get injured like that. But that's the way it goes. I think everybody gets injured as part of the game. I think this help you to be more – to take care more of your body, and I would like not to have it again.

Question: You practice with Alex Corretja. Why do you think he struggled a bit at the beginning of this year? What do you think are the weaknesses and strengths of his game?

Marcelo Rios: Why you ask me about Corretja?

Question: If you don't mind, I'd just like your opinion.

Marcelo Rios: Why?

Question: Because I'm doing a story on Corretja. I wondered if you had any opinion on his game.

Marcelo Rios: I think he's a top player. He's been doing pretty good. I think maybe he have all the shots. He have all the shots in the game, but I think he fight a lot, and that make him win.

Question: Do you see yourself getting back to No. 1 in the world again ever, when you're healthy?

Marcelo Rios: If I'm keep healthy and I do things good, I think I have chances.

Question: Has it been difficult to kind of lower your sights after challenging for No. 1 last year, now you just want to be healthy, get back out there, stay in the Top 10, those kinds of things?

Marcelo Rios: For sure when you're at the top of the game, you go down, I went down because I didn't play. I was 1, 2, then I got injured and that's why I fell from the ranking. But obviously if you're a little bit bad, you couldn't recover your points. Like I say, I was #1 one time, I can go back.

Question: You say you prefer hard courts now, and your record is very good on hard courts. Is the French Open more important to you than the U.S. Open?

Marcelo Rios: Grand Slams are really important. I always like French Open a lot, but I like to play on clay. It's not that I only prefer to play on hard court. I think I play pretty good on clay. As I say, I've been doing much better on hard courts.

Question: Do you expect Sampras to end this year as #1 or do you think we're going to see a new player?

Marcelo Rios: I don't know. I think it's going to change. I think there's a lot of players coming right now, top players. I think soon somebody's going to replace him.

Question: Do you see other South Americans who are able to come to the Top 10?

Marcelo Rios: It's tough to say. I don't see a lot of South American players coming to be Top 10 guys right now. But maybe in a while, they have a lot of chance.

Question: What aspect of the game did you miss the most when you were away? The competition? The tennis itself?

Marcelo Rios: I think we used to compete. I think that's a little bit you miss being on the court, win the matches. Running, playing your game, playing good more than anything.

Question: Have you been watching a lot on TV?

Marcelo Rios: Didn't see any tennis in two months.

Question: Was that out of choice? Did you decide, If I can't play, I don't want to watch?

Marcelo Rios: I didn't have TV where I was. That was the only reason I didn't see.

Monte Carlo Open

April 20, 1999 Marcelo Rios d. Andrei Pavel 0-6 6-4 7-6

ATP: Questions for Marcelo.

Question: How is it to win a fight like that?

Marcelo Rios: A long time ago, I didn't play matches like that. Come to play a match like that and winning I think is going to give me a lot of confidence going to the next match. That's good. What I was looking for is play a big match and win it.

Question: What happened in the first set? Was it the ceremony that put your mind completely out of the match?

Marcelo Rios: No. I think I start playing too defensive. He start playing really good. I think once I started stepping in the court, playing much offensive, I think he have less chance. I think I play the best match of the year. I've been hitting the ball much better today.

Question: Are you completely rid of your problems of your back, things like that?

Marcelo Rios: Well, I think from the injury, I'm okay. Maybe after I play, get a little bit tired, a little bit sore. From the injury, I think I'm a hundred percent on that.

Question: How is this victory for you mentally?

Marcelo Rios: It's really good going to come here and win matches like that, 7-6 the third, first round. It's really tough. It's going to give me a lot of confidence for the next match, for the tournament, for my tennis.

Question: Were you hurt at the end of the first set when people were whistling? Were you upset?

Marcelo Rios: Why should I be upset?

Question: They were not very happy.

Marcelo Rios: That's the way it goes. I think when you're a top player, and you go there and lose 6-love, people want to see some more. For sure they go like that. I finish the match, everybody was with me. I think there's parts of the match that people want to see more tennis.

Question: Was it a little bit weird to get an award for being #1 when your ranking is as low as it's been for the last couple of years?

Marcelo Rios: I don't think so.

Question: Do you feel ready to win such a big tournament like this, or would it be a surprise for you to be already in the final?

Marcelo Rios: I think I'm playing pretty good. If my back still go okay, I think I'm mentally prepared, I think I have a chance.

Question: How much do you feel you lost in those couple of months that you missed in terms of match toughness and mental strength?

Marcelo Rios: I think I lost a lot.

Question: What are your expectations now in the next few weeks and for the French Open?

Marcelo Rios: I'm looking forward to play a lot of matches and be a lot of hours on the court and get my confidence back. I think I'm serving much better than last week. Just get ready for the French Open.

Question: That's what you need?

Marcelo Rios: Yes.

Question: What do you think about the balls here? Many players say they're like stones, very heavy. Is that your opinion?

Marcelo Rios: I think the ATP make a big mistake every week of changing balls, every week different balls. But I think they're okay. They're a little bit heavy. I think there's a lot of injuries because of that, elbow injuries. I think the ATP should do something, but it's tough to talk with them, they have the last word always.

Question: Did this match impair you physically or leave traces physically for you for the next match?

Marcelo Rios: I think I'm playing pretty good right now. I don't think it's going to affect me. Maybe it will give me a little confidence. Physically I think I'm pretty good right now.

Question: Do you feel you're one of the big guys on clay that players want to beat or are you feeling a little lower with this situation?

Marcelo Rios: I think everybody wants to beat everybody. Once you get in the court, even if the guy's No. 1 or 20, you want to beat him, as well.

MIAMI, FLORIDA

March 28, 2000 Marcelo Rios lost to Tim Henman 1-6 6-1 6-7

ATP: Questions, please.

Question: That was a strange match. How did you see it?

Marcelo Rios: I think I played a really bad first set, and he play a bad second. But I think it was a good match, just missing too much. Got a lot of chances, but never feel good on the court. It was windy. The only thing I got to do is return the serve, and that was it, but I couldn't even hit the return. It's another match.

Question: Is that the longest and most tiring match you've had since you've been back?

Marcelo Rios: Yeah.

Question:. How did you feel your fitness held up?

Marcelo Rios: Right now I'm feeling good. Last night I was a little bit tired. But I think that's good to feel a little bit in my legs so it can get used to it. Right now I have no pain. Maybe moving a little bit bad; sometimes it's tough to move. But that's going to come with time.

Question: Tim (Henman) plays Agassi next. Do you see him having any chance in that match?

Marcelo Rios: I don't think so. I think Andre, he's playing pretty good. I think he like to play guys that serve-and-volley. I think Andre should win pretty easy.

Question: What should Tim's tactics be to go out and play him?

Marcelo Rios: I have no idea, man. You've got to ask him Tim, not me.

Questions: Where do you think you are at the moment in your comeback?

Marcelo Rios: I think some days I'm hitting good the ball. All depends how my leg is feeling. Sometimes I'm a little bit tired, and it's tough to move. But just time, just time. I try to put a lot of me to try to hit the ball good. I think it's going to come by itself.

Question: Are you restricted in how much time you can practice?

Marcelo Rios: I try not to play a lot of tennis. I try more to exercise, to like get stronger, the leg more than I'm playing tennis.

Marcelo Rios Answers Readers Questions for BBC Sport in 2006

How did you pick up tennis in a nation and continent obsessed with football? Devasheesh Mathur, India

Rios: "Well, it was tough because when I started to play there were no tennis players. It was a sport no one used to play so it was pretty tough."

Marcelo, Which of the four Grand Slams did you most enjoy playing in and why? Kev Foster, UK

Rios: "I liked French Open a lot since it's on clay and I grew up playing on clay. All of the Grand Slams were pretty nice though. But don't ask me for the one I hated because the one I hated was Wimbledon."

Why did you retire so suddenly from the professional circuit? A. Horvatovic, UK

Rios: "My back was troubling me a lot and I had a lot of back surgery. That was one of the reasons for retiring. I would love to play professionally but I'm not fit enough to do it."

What do you miss most about life on the tour? And what do you miss least? Vicki Blackburn, England

Rios: "Nothing really. I only missed playing the game. The thing I miss least is practicing every day. I was really sick of practicing and traveling and doing all the stuff you have to do to be a professional player."

I was a big fan of your tennis during your pro years. I just wanted to ask if you have any regrets about your tennis career? P Sundaralingham, England

Rios: "I have no regrets. I'm pretty happy with what I did but obviously I would have loved to have won a Grand Slam."

Who was your toughest opponent? S.B., England

Rios: "I think the baseline players were the toughest to play. All the Spanish guys were tough but I can't single out one particular player."

Do you think that Fernando Gonzalez could go on and win a Grand Slam at some stage in his career? Daniel Bissett, Wales

Rios: "Oh, it looks pretty tough. But he is a great player and if he is confident enough over two weeks he could do it. I certainly hope he can do it."

Can you name any up and coming new players from Chile who we can expect to see on the ATP tour in the next few years? Mr Hitul Mistry, England

Rios: "Nobody. After Gonzalez and Massu there is really nobody at the moment."

A lot of players have mentioned how fantastic playing at the Royal Albert Hall is. Is this a venue you are looking forward to playing at? Katie Andersson, England

Rios: "I've never had the opportunity to play at the BlackRock Masters and I don't know the venue. But the other players have told me that it's a great tournament and a great place to play tennis so I'm looking forward to playing there. Being back in tennis on this tour has been nice - I didn't know how competitive it would be but everyone wants to win."

What are your thoughts on the career of Andre Agassi who retires at the U.S. Open later this month. Would you be happy to play against him on the Merrill Lynch Tour of Champions one day? Mark Witchell, United Kingdom

Rios: "I would love to play him. It would be really nice if he would join the Merrill Lynch Tour of Champions. I don't think he will do that for a while though but it would be nice."

People compare your style of play to Rafael Nadal's. How do you compare yourself to him? Mano, Canada

Rios: "We both play double-handed backhand and I think we are both pretty fast around the court. But we have also different styles of playing the game."

Greatest of all time: Sampras or Federer? Eileen, Scotland

Rios: "Federer by far. At the time when I was retiring from the ATP circuit he was only playing serve-and-volley. He didn't play that well from the baseline back then. Now he just won Wimbledon from the baseline and that shows that he is a really complete player."

Ilie Nastase was very critical of your behavior off the court during your career, and you didn't have a very good relationship with the media. Why did you behave the way you did? Did the world have the wrong impression of you? Jonathan, England

Rios: "I don't care what Nastase said. I don't even know him and I couldn't care less about what he said. I have good and bad relations with different people like everyone. That's the way people are. I was never fake with anybody."

Hi, I've followed your career for many years, and went to my first seniors event in Portugal specifically to see you play. It was wonderful to see you back on court and you seemed to be enjoying yourself. I would like to know if you feel less pressure at the Senior events? Jena, Wales

Rios: "For sure there is less pressure and the atmosphere is more relaxed on the Merrill Lynch Tour of Champions. Life is more relaxed and we definitely try to put on a good show for the crowd. But I think everyone still wants to win. I didn't really know how to approach this in the beginning but I realized when everyone steps on court they try to win. It's been a great time and nice experience and I will try to enjoy it as much as I can."

Is there any way you could ever play any ATP main tour event? Jena, Wales

Rios: "I don't think it's very likely that I will return to the ATP circuit. To have an ATP ranking you have to play all year and I'm not fit enough for that so I don't think I will make it."

Do you still have to carry out special exercises to take care of your back problem? Jena, Wales

Rios: "I'm sick of doing the exercises so I'm not doing them anymore. During a couple of years I was doing a lot of exercises getting my back fit but I'm done with that."

What kept you from winning a Grand Slam? David Eisenbud, USA

Rios: "I think it was pretty tough to focus for two weeks. It was too long a tournament and I also think I maybe had a little bit of bad luck. There were better players than me back then as well."

What do you think of the young guns at the moment-Berdych, Monfils, Gasquet, and what do you think of Andy Murray? Shane Roche, UK

Rios: "I don't know the youngsters that much. I know them by name but I haven't been following the ATP circuit that closely lately. But from what I hear they are pretty good and hopefully more young guys will come up. I think Federer is the best player though and he is going to be the best player ever and hopefully he will. I saw Murray play Massu at Wimbledon but I don't know him that much. Was I impressed by his game? No."

David Law (ATP Communications Manager): "I have worked with Marcelo since 1998, first in my capacity as an ATP Communications Manager, and now on the ATP Champions Tour. I believe that Marcelo is an innately shy person - he doesn't like a lot of fuss being made around him, and I don't think he has ever understood why people might be interested in talking to him when he has played badly and lost. Those are the main reasons why I think he has sometimes come across as difficult during his career. I have had instances where he has looked at me as if I'm crazy for asking him to go to press conferences. And while it wasn't much fun at the time, I understand that a.) Players are not happy after they lose and the last thing they want to do is talk about it. And b.) In Marcelo's case he just doesn't understand the point of talking when he has lost. Had this been explained to him very early on, perhaps his demeanor would have been different."

"Having said all that, even though we had the occasional run-in, he is not a bad guy really. Spoiled, yes, but I quite like the fact that he tells you what he is thinking, no matter how uncensored or un-PR that may be. It can sometimes upset and offend people. But if you actually listen to the words, he is just telling you what he thinks. I once asked him 'Marcelo, why can't you be a little bit nicer to everyone?' He told me 'Because I don't want to be fake. If you are nice to everyone the same no matter what the situation, it's not real, it's fake.' To some extent I can understand and agree with that."

"I think the other thing that people don't always allow for are the crippling injuries he has suffered. He looks in great shape right now - bulging muscles and not an ounce of fat, but his back really inhibits him, and he has had a lot of injuries. That's why he stopped playing and why he doesn't come back to the ATP Tour."

"As you saw in his (late 2009) video interview though, he has kids, and they seem to make him really happy. He doesn't socialize with the other players that much, although he gets on really well with guys like Fernando Meligeni, but as I said, I do think he is a shy person, and it sometimes makes him seem very unapproachable. McEnroe has some of that as well. He is a genuis though - some of the things I've seen him do with a tennis racquet seem to defy physics."

Marcelo Rios Interivew September 2009 Courtesy of ATP Champions Tour

Catherine Whitaker (ATP Senior Tour): Describe your life on the ATP Champions Tour?

Marcelo Rios: "Everybody wants to win. We all obviously want to have fun. It's totally different from playing professional. I did my job already professional and this is like my second chance too play tennis - but enjoy it (this time)."

Catherine Whitaker: How do you fit it around your family life, you have another child now.

Marcelo Rios: "Well it's tough. It's tough because it's tough to travel with kids. It's tough coming from Chile (because) it's pretty far. It's good because I knew today I'm gonna have another baby (third)."

Catherine Whitaker: Oh, congratulations!

Marcelo Rios: "Yeeeaah! So it's pretty nice."

Catherine Whitaker: What are you doing these days away from the tennis court?

Marcelo Rios: "I work with my dad. I have a construction company, we're doing some subway parking lots. We do building, we have some concessions for airports. We work around with things with construction."

[Suddenly a daredevil airplane flies loudly overhead, diverting the attention from Rios who looks up curiously.]

Marcelo Rios: "What was that?!"

Catherine Whitaker: Which players have you played that are on the Senior Tour that you did not get to play on the regular circuit?

Marcelo Rios: "Muster used to play with me. But Leconte - he was from other time. It's pretty fun to play with guys who never played with me (before). Because they're older, it's very fun to come up with guys that you didn't have chance to play. Leconte, McEnroe, Wilander, Borg, Vilas - I did not play."

[Plane flies back over again, this time closer. Rios again is fascinated by it.]

Marcelo Rios: "That was close!"

Catherine Whitaker: Would you like to do that, fly a daredevil plane like that?

Marcelo Rios: "I'd love it! YEAH!"

[Interview ends but a producer in background comments aloud to a smiling and pleasant Rios that it "was the best interview you ever did."]

Three Rios fans comment on this interview:

"I don't think he has changed like literally. I think when he was trying to make a career out of himself, he probably felt the pressure and hence why he came across as an asshole. But now that he can just relax, I think that competitive flair he had, has slowed down a bit, allowing him to just be more happy."

• • •

"My favorite player of all time. Amazing talent. He really does seem more relaxed and positive now, wow. His English has also improved a lot."

• • •

Jena (Tennis Fan): "I did see that interview clip from Portugal - and I was actually at the food court watching the same plane. Unfortunately, Marcelo played the worst tennis I've ever seen any player play at that Senior's event! He was dreadful, and had clearly not picked up a racquet for months! It was such a shame. He does have a playful side, which I've seen at his practice sessions. He rarely shows that on court. The other two biographies, Well, the first, Marcelo cooperated with to start, and then his first marriage to Giuliana hit a bad patch, with some of the Chilean press blaming the book. Apparently, she didn't like his past girlfriends being talked about, so Marcelo withdrew his support for it. It is a good book, in that his early life is very detailed and you see how supportive his family were. It made a refreshing change to read about tennis parents who actually tried to stop their child playing tennis! It seems Marcelo wasn't doing well in school, and his parents used his love of tennis as a reward to do better at school - they never dreamt he would be able to make a living from playing the tennis Tour. The book also gives an insight to the clash with the Chilean Tennis Federation which led to him getting a mauling in the Chilean press, which may have shaped his adversarial attitude to the media. The other bio was written by a former Chilean journalist who accompanied Marcelo on the tour in his junior days. It has some great anecdotes, but also contains the journalists views on other players a bit too forcefully. He really likes Becker and really dislikes Muster, and he's not objective in discussing them."

Marat Safin on Marcelo Rios in 2005

Question: How do you treat the opinion that your injuries are a result of your tennis routine violations?

Marat Safin: "I am already 25 and not 18 when I could have gone out to play after a party and treated tennis differently. Knowing what kind of money I earn people tend to think that I party every night and don't give a damn about tennis. This point of view is not only stupid but it is also an insult to me. It is very unpleasant to communicate with people who think like that. It means that this person is 'spitting in my face' thinking that I am just lucky because I have the talent. How many of these same talents weren't able to remain in professional tennis! Take Marcelo Rios for example. When he worked - he was the first (#1), then he stopped taking the business seriously and had to leave. And if I treated tennis in the same manner I would not be around."

Chapter 4
The Many Faces Of The Diamond

"There is no joy but calm." –Tennyson

Roger Federer hasn't forgotten the inspiring effect Rios has had on his career as he answered this media question at the 2010 Australian Open:

Question: As a fan, who is your idol apart from Roger Federer?

Roger Federer: "No, I think idols for me were the ones sort of reaching for the stars I thought were untouchable, such as Boris Becker, Stefan Edberg, Pete Sampras. You know that. I liked also Marcelo Rios' game as well when I was coming along. I was lucky enough to play him a few times as well."

Joshua T. Rey (Former Ballboy): "I ballboyed a few of his matches in Key Biscayne. I remember watching him wipe the floor with Taylor Dent in 2003. In a clash of styles, Rios crushed the serve and volleyer (6-1 6-1). It appeared no matter what Dent did with his serves and approaches, Rios had an angle and an answer.

As a ballboy, I thoroughly enjoyed watching him play because he could hit shots that other players only dreamed of. I was also on court when he whacked Alex Corretja 6-2 6-2 in 2002. Rios had the ability to make the best players look bad. But he could also make mediocre players appear great when he wasn't motivated."

. . .

I approached Larry Stefanki at the 2010 U.S. Open, at the player's locker room area, to discuss Rios. He was on his way somewhere with Andy Roddick, and gave me an annoyed look upon hearing my request, as if the bitterness of being fired by Rios still bothered him, some 13 years later. "I'm not sure if I want to talk about Rios," Stefanki replied with hardly a smile, and a hint of aggravation.

A journalist colleague gave me Stefanki's e-mail and phone number, so I attempted to contact him numerous times after the tournament but Stefanki would not respond.

In March of 2011, Chile hosted the U.S. in a Davis Cup tie and during the telecast on The Tennis Channel, and Stefanki made an appearance as a phone call-in commentator for about ten minutes. It seemed like an excellent possibility that Stefanki might make some kind of statements or comments about coaching Rios but, surprisingly, Stefanki did not. He spoke about coaching Yevgeny Kafelnikov, John McEnroe, Fernando Gonzalez and Roddick but did not say a single word about or even mention the name of Rios.

"You have to take the element of fitness out of the equation. Be fitter than the other guy no matter what. All the guys I worked with, worked very hard," said Stefanki to Tennis Channel commentators Justin Gimelstob and Sam Gore. "They had that element with fundamentals and a lot of talent. I think all of my guys made big improvements on fitness, not just with footwork and taking the ball on the rise. But it's a big puzzle. There's a lot of factors in the equation."

A month later I was in Key Biscayne for the 2011 Sony Ericsson Open and approached Stefanki as he departed the court after an early afternoon practice session between Roddick and Jurgen Melzer. I tried one last time to persuade Stefanki to talk about Rios. Once again, it was fruitless. "I'm not interested in talking about him," he said.

• • •

Brett Connors (The Tennis Channel): "I don't know Marcelo that much, I met him once in Dallas Airport waiting for a flight to Cancun over ten years ago. I think it was when Larry Stefanki was coaching him. He was okay. Seemed to be a little cocky, but then again, what tennis player isn't? One thing that stuck out was how much attention he was paying to the way he looked, constantly playing with his hair and checking himself out to make sure nothing was out of place. I feel this also explains why he underperformed as a player and never lived up to his potential. Yes, he was #1 but I felt he had the game to win at least one major."

Dan Markowitz (Journalist): "I did a cover story on Agassi for New York magazine in 1995. In New Haven or Cincinnati I asked Marcelo Rios, Can you tell me something about Agassi? What do you think of Agassi? And he said, I won't talk about anybody but myself."

Stephen Wake (Photographer): "He won the Monte Carlo Open years and years ago. He wouldn't pose with the winner's trophy for the photographers. He held the trophy up for about one or two seconds. Then he put it down and stormed off the court. Photographers got one frame - if they were lucky. The tournament director was trying to get him to come back. He just blanked the guy, he didn't want to hold the cup."

David Mercer (Eurosport and BBC Sport TV Commentator): "I got the impression that Marcelo Rios had a very low opinion of the media and he was neither very cooperative or forthcoming at press conferences or in interviews. In terms of interaction, I remember the tournament in Amsterdam in 1995 when he won singles and doubles. I was commentating on the tournament for Eurosport and we were staying in the same hotel as the players. By sheer coincidence I shared a car between the hotel and the courts with Marcelo on three successive mornings. On the first two I tried to make polite conversation with him. His responses were little more than grunts. On the third day I did not bother. I admired his talent as a tennis player. I did not admire him as a man."

Ezio Prapotnich (Journalist): "This guy is like a diamond with many faces, and all of them are a part of him."

Franco Davin (Coach and Former ATP Player): "He was one of the players I would buy a ticket to see the matches. I play with him, I win and lost I think. But I win for sure [laughs]. Won in Palermo and lost in Davis Cup. I remember the match when he play in Miami with Agassi. I like a lot when Rios play. I pay for the ticket."

Jimmy Connors (Hall of Fame ATP Player): "I didn't really see many of his matches."

Nenad Zimonjic (ATP Player): "He was one of my first big matches, former #1 in Doha. After losing the first set, I won the second, ended up losing in three. It was a great experience, one of my best matches. He ended up winning the tournament. Very talented, plays very easy, returns well. And me, a player who likes to attack, play serve and volley, it was a tough opponent. He was one of the playes that I enjoy watching as well."

Sven Groeneveld (Coach): "When he was coming up in the time Peter Lundgren was working with him, he had such an ability to open the court, his ability to maneuver the ball. It's a shame he stopped early because I think he would have done well, I think he would have won a Slam eventually. He was unliked in the locker room, no one really liked him. I felt that he was very young when he came out and it was kind of his way to protect himself. To play his terms. I'm sure, looking back, he would agree with that and his behavior was unacceptable. He's playing some of the Senior events. I don't know if he's changed or not. He maintained a certain level of distance from the other players. And the locker room is where the players stay together and they bond a little bit. But he was always a bit of an outsider. I think the first time I saw him was at the U.S. Open. I would say '94. I remember when he came up I was just amazed, he was just a short guy, not very strong. He got thick legs after a while when he built up, but his ability was just astounding, to maneuver the ball so easily. Besides that, it's been a little bit of a mystery from the outside. I think he was a magnificent player with a lot of flair in a way. But I think it's great that you're writing a book about him."

Enrique Cano (Journalist): "Rios was sitting inside the car with his girlfriend in Miami, a blond model from Chile. A little boy asked him to sign his paper. And he signed the paper. And throws through the window the pen and the paper, 'Thank you.' And another time in Miami in '98, a journalist (Roberto Nappo of BBC Latin America) went to ask him three questions because the journalist arranged with ATP the three questions after the press conference. And Marcelo Rios disliked to do this and shouted with the ATP contact, 'Why? Why? Do I have to talk with the journalist? I made a press conference.' So we have to answer three questions. Rios says, 'Okay, I will do.' So the journalist asked him. He looks to the journalist and says, 'Yes.' The second question the answer was, 'No.' The third question the answer was, 'Yes. Thank you.'"

Michael Sell (ATP Player): "I'm sitting in the U.S. Open junior hospitality room. And just before the meeting - I was sitting with Eric Taino and Cecil Mamiit - just sitting around. And Eric Taino leans over and says, That guy over there with the hair pulled back and the pony tail is your future #1 in the world player. He was leaning back in his chair, nice and relaxed. Eric knew right there and then."

Anonymous: "You remember Bob Hewitt? He got knocked out by Roger Taylor in the locker room. I can't remember who it was but there was a confrontation with Rios almost similar to Roger Taylor and Bob Hewitt. That's all I'm gonna say."

Cedric Pioline (ATP Player): "He was a very, very good, talented player. I played a few times against him and it was a tough opponent. And off-court he was not really the kind of person joking around, talking to everybody. I don't know if he was a nice guy or not because I never really talked to him. Because he was not open to us or not open to us to talk to him. I think he was really shy. He was really quick on the court, he was seeing the game really well, taking the ball early. Make you run. Sometimes I think I'm playing well and he's hitting winners. He was really a top player. Probably deserves to win a Slam. But he didn't, so maybe there was something wrong with him."

Lou Noritz (Tennis Fan): "Marcelo Rios is the biggest jerk in the whole sport. In one incident with me in Miami, we were walking from the lounge down the stairway in March of 2003, he intentionally bumped me. And the reason, in my estimation, was because I supported the opposition in a recent match in Indian Wells. I did report this to Gayle Bradshaw who was supervisor at the time. Marcelo Rios is absolutely ridiculous as a person."

Gabriel Matteazzi (Coach and Journalist from Argentina): "At the tournament in Buenos Aires. I saw a girl, about 12-years-old run up to Rios on the practice court. She asked for the autograph. Rios took the paper and pen and was about to sign. Then suddenly he threw it on the ground. He said, No. The girl started to cry and she said to Rios: 'I hope you break both your legs and never play again.' Rios said, 'Motherfucker' in Spanish. Then he said, 'Don't cry. What are you crying for? Be tough.' I don't know why Rios would do that. Why do that? Why not just give her the autograph? He could be so illogical."

"Rios is Rios. Very complicated. Very hard to figure out a guy like that. He is his own person. His way of seeing the world - he's not willing to change. He has his own ideas. Are they right? Well, he will justify them [smiles]. The main thing about Rios is that you never knew what was going to happen. And not just in life - his game was like that. You never knew. He could he happy the next minute, the could be upset the next minute. And he could play - you never knew. You never knew. He did things that were not following the normal, logical. He didn't follow people's logic."

"You have a normal scheme of human relationships and conversations in tennis and I think it's all the same what he did. It was all the same. What he did on the court and outside the court. He didn't follow a logical process. He followed his instinct and whatever, I don't know. Maybe it was emotional, maybe it was he was playing by his own tune. It didn't matter what anybody else was saying or doing, he had his own reasons, he would go full-speed ahead with what he wanted to do. And sometimes it was genius, sometimes it was crazy, and you never knew. And I can tell you, to me, he was all of that. He can be a genius - he is a genius - and sometimes he tried something a little too wild and he looked silly. Like in a match, he would quit a match. And he wouldn't explain to anybody watching why he did it. Sounds like an artist, but this is a competitive sport."

"I didn't know him too much. I saw him playing. To me he was a talented guy, a genius. Inconsistent but genius. And I thought he was going to mature. And I thought: This guy's gonna be amazing, because everybody matures. People have silly ideas. But then you realize it was wrong and then you mature. I'm not saying he didn't mature. I think he matured in his own way. But it was not good in a way to make his career more productive. You have to think of how to progressively keep getting better. And in his case, I don't know if he was better, but not to the world, to himself maybe, I don't know, I won't judge that. I'm not judging but I'm saying, as a player, he didn't really better himself. He never did really. Can I say that's wrong? I don't know."

"I've been with him on the court with his coach Luis Lobo. I heard him talking and the main thing is Lobo had to be very patient. Very patient. Lobo is a very good guy who is very understanding of people. A person who doesn't just listen but helps you a lot. But there's only so much you can do. There's a saying: You can take the horse to the river - but you can't make the horse drink. As a coach, it could be a rollercoaster with Marcelo, with so many unexpected turns that it's ridiculous. He could come one day and say, 'I don't want to play.' Just like that. Like with (Juan Martin) Del Potro - he's thinking long term, let's make plans, long-term approach. That's Del Potro. You're secure. With Marcelo, it could be a long trip - or you could crash into the wall in the next second. He could crash you. The wall could be behind you and he would turn around and crash you against the wall, you and him. A very interesting personality."

Horacio Morales (Chilean Tennis Fan): "I don't know where to start these words. I think I should mention that I clearly recall the moment I first found your original Rios article back in 2008 on www.TheBiofile.com after a Google search. Every two years roughly, I don't know why, I am back in my obsession with Chino Rios. At the time, I found the article was so moving because it somehow exposed why tennis can be seen as an art form, where there is something undecipherable about some of their characters. It's that extra bit that we followers with lack of knowledge sometimes can't see but somehow can feel. David Foster Wallace took this further when writing about Roger Federer."

"For some Chileans like me, El Chino is a hero of a generation. Growing up alongside his takeover of the

ATP Tour. We were just kids when he faced Sampras in Roland Garros 1994... teenagers when he struggled but finally overcame Muster, Ferreira, and all to become a Top 10 in 1996. The last year of high school, we were feeling at the top of the world in '98 at the same time Rios became world #1. And so on until his retirement in 2004. And now, of course, I feel deep nostalgia."

Karel Novacek (ATP Player): "I played him myself (d. Rios at 1994 Hilversum SF 3-6 6-3 6-4). He was one of the players - as a tennis player you don't go out much to watch the other players, because for reasons, our egos and what have you. He was one of them I went out to watch him play. He was so much fun to see him play. Even with his outbursts and what have you, it was fun to watch him. That's pretty much what I want to say because at the time he was one of the players that was needed by the ATP - because you need a player like him all the time. He was entertaining, he was unbelievable talent and all his other things which were negative probably for you guys from media. He was fun to watch. You need a character like him in tennis. I really liked him, the way he played. Cocky, but at the same time I understand where the cockiness came from - because he was so damn talented. And maybe he was misunderstood by some. I don't know him much. I'm limited, we said hi here and there, few exchanges, but he was private. He didn't let anybody close to him. But he was one of the players I would come and sit and watch. For different reasons. He was #1 in the world, right? He never won a Grand Slam. But he was giving something which you would say, If I would have his backhand - many people would take his strokes, put them in their game and be #1 in the world. You know what I'm saying? It was either a coincidence why he didn't win a Grand Slam but he was # 1 in the world, so he achieved that."

Nicolas Escude (ATP Player): "I play him in junior in the French Open and here in New York, in Armstrong and beat him. He was strange. Sometimes he say hello, sometimes nothing. Strange man. I remember in junior I beat him, I play against him and always on the changeover he bust his racquet into the chair. I don't know why. I don't know why."

Alese Pechter (Photographer): "I photographed him many times in Miami and also at Delray Beach. Fantastic tennis player. He really got the crowd to go with him. When he walked into the stadium in Key Biscayne, everybody was cheering and screaming. And they had the banners and the flags and everybody just cheered him on when he got a point. The only other player I can think of who could excite the crowd like Rios was probably Jimmy Connors. When Rios played here he really drummed up the crowd. It was great. Always exciting. He was one of my favorites at the time. He was one of the favorites of the media and photographers who went out to photograph. He always brought life to the court."

Rodrigo Hernandez (Jefe de Deportes Radio ADN Chile): "My first memory is playing against Rios. I was 19. At a tournament. Rios was 14. He won. It was a tough match but he won 7-6 in the third. And the next year he won his first professional tournament Satellite in my country. At 15-years-old. With those points he was 500 in the world. I remember that. He was a very talented player. He play everything very easily. I was going to the university, I was practicing for many years, playing tournaments in my country. I was a good player, he was a child. I was taller than him. I have stronger hits than him. But obviously he has more talent than me. I didn't know about him before the match. I played many matches, he was one more match."

"After the time of the match I went to university to study to be a journalist. I take the memory. I can remember it as something important maybe. I remember that he was very serious. He don't like the jokes. At that age I know I can't be a professional player. I really like it but after a while you know that you can't be a good player. He was very serious on the court. Just focusing on the tennis and trying to win. He tried to win everything, all the balls. When he lost the point he was very angry. And he looks at his mother. At that time she was his company, outside the court."

"I ask him about the match eight years later and he says that he doesn't remember the match. But we have a very good relationship at the beginning. After - he was very angry with me. I really don't know why he was upset. I tried to talk to him to ask what's the problem with me. And one year after the break in communication, he then tell me, 'No, it's okay. Everything okay.' He begin to talk to me and give me interviews again. It was one year we did not talk and I never know why he was upset. It was difficult for me, for my professional work because that time we didn't talk was in his best moments on the ATP Tour. And I was the only one Chilean journalist following him in the world, in many tournaments I remember."

"It was incredible because, in my country, it was difficult to understand why in the press conference I sent my boss Rios talking in English and I remember that I must do the translation. And my boss and all the people ask me, 'Why don't you do the interview in Spanish?' And I have to explain that he's upset with me and he won't answer. That was for one year. When he became #1 in Miami in March 1998 we had regular relations. But a couple of months after he begins with this attitude."

Question: You have no idea why?

Hernandez: "Never, never. I ask his trainer Manuel Astorga, he was very close friends with me and he never understood why Rios take that position. And me - I always did more technical reports - because I play when I was young. I never take care about his private life. I never was very critical about his behavior. Sometimes you have to describe what happened but I never was the most hard critic about him, like many other journalists in my country. I never had an explanation from him. And then we recovered the relations one year after. And he's been cooperative ever since."

Question: Why do you think Rios was the way he was?

Hernandez: "Probably shy. Probably the example of his father because he's a very serious person. The father is hard to take a conversation with him. I remember the time when he had the relation with the directors with the Chilean federation. Once, the people told me it was difficult relations with Mr. Rios. He was very difficult, very serious. And probably Marcelo get the same personality that the father has. Some people said that when the father begin to work when he was young, he was in the middle class, social-economic. And when he have a lot of money, he changed. Some people said that but I'm not sure. But it could be one factor."

"I think that maybe if Rios was not like he was, I mean, a hard personality, a guy with few friends, maybe he probably never goes up in tennis. He would not have been as successful. It's hard to describe. It's a factor that the family has to explain. When he was traveling for the Tour, normally he was with his father and his mother. They are okay. I remember when Marcelo was very young, the father told everybody in the Tour, the #1 rule is that you don't have friends. No friends was the most important rule for him. And he applied that rule in all life maybe. Outside the court also. At that time he had like a challenge with his father. Because the father, I remember, told me that Marcelo must go inside the top 100 or he go to the university to study. The father defined very, very high goals for Marcelo. And Marcelo gave a good response on the court. Maybe that pressure makes that he will be a special personality."

Question: Now how is Marcelo?

Hernandez: "There are some problems with the kind of media that follows actresses, celebrities and that kind. He got married for third time. And he is more quiet now. He will be father by third time but second time with same girl. And he was studying business in order to manage his money. Because the father is an engineer, oversees all the business of Marcelo. But now Marcelo has a lot of free time and he's trying to be involved about his money. And also he plays the Senior Tour. And in September 2009 he's assistant coach for Chilean Davis Cup team, because we're gonna play against Austria. He's going to be a sparring assistant coach because he plays with the left and we need good sparring with the left (to play against Jurgen Melzer, Stefan Koubek and Julian Knowle). In order to train with Massu and Capdeville and other players."

"Marcelo keeps a low profile now. Because he had bad moments with paparazzi and the rose press. In the free time he plays golf and a couple of exhibitions in my country. He play against Sampras and Agassi, he won both. Sometimes he's also a TV commenator for the ATP event which is moving to Santiago."

"I think the injuries stopped his career. Agassi and Sampras played 18-20 tournaments a year, no more. The top players take a lot of care about their bodies and take this important period to relax. Rios played about 32 tournaments a year and many exhibitions in my country. He plays against Moya, Muster, Chang, Kafelnikov. I remember that he plays three or four exhibitions because he receive a lot of money -

$100,000 or $150,000 for each match. And also Davis Cup. He never gives the necessary relaxing that his body need. And in two years of overplay, his body did an explosion. He started to drink more when he suffered the more injuries. It was a response to the injuries."

Anonymous: "I remember hearing people say after he made the final in Australia that he took half his check for making the final and lost all of it in the casino."

Anonymous: "I remember one time I was in an elevator with Rios. And there was an old lady. And she asked him for an autograph. And he ignored her. He wouldn't even look at her. There was no reason to do that."

Brad Gilbert (Coach and Former ATP Player): "One of the greatest matches I ever saw anybody play against Andre was in the final of the '98 Key Biscayne. Andre played Rios and I was thinking Andre was gonna be pretty straight-forward, just take care of business. And this guy hit angles and he hit shots and he served and played - like, I thought he was destined to win at least five majors the way he was playing. A lot of talent. Andre walked off the court and he said to me, 'Geez, I thought I played okay.' And he lost - it was a best of five final - and he lost 5-4-3. I mean, he was never in it. It was an incredible match by Rios. (Was Andre sharp then?) He was coming back from his '97 season. He was playing well, he got to the final of Key Biscayne. He plays well there. But that was an amazing match by Rios."

Richard Pagliaro (Journalist): "I was at that Rios-Agassi final match in Miami and the one a few years later when Rios retired after the second set. In both cases, Agassi had those eyes as wide as silver dollars, almost like he was trying extra hard to see the ball because it was coming at so many different angles. I have seldom seen the A-Train wrong-footed as much as he was in that match and Rios had such loose, easy, fluid swings in those matches. Like he wasn't even trying to put extra pace on the ball but was able to do it. He was breaking out the swinging volleys big time then too. Rios was the very first player I recall ever doing that leaping two-handed backhand where he would jump to catch the ball at the peak of its height and then drive it down into the court while in mid-air. It was like seeing a guy leap off a mini-trampoline and smack the star right off the top of a Christmas tree. I remember Safin started doing that after Rios did and the funny thing was Rios was listed at like 5-foot-9 and Safin was 6-foot-4, so he could obviously handle the high ball much better without leaping anyway. I think Safin thought it looked cool. Safin was clearly a big Rios fan based on his answer at the U.S. Open press confernece about how many Slams Rios could have won. He said Rios had the talent to win ten Slams."

Paul Capdeville (ATP Tennis Player): "I never play with him and I never train with him. He don't like to play with Chileans. (Why not?) Marcelo Rios [laughs]."

Pia Gutierrez (Chilean Tennis Fan): "Un orgullo Chileno. Thank you Marcelo Rios for the crazy days spent in the streets of Chile waving our flags and chanting your name. I still remember the day you became #1. I was 10-years-old and my dad and brothers got in our car and honked our horn till late hours of the night only because of Marcelo Rios. People running and driving their cars like crazy people! How I miss celebrating in my native land. I watch tennis often and not one player has been able to transmit so much emotions on the court like you did. Grande Rios! Deportista del Bicentenario!"

Caroline Merino (Tennis Fan): "I have watched tennis on TV for many years but have never enjoyed watching anybody as much as Marcelo Rios. He was such a beautiful player. I know many things have been said about him but I always felt that Western journalists were unfair to him. If he had been interviewed in Spanish then maybe they would have understood him better."

Anita Klaussen (Journalist): "He was a disgusting person. It was horrible how he treated Bud (husband, Collins). People told me he would break the kids' pens when they asked for an autograph. Or sign his name over other player's names. He was just terrible. One time at a press conference at the Estoril, Portugal tournament, Rios was on the podium being asked a question. And Bud asked him a question. And he just said to the ATP rep, maybe it was Greg Sharko, he said, 'I won't answer questions from that man.' And everybody in the audience, all the other press corps just gasped at that anybody would be so rude to Bud

Collins, of all things. And 36 papers wrote about it the next day, about how rude Marcelo Rios had been to Bud Collins. (Why did Rios do that?) Bud had made a comment to Rios' ex-girlfriend who was his girlfriend at the time and then became his ex-girlfriend. She was a TV reporter and had interviewed Bud. Bud had said something like Rios should pay more attention to his career, he has so much talent, but he's wasting it. I don't know how he phrased it. But that was the message, so, anyway, he didn't like that."

Jennifer Capriati after hearing Rios slammed women's tennis and it's lack of depth, calling it a joke: "Stupidity really deserves no answer back."

Todd Martin (ATP Player): "I played him twice. I beat him twice. I had a good way against him. I was coached well to play against him. By Jose Higueras. Jose helped me a lot against him. But with Marcelo, in my opinion, I think it's really sad. I mean, he's a sad story and I hope eventually there's some peace in his life that allows him to be cordial and interactive. We never got to see that. We only got to see the talent. We never got to see what else is possibly inside."

Russ Adams (Photographer): "Very photogenic as far as action shots. On his body, the way he hit the ball. Some of his best action was before the ball arrived, because he'd wait to the last second to come around and hit it. He was very quick to the ball."

Mary Carillo (TV Commentator): "I never really had any interaction with him. I didn't always like the way he competed. But I thought he was a magnificent talent really. In the McEnroe lefty artisan style."

Chris Chaffee (Tennis Fan): "I remember a fan at the U.S. Open told me he tried to have Rios sign a tennis card for him and he took it and drew a giant X with the Sharpie over the card and gave it back."

Chapter 5
The Magician

"The object of the superior man is truth."
-Confucius

One night, on the media bus ride back to New York City after a night session at the 2009 U.S. Open I plop down on my seat. It's late. But suddenly I have new energy. Sitting to my immediate right is the Hall of Famer Todd Woodbridge. After some tennis conversation I decide to ask if he has any memories of Rios. The affable and friendly Australian seems a bit surprised that I'm doing this book but he becomes interested and recalls his unique experiences involving Rios...

Todd Woodbridge (ATP Player): "What prevented him from winning a major - week in and week out, he wasn't willing to put in the work. He'd tank a tournament here and there. And you'd never see the guys like a Federer or a Hewitt - they never behaved that way. If they lose, they lose trying. So there were some weeks, he'd turn up and he didn't want to play. And that made it hard for him, I think, to go that last, little percentage - that made a Grand Slam difference. But probably one of the most smooth ball strikers of the last 15-20 years. He could play looking like he wasn't hitting the ball very hard but it came off the racquet with interest. He had a great understanding of the different angles because of being left-handed, he could create and move you around to different places that you don't normally see right-handed players do. I think it was a bit of a shame. I don't think he achieved as much as he could have out of the game."

"We played, I was 2-1 up I think. One of those times we played was in the semis of Toronto ('96). And I won like 4 and 0 (actually 6-0 6-3). And I thought that was one day he decided not to turn up. Maybe I had a game he didn't like playing. I had a slice backhand that I used effectively, that not a lot of people would hit the ball like. Put him in places of the court he didn't like. Talent-wise, he was the better player. So he should have been able to handle me."

"I felt you could beat Rios by outhustling him, keeping him off balance, mixing up your angles and speeds."

Francesco Ricci Bitti (ITF President): "Rios was, in my opinion, one of the most talented players I've ever seen. He could have done more. But his character was not exactly helpful but he was a great player. I gave a trophy in Rome when he won the Italian Open - he was not as easy guy. He has his own opinion, his own character. But he was not bad I felt. I gave two trophies, in fact, to Marcelo Rios. One in New York - the

U.S. Open junior championship. I was chairman of the junior committee of International Tennis Federation. The second time was at Italian Open. (Remember his reactions?) Surely, the first time he was very shy. It was not great communication. He was very shy. The second time in Rome he was already a big star, so."

Toni Nadal (Coach): "His game was spectacular game. He played extremely good. (Was he an inspiration. model, as a lefty, in developing Rafael?) No. Inspiration for me was people who are very thoughtful and correct when they're on the court. Rios was a very good, talented player. But he is not my player, not my dream model player. Rios was very good. I spoke with all the people who play with him, they say he has a very good talent. But truth, I like other kind of players. (Like who?) Many. Like Federer. Like Borg. Like Santana. Many, many players."

Rene Stauffer (Journalist/Author): "He used to play in Gstaad and he was really a figure which made a lot impact in the nightlife then. I remember he was in the Palace Hotel which is very famous, and they had a nightclub which is called Gringo. And he used to enjoy his nights over there. I remember when I saw him play there he didn't seem like a real ambitious guy in the tournament. It was just - enjoying his days and doing whatever he wanted. So I know Rios had a huge talent, I always admired him, to see him play. But when you saw what he could have done and what he did, then you really get a feeling that there was a gap. And in small tournaments like Swiss Open in Gstaad you see it was very evident that he could maybe have gotten more out of his career if he was a little more ambitious or professional. Like everybody knew that Rios was a great player. It didn't matter where he was standing in the rankings."

"Rios played seven straight years in Gstaad - 1994-2000. He got to the semis once. In 1994 he got a little breakthrough in Gstaad when he went to the quarters. After that, he got his first sponsorship deal. In 1994 Rios said, 'Gstaad is a very beautiful tournament, a beautiful place, and has one of the best tournament directors on this Tour.' It was Jacques 'Kirby' Hermanjat, a legendary figure in Swiss tennis. Then Rios said, 'Gstaad is too high up in the mountains. That's why the balls are too quick for me. It's tough to control the balls and they should use slower balls. Then I would have more control.'"

Michael Chang (Hall of Fame ATP Player): "Why are you doing a book about Rios? ...Very talented, great player, as I'm sure all of the other players have told you. A great shotmaker. We had a lot of great matches including a five-setter at the U.S. Open. (Did you enjoy to play him?) I knew that every time I play against Marcelo, it's going to be a tough match. He takes the ball early. Then, being a lefty, on top of that, doesn't necessarily make it any easier. But I think I played him at the U.S. Open, played him at the Australian, a bunch of other times. I didn't get a chance to really play him on clay. I have a good record against him. Off the court, I don't know Marcelo that well. I don't know if a whole lot of guys really know him that well. He's pretty private, more on the quiet side. He was a little bit tough to get to know. But I don't have anything against him."

Question: What was your strategy against him which gave him trouble?

Chang: "I think his game just matched up well against mine. I know obviously he's very sound off the ground. The times that I played him I was at the peak of my career. And I wasn't afraid to play him or go toe-to-toe with him. So I think that in itself was helpful for me. Marcelo obviously has had a great career, reaching as high as #1 in the world. He accomplished a lot of great things on the court."

Question: What was difficult about playing him?

Chang: "Well, he's a shotmaker. He takes the ball very early. He's a shotmaker. Good cross court backhand. Good kind of hook forehand cross court. And he didn't come in that much but he could hit decent volleys and had a decent serve. I think for me, it's a matter of going out there and really staying tough in the point. More times than not it was good enough to enable me to come out on top."

Jose Higueras (Coach and Former ATP Player): "The best player I think that never won a Grand Slam. I think very talented. (What was your strategy for coaching Todd Martin to a successful record vs. Rios?) I worked with Todd Martin for a long time. Marcelo was a very good player, but the more you opened up the court, the more you run, normally. So he had a very good form, he could run. His passes weren't very, very good. Kind of weaker serve. I felt like you had to play him a lot - instead of just trying to make him run. The more you try to open up the court, the more he punishes you. Hit right down the middle quite a bit. Or sometimes if you open him up to one side, you keep him there - instead of making him go back and forth. His quickness and hitting the ball so early - that would get you in trouble. And his return of serve was very good."

Rios vs. Alberto Berasategui in Rome 1997: Match Study

Semifinal match. Rios is 28-10 on the year while the Spaniard is 22-11. Berasategui is 2-1 this year vs. lefties, beating Meligeni, Rios in Hamburg, while losing first match of season to Kenneth Carlsen.

Rios holds at 15, 1-0.

Eurosport commentary: "Berasategui doesn't seem to have settled into it yet." But he hits an inside out forehand winner to level the score 1-1. "These are the type of shots that might drive Rios to despair."

"Rios is not a great player of drop shots but it's something to keep in mind against Berasategui."

"That point illustrated what Larry Stefanki said before the match: Sometimes you have to go to your opponent's strength to open up the weakness. Rios went wide to the Berasategui forehand to get to his backhand."

"Berasategui's serve is not as strong as Courier's. Rios was able to break the American five times in all (in quarterfinal). After the match Courier had an interesting exchange at the press conference with an American journalist who asked, 'You used to win matches like that.' And Jim answered, 'You used to ask better questions than that.'"

"Strange few points here for Berasategui, under a great deal of pressure. Three errors. A break point for Rios."

"And there's the break. Early advantage to Rios, he leads 3-1."

"Lovely placement of the volley for the Chilean fans to savor."

"Marcelo Rios really is pushing on the accelerator pedal, 4-1 after 21 minutes of play."

"That's the shot that's making the difference at the moment. That two-hander, taking it early with the right hand over it, he's able to get the snappy crosscourt angle on it."

Rios makes a nice touch volley: "Beautiful instincts by Rios."

"Second ace for Rios, so far, just conceding four points on serve to this point, 5-2 Rios."

"Yep, nice combination of punches there for Alberto Berasategui including the clean winner, dragging Rios all over the place."

"Rios serving for it. Rios lost his serve serving for the match against Courier yesterday. Three set points. Terrific serving set for Rios. He has the set, 6-3 after just 31 minutes."

Second set:

Rios forehand long, he's broken. Berasategui takes a 3-1 lead.

"Very lackadaisical swing by Rios."

"Rios sparked back into life with that one. It's an absolute beauty of a shot."

Rios nets a low backhand volley. "This is good work by Berasategui, making Rios investigate those shoelaces again that he just tied up."

"Rios looking to the sky, just missed that one."

5-2 Berasategui. "Another one of those scorching backhands. Jim Courier said that's what he thought was the difference yesterday."

"Rios backhand down the line, that's the seventh love game of the match. 5-3."

"Mirror image of the first set. One break decides it, 6-3. One set all."

Third set:

Rios sits in chair and decides to change racquets. He pulls a new Yonex out of his blue Yonex bag and taps the strings a few times but doesn't like the tension and pulls out another.

Berasategui strikes first. "Big forehand does the damage, 1-love, Berasategui."

"Another love game, this time against the serve. 1-all."

"Ad Rios. Rios stands a bit wider on the first serve. He takes the 2-1 lead."

"A little clench of the fist for Rios, 3-1 Rios."

"A comedy of errors but it made for an exciting point. Four games in a row now for Rios, he leads 4-1."

"Byron Black and Alex O'Brien watching play, they're in the doubles semifinal."

"There's quite a bit of vigor now in Rios, the end is in sight."

"Rios has two points to lead 5-1 with his serve to come."

Rios connects on an inside out forehand winner. "Oh, that's simply too good. He looks to his coach, clenches his fist, as if to say, I've got him."

"5-1, Rios serving for a place in the final."

"Three match points for Marcelo Rios, who's run away with the final set after dropping the opening serve of it."

"That's it. The winner in Monte Carlo could be on track for another Super Nine title. He'll be a favorite at Roland Garros. He's got the talent to do it. But to win seven matches is a lot to ask."

Rios wins 6-3, 3-6, 6-1

Rios interview after the match with Heinz Gunthardt. He seemed bored having to answer routine questions but somehow got through it, even if he only offered minimal, basic responses:

Question: Another three sets, comeback win, you had an epic the day before (6-3 3-6 7-6 vs. Courier in quarterfinal). How did you feel today, physically?

Rios: "Well, yesterday I played Jim, of course I knew it was going to be a tough match, he's a great player, even if he doesn't have a good ranking, he's always tough. I think we played some good points, was one of those matches you can win and have a break. I think I played really good."

Question: It's almost like you played a similar player two days in a row, two guys that are almost quicker going backwards than forward, wanting to hit the forehand all the time. Was it almost the same thing, playing somebody that plays similar today?

Rios: "Yeah, both have good forehands, very big forehands, every time I hit like cross to the backhand or most of the time, win the point. It's tough to play a guy like that, really quick and they always think for it."

Question: Yesterday it seemed like you had all these rallies where Jim was going around and hitting to your forehand and you kept hitting crosscourt, crosscourt, crosscourt. And we watched the replay, geez, Jim is so far over that down the line is way open. Yet you never went for the down the line. Today you hit it much more often. Was that something you were thinking about?

Rios: "Yeah, I was thinking I lost last week with Berasategui in Hamburg. I was thinking about serving more, going more to his backhand and also play more down the line."

Question: It seems like in the third set you started to slow it down, hit a lot of those soft serves wide, he kept on missing that return.

Rios: "Well I was not making a lot of first serves, I served good first set, but he broke me first game of the third set, then I tried to go more for his backhand."

Question: You had some terrific rallies at the end, you guys were running all over the place. Now, the Spaniards practice a lot, Corretja, for example, said he practiced for up to six hours a day. How much do you practice?

Rios: "Well, I've been doing more physical, play tennis, practicing two hours a day. But I know the Spanish guys practice a lot, that's why they're tough to beat and they're really fit and they play a lot of balls."

Question: A lot of people feel sometimes that you don't show so many emotions. Yesterday after the match you raised your hand and it was like, Wow, it was huge. I've never seen you do that after a match. And it wasn't the finals or anything. What happened out there?

Rios: "Playing with Jim, I knew it was going to be tough and if I win it was going to be a great win. So I feel it in the, 7-6 in the third, you always feel the emotion."

Alex Corretja (ATP Player): "Very talented. Very good player. Probably the best player to never win a Grand Slam. Very inspiring. Nice forehand. Very nice return. And very nice backhand cross court. (How was Rios inspiring?) He was a very inspiring guy, he could make you improve a lot. (Enjoy to play him?) He was tough but yeah, I did enjoy to play against him."

Art Seitz (Photographer): "Acrobatic player. He had one signature move. After he won, he did a cartwheel."

Tommy Robredo (ATP Player): "It definitely was great to see him play. I think he was a very talented player, no? He was a charismatic guy. He was a different guy with a lot of talent on the court. Was loved and hated and I think that's great for the show. I remember beating him one time. But I remember playing him a couple of times. I'm not good on remembering head-to-head. But he was tough to play because he was world #1 and he was a great player, always playing on the line and hitting the ball everywhere. If you wanted to beat him you had to run, run, run all the time. So but anyway, it was fun to watch him play. If you play a guy that is talented like him, you enjoy the match."

Rafael Nadal (ATP Player): "Sorry, but I wasn't on the Tour when he was on the Tour. If I say something about Rios, I gonna say some lies. Because I didn't remember him or his playing style. So is better not say anything."

Greg Rusedski (ATP Player and TV Commentator): "I think Marcelo is an interesting character. I think he was a little bit misunderstood on the Tour. And you didn't always get to know all the guys on the Tour. But his accomplishments are fantastic - getting to world #1, the first South American to do that. And I've seen him a few times on the Senior Tour. It's always interesting.

And you kind of describe him as a little bit of a rebel and that's his personality. I saw him in Portugal in 2009. We played a Champions Tour event. His wife just found out she got pregnant."

Question: Tough to play Rios?

Rusedski: "I think he will go down in history as the only #1 never to win a major. And if you look at him talent-wise - phenomenal talent. The guy could take the ball early on the rise. Wonderful hands. It's a shame he never got that Grand Slam. Because he was such a good player. He won Indian Wells and Miami back to back to get to world #1. And on his day he could beat anybody, whether it's Agassi, Sampras or any of the guys, on his best game."

Sandra Harwitt (Journalist): "The only thing I remember that much about Rios is he beat to his own drummer. I remember when he won Indian Wells - and I believe gained the #3 ranking with that win - he came in and said something like, I know I'm not well-liked in the locker room and by people in the game, but I don't care. People were horrified. But I recalled having a conversation just before that with people complaining everyone in the game had a bland personality and here was a guy showing a personality - good or bad - and then people were annoyed with his attitude."

Fernando Vicente (ATP Player): "He was one of the most talented players in tennis, amazing shots both sides. He was crazy a little bit outside off the court but he was a nice guy. He was a nice guy on inside he was very professional. I played him two times and lost both - in Lyon and also in Chile, it was a tough match. I remember the guy was too much talent, he move me around the court. I tried to fight. A lot of talent. He was #1 in the world, so nothing to do."

Anonymous: "I remember we had a photo shoot with Marcelo on the beach after he beat Agassi to become #1 in Miami. He was one-hour-and-a-half late. When he got there it became cloudy and a storm came, while before it was perfect sunshine. They said he was watching a replay of the match."

Charlie Passarell (Former Player): "He won my tournament at Indian Wells one year. He was probably the least happy person I ever saw win the tournament. Like it meant nothing to him. That's really the first thing that comes to mind when I think of Marcelo Rios."

Michael Llodra (ATP Player): "I saw him many times in the beginning of my career and he didn't too much smile. And he was strong, good eyes, he always thinker, focused on what he want to do. Difficult to talk with him. His game was unbelievable."

Manuel Santana (Hall of Famer): "I say hello, how are you doing, that's it. I met him and saw him play in New York and Roland Garros. I saw him playing in Europe. He went up in the tennis game very quickly. He was a talented player with an easy way of playing. I like to see him play."

Roger Rasheed (Coach): "He got to the top without winning a major. Extremely gifted tennis player. He was a player that if you knew you hung around in the match, that you'd have plenty of opportunities eventually. Of course, he was very good at times. But he could move away from his platform and it was just a matter of staying the course and then you felt like you'd get the job done. Lleyton never really had any problems with Rios. Hewitt's a very mentally strong person. When you've got his mentality vs. Rios, I think you always go with the person that is stable over the person who probably wasn't a crowd favorite throughout his career. Not sure, but if he could do it again, he'd have done it with a different style. Extremely gifted, no doubt about it. At the end of your career, you're judged on Grand Slams."

Richard Williams (Father and Coach of Venus and Serena Williams): "Oh yeah, man. He was the type of guy, when he came up, I think no one thought he was real. But he was more than real. He would come out, he didn't have his racquets in a bag like everyone else. He'd put his racquets across his shoulder. Left-handed guy. He played Eddie Herr and wiped the tournament out. He was a great player. He was a great player out here too. Unbelievable human being. Trained over at Nick Bollettieri's. But I thought he was great. I think he came around and had one or two bad years maybe. But as a human being, I thought he was a great, great person. From the juniors to the pros. He was fast, he had great groundstrokes. Where they hit the ball, he understood where you were gonna hit the ball back to.

It's like he had studied the whole game. He was a great person. (Ever talk with him or have lunch?) I don't have lunch with no one. Because people don't eat where I eat at. But I did not have lunch with him. But yeah, I talked with him several times. I always thought he was very polite and very quiet. Very reserved from what I can see of him. But he was a great tennis player. I just think he did a lot for tennis. He was #1 in the world. And he was #1 very fast. It's not like it took him a long time. But I just think he was a great player. And from what I've seen, and what I thought about tennis, I thought Marcelo Rios was a terrific player, a terrific person."

Gabriel Markus (Coach and Former ATP Player): "I practiced with him in Athens in 1994 or '93. He was young. He could make any shot from anywhere on the court. Every ball from him was difficult to read. This is a quality that not so many players have. That's why he was so good."

Randy Walker (USTA Communications): "I remember when he was a junior, like 17-years-old, I tried to get his basic biographical information. He was going out on the court. I said, 'I'd like to arrange a time for us to talk so I can get biographical information for USTA information'. He was at the time a #2 junior player and also ranked about 300 in the world. I remember him looking at me weird and brushing me off. And then his agent Jeff Schwartz immediately came up and said, 'Let me help you'. And then he kind of whisked Marcelo off. I think you were the reporter who actually might have been the guy where it was someone asking him personal questions. It was nothing about the match, just like, 'What's your favorite movie?' Was that you who asked those questions? (Yes.) That was the funniest transcript in the history of the U.S. Open. The funniest interview. I think I made a bunch of copies because it was just so funny. I mean, people were falling over laughing when they read that. Where he was like, 'Come on man, I don't want to answer this.'"

Fernando Gonzalez (ATP Player): "He showed us the way to do it. He was so talented. He was the one that you would pay a lot of money to go see his match. Sometimes you see the top player and they always do the same, and then Marcelo, you don't know what is going to happen. It was really amazing the way he played. It's really fun to watch, he was a different player."

• • •

Rios vs. Andrei Pavel Monte Carlo 1999: Match Study

Second-round match here. ATP #13 Rios leads the career head-to-head 3-1 over #73 Pavel.

Eurosport commentator: "The doubt about Rios is, what kind of mood is he going to be in? Will he want to play today? At his best he's just phenomenal, as anybody who saw the final last year in Miami would attest. For me that was one of the performances of the 90's, if not THE performance of the 90's. Agassi was just brushed aside."

"It hasn't taken long for Pavel to show Monte Carlo his credentials."

"Rios is looking decidedly second best here so far. Is it going to be one of those days?"

"Every shot in that rally was directed by Rios to the strength of Pavel - the backhand."

"Already some delightful little touches on the volley by Rios. Cutting across it to put some sidespin on the ball that slid away from Pavel."

Pavel connects on a backhand winner. "Aw, take that. That's outrageous."

"Rios looks a little shellshocked by it all. Three break points...broken to love. 4-love Pavel."

"The French have a bit of a love/hate relationship with Rios. He's won five points. It's 5-love."

"The crowd may start to boo. He's such a mercurial character. Set point Andrei Pavel in 19 minutes. 6-love, Pavel played extraordinarily well. Rios won six points in the first set. Will Pavel be able to keep it up? How will Rios react? He could say, Uh, I'm out of here. Let's hope he will react the other way."

Second set:

"Well that's fantastic. The early signs are encouraging. Rios getting down to business. Two excellent points. He's starting to have a little spring in his step. Three break points."

"Very pretty. Rios never looks alarmed or surprised."

"One thing is for sure, this match will be broadcast in Chile. I think if Rios sneezes, it's something of a national bulletin."

"3-1 for Rios, the man who 13 months ago was virtually unbeatable on any surface."

"Again Rios being suckered into these macho exchanges - and he has the subtler skills."

"Oh yes, Rios does well to counter the raging bull there."

Rios hits a forehand winner on set point. "Oh, how about that to finish the set. About the best player in the world and he's got some impish qualities. Fabulous way to end the set. Two rapid sets, just 54 minutes."

Third set:

"Rios continuing to work hard every single point. Now he's playing like the man who was the world's best last year."

"Oh, a fabulous shot. Wonderful way to get the break. He finished the set in style and that was even better."

"His expression never changes."

"He's a magician when he plays like this. This is Rios now very near his very best. And isn't he a delight?

"The short angle forehand wide to the backhand set it all up. Pavel forced to hit defensively on the slice. And Rios having opened up the court isn't going to miss. 2-1."

"You would expect him to go on and win. But you can't really expect anything from Marcelo."

"Two absolutely dreadful errors. 2-2."

"His timing seems to have deserted him again. Pavel has moved ahead, 3-2."

"He is a complex character. The players like him - the top players. Tim Henman speaks very warmly of him. I don't think he respects many people in our job, the media. I think he regards us as like parasites, living off his skills."

"The players like him, they believe he is somewhat of a rebel. He goes about his own way. If Rios doesn't want to do anything, he won't do it."

"He suddenly stopped moving his feet. He's suddenly gone a little flat."

"Unbelievable rally, phenomenal reaction by Rios. But he's been broken and Pavel leads, 4-2."

"Here's Rios with a chance to immediately break back... and he's got it. Four breaks in five games."

"And Rios is back on level terms, 4-4."

"And again, hurling himself into that double-hander. Rios is stepping it up again. And it's bad news for the Romanian."

"The great escape. Can he take advantage? We're into a tiebreaker. I still fancy Rios but I wouldn't put a penny on him."

"What a beautiful volley by Pavel. And Rios is gonna have to play catch-up."

"OH! People are standing up around the court. It was that good. Incredible shot by Rios to play when he's down a mini-break. Exploring corners of the court that nobody knew existed. 2-2."

"Boy, this is some breaker. 3-2, Pavel."

"Rios, he's got the corner. Of course he would. 4-3, Rios is ahead for the first time in this tiebreak."

"Pavel just stared down the court at Rios, that he could pull off a spectacular winner like that. Two match points for Rios. You don't want it to end but it might here."

"Fantastic backhand! Given the situation. Another backhand winner by Pavel."

"Pavel's first double fault of the match. Third match point."

"He's got it! The match that starts with a whimper, ends with a roar."

Rios wins 0-6, 6-4, 7-6 (8-6).

"A truly wonderful match. And no coincidence, Prince Albert leads the cheerleaders at the top there. So much of it was just breath-taking."

• • •

Andrei Pavel (ATP Player): "For sure one of the most talented players on the Tour. He was an amazing talent. He played very fast, like an Agassi with a left hand, angles. Like, kind of John McEnroe but playing much faster from the baseline. He had that talent to hit the ball really fast and close to the line with the left hand. I remember him when we played French Open juniors. I had him that time then I beat him one time on Tour and then he beat three times. So it was 3-2 for him (actually, the final head-to-head tally was 7-1 in favor of Rios). He beat me one time in Monte Carlo 7-6 in the third. I liked to play against lefty because he was always playing to my better side, the backhand, so I could hurt him. But I think one time he really kicked my ass, I think it was in Sydney (2002), 1 and 4. He was a little bit strange guy, very quiet, he didn't like so much people coming up to him. I guess he was a little different from the rest. There are a lot of players very talented and they don't win a major. He reached #1. At the time, to be #1 without winning a major is pretty strange. That means maybe he put too much pressure on himself in the big ones."

. . .

Rios vs. Albert Costa French Open 1998: Match Study

Round of 16 match. Costa is serving up a break at 4-3 duece.

Eurosport commentator: "Rios got booed when he came on the court."

"A lot of people think this match could determine the destiny of the men's title."

"Rios has won two of their three previous matches but it's one-all on clay."

Costa wins the first set, 6-4.

Second set:

"Marcelo Rios has only lost four matches all year. But he's now in danger of falling a set down and a break. It's love-30."

"Love-40."

Rios looks extremely disgusted with himself and spits on the court.

Costa breaks after four deuces, and leads 2-1.

"Marcelo Rios has asked for the trainer, Bill Norris, who has arrived to the corner of the court. Rios tells Norris,

'It's tough to breathe.' Bill Norris basically gives Rios smelling salts under his nose."

"Difficulty in breathing is a suggestion of high tension."

"This is not the same Rios we came to admire so much this year. Snatched at that one."

Costa leads 4-3 with the break.

"Another drop shot that goes long for Costa. Two break back points for Rios."

Rios hits a forehand winner up the line. "And he seizes. The match is even at four all."

Someone in the stadium shouts: "Come on Chino." "Chino is the nickname of Rios but not one that he particularly enjoys."

"Suddenly Costa is looking very edgy and very tentative."

"Bill Norris is back again."

"He's playing pretty well for a man who's finding it difficult to breathe."

"Brilliant shot by Rios and it's one set all. I have to say Costa let him off the hook there. That stupid drop shot. That's the first set Costa has lost in the tournament."

Third set:

"Momentum of Rios grows - five games in a row. One-love Rios."

"He's finally made a drop shot. If he missed that one his racquet might have landed in Barcelona."

Rios throws racquet after a miss and the crowd jeers him.

"He's becoming the man they love to hate."

"That's an incredible drop shot by Rios."

"Be interesting to see if Costa can re-develop the aggression, seems to me he's lost the muscle. It's Rios now very much the dictator."

"It looks like Anna Kournikova has come out on the player balcony to watch. Todd Martin's out there as well."

"Rios in front, 2-1."

"Third ace from Costa. What a set. Two-all."

"Marcelo has called for the trainer again. He says he's pulled a leg muscle."

"Oh, Rios launches himself (hits his trademark jumping backhand winner cross court). And he'll serve for the third set, 5-3."

"He's the genuine article when it comes to honor on the court."

"And he's getting really pumped up now. Three set points for Rios. An ace. He wraps up the set in style."

Fourth set:

"It's raining but we're still playing."

"Costa breaks, it's 2-love. It seemed to come from nowhere."

"Rios gives it his all, no sign of any strained thigh there. A break of serve to love. Just when you thought Costa got himself back into it."

"I cannot understand this fatal fascination with dropshots with Costa. Break point Rios."

"Rios has won three successive games."

"Bill Norris coming back out, yet again."

"Too good. And Costa does break, 3-all."

"With all the talk of Sampras having the best forehand in the game, Rios has shown recently his matches the American's. 4-3, Rios."

"Bill Norris is on again. This time it's the other leg."

"Oh, that's wild from Costa. And Rios moves to within one game of victory."

"Ever since the second set he's allowed Rios to be the aggressor."

"Match point for Rios."

"Rios has taken a big step, he's one step closer to his first Grand Slam title. He needs to win one more match to re-take the #1 ranking."

Rios is ecstatic with the win, smiling and raising his fist in triumph. It almost looks like he feels this was the final and without any doubt he will win the tournament. He continues to smile on his way back to the locker room. He'll play Carlos Moya in the quarterfinal.

Carlos Moya (ATP Player and 1998 French Open winner): "I think the best match I ever played was when I beat Rios in French Open in '98 in quarterfinals. I beat him in four sets. That's one of my best memories. He was the favorite. Not #1 but the biggest favorite to play. And I never won a Slam before. It was an exciting match with many exciting points. So I think after I win that match I realized that I was gonna have a good chance to win the French."

Bill Norris (ATP Trainer): "A very misunderstood man. A man with deep compassion. He was a quiet guy, very strong beliefs, and a guy that I consider a real friend. Sometimes didn't have patience for some people.

But he was a very complex individual. And I think he looked at tennis as a real challenge. It's a pity, he had such great feeling and compassion for the game, it saddens me that that fuel for that fire that he had wasn't fueled better. But, you know, he had a good run. You don't have to play 10 or 15 years to be a great player. You could have moments of greatness. And he definitely could do it when he wanted to...I sort of took him under my wing, counseled him on a lot of things. Had he stayed around, he would have been like another Agassi, and re-invented himself like Andre has, who is also a great competitor. He played his heart and soul out many times. He had a real soft spot for less fortunate people. I saw him really help some people in Santiago. I think the lasting image of him was Key Biscayne, when he won down there and the Chilean people - there's a big population of Chilean people in South Florida - I live in Boca Raton - they picked him up and brought him around on their shoulders in the stadium, outside, around. It made me think of that 1977 win when Jimmy Connors was defeated by Vilas in Forest Hills. I was there as well."

Jerome Golmard (ATP Player): "I played three times against him. And every time it was a strange feeling. Because the first time I was injured, the second time I beat him in a strange match - he was leading 6-1, 3-0. So, I don't know, I never really play a real match against him. When you play against him it's like you play a video game because he play so easy and every time he touch the ball, he can do a winner. After two or three games, he knew your game. So when you do your best shot, he know. And you kill yourself. And then you start to think, why should you try to end the point? When you need easy points when you're in trouble in an important game, you try to play your best shot to win the point. After two or three game, he knows and can do a winner on your best shot."

Nicolas Massu (ATP Player): "He's a great friend of me. I learn a lot from him. In the four or five years we are in Davis Cup, I travel a lot with him. He was a great player."

Richard Evans (Journalist and Author): "(Excerpt from his story "Playing to the Nines" in the Nov. 26, 1998 issue of Tennis Week magazine)...we were presented with the sight of Rios in a press conference telling us he had decided he was not fit enough to play Kafelnikov (Stuttgart, QF in 1998) in a match that had been due on court in thirty minutes. He had pulled a muscle again, this time playing soccer with a tennis ball. A little twinge, apparently, although he wasn't really sure because he hadn't even had it properly examined by the trainer at that point. No good trying to fathom Marcelo. He lives in a world of his own."

Question: Did you ever have any personal memories interacting or interviewing Rios?

Richard Evans: "No. Thank God. I stayed as far away from him as possible."

In the chase for the year-end #1 ranking, Rios surrendered the chance to earn at least 80 ranking points by defaulting to Kafelnikov at the Eurocard in Stuttgart. A week later at Paris Indoors, Rios met Kafelnikov again in the quarterfinals but this time they played the match and the Russian defeated Rios 6-3 6-2. After Paris, where Sampras lost in the final to Rusedski, Sampras maintained the #1 position over Rios by just 3703 to 3670 - a margin of 33 points.

Two weeks later at the ATP Tour World Championship in Hannover, Germany, Rios was defeated in his first round-robin match by Tim Henman 7-5 6-1 and then abruptly withdrew from the event, citing a back injury. Sampras, who was the defending champion of Hannover, defeated Kafelnikov, Moya and Kucera (each in straight sets) in round-robin action before losing to Alex Corretja in the semifinal 4-6, 6-3, 6-7 (3).

• • •

Stefan Koubek (ATP Player): "Played him once in Austria and I lost pretty easy to him. And he was always the kind of guy I love to watch, I like to practice with, and he was kind of an idol for me. Because he was like a genius on the court. It was amazing what he can do with the ball and the talent he has. For me, it was very surprising when he stopped. I thought he had a few years in front of him. But he was like a kind of guy I could watch every day."

(Why did you enjoy to practice with him?) "I like his game so much so every time you can practice with guys like him - he's been #1 in the world, at the time he was one of the best - it's always good to practice with top guys. And especially he's a lefty, I'm a lefty. I can watch him, what he was doing on the court. And see how he is playing when I'm playing him. So he was awesome just practicing and watching him."

"I'm the kind of guy who walks around and asks a player, 'Do you want to practice?' Least they can say is no. Which is no problem at all. But a lot of times I practice with the guys, they know me, I'm always playing hard in practice. So I guess I'm a good practice partner. I practice well. I was around a long time. It's easy for me to practice with the top guys because they know me."

(Talk with Rios at all?) "Not at all. He was the kind of guy nobody really liked because he was a little strange, in his own world, but I never had a problem with him. We basically say, 'Hi, what's up?' That was basically it, as far as talking with him. But it was always fun practicing."

"He beat me, I think it was 1-1 or something. Kind of close, a lot of close games but he won all of them. And he was just a better player at that time. He was definitely talented enough to win several Grand Slams. He was not a hard worker. So if he would have mentally been more prepared to go out there to work his ass off and stay in there consistently, definitely the talent was there. But it's not all talent."

Nicolas Pereira (ATP Player): "I remember when he was 14 he came to Caracas with his coach and we played a set and I was on the Tour, I was 22, 23. I was really impressed how he could handle the ball at that early age. Very mature. And we played doubles a couple of times, in Bogota, the finals of the ATP. Then in Santiago. I had a good relationship with him. He was a bit misunderstood and on the otherhand, a bit of a rebel in his own way. But a beautiful player. It was a misfortune for all of us when he got hurt. He had an amazing control of the ball for that age and that size. The guy was five-foot tall or something. Very small. He had incredible racquet control. That struck me as odd. It caught my attention. He was actually traveling with Hans Gildemeister, who was one of the great masters of Latin American tennis. That said a lot. For Hans to leave home and travel with somebody. The kid had to be good. It was incredible to play doubles with him. The control he had, the few returns that he missed. He would always make the return. I was always playing the ad side. It was hard to keep up with him. But it was a great experience and I was glad I shared it. It's something I'm fond of. He's always been very kind to me. I last saw him about two years ago."

Juan Coronel (Coach): "I had the opportunity to watch him train for four days at Saddlebrook. Because I know Luis Lobo. And Marcelo was always giving you 100% and more. But his reputation was that he didn't want to work hard. But he had everybody fooled because he was a hard worker. He was trying on court but it appeared to the public that he wasn't. That was his style of play. Deception. Very, very talented young man."

"And there's a reason why he was #1 in the world very briefly. I remember he never stopped working on any of his deficiencies, which were, he was a little lax with his backhand. And he wanted things repeated over and over and over and over again until he got it right. So I remember that. And he was a great guy. Once you were in his corner, you were in his corner for life. A lot of people, like, tried to get close to him, but very few got close to him. That's why he was not the most popular guy on the circuit."

Donald Dell (Hall of Famer): "Wonderfully gifted player but he was very talented at a very early age. And I don't think he really adjusted really well to the people around him. I thought he was difficult to deal with and that hurts him today. I liked his tennis but I didn't like his attitude. He had a bad attitude about the sport and about people. You gotta understand, relationships are what makes the world go round. One time we were doing a television show. He did the match - finals of the tournament - and we sent Barry McKay down to interview him live on national television. And he was talking to a friend. Barry McKay said, 'I'd like to interview you for NBC.' And Rios blasted Barry, 'CAN'T YOU SEE I'M BUSY, I'M TALKING TO HIM? DON'T INTERRUPT ME.' We were live, on a schedule, and we went live. So that really hurt him, that really hurt him."

Pancho Segura (Tennis Legend): "Oh shit. I saw him as a junior when he won the U.S. Open juniors. I saw the guy had potential but a lousy temperment and a bad sport. I don't have much admiration for him but I like his tennis. He should have been a great tennis player. I saw him lose to Korda in Melbourne, Australia - it looked like he didn't try. I saw him throw a match at Paris - he was aiming at the alley. Lousy sportsman. But a great tennis player. A great touch. He had the best forehand on lowballs from the center of court. He could hit angles. He moved so well. A different Chilean. He got upset because I called him Chino. (Was he nice to you?) I just barely talk to him. Really hard to communicate (with) this generation. They think they know more than you. They think we never play good tennis. The court doesn't change but the equipment has. And the competition has. And the money has."

Rainer Hofman (Coach): "He was playing unbelievable but he lost 2-2-2 to Korda in the final of Australia. He loves tennis. I worked at Bollettieri, I hit with a lot of players. I hit with him when he was 14 in 1989. He was very special. I remember the first time I see him, he had on the white shirt but he was very dark. His look was very interesting. He was unbelievable talent, unbelievable. Some people play tennis, but the way he play it, it's like another word. I was with him at his first tournament in Dresden, Germany ('94) as a hitting partner. He got a wildcard into the tournament and then he won the tournament (d. Oliver Gross). Everybody was asking, Who is this guy? Nobody knew him. He had the ponytail but not as long. Then later he grew it longer. Then I was with him when he won his first ATP event in Bologna, Italy (d. Marcelo Filippini in '95)."

"Monica Seles was in the cafeteria and Marcelo goes right there behind her, he said, 'You're too fat to play tennis.' Seles was like, 'What?' When we went out to eat, if the waiter ever made a mistake on his order, he would get so angry. He was arrogant but in some ways for tennis you must be. Like (my wife) Patty (Schnyder) today. 6-5, match point in the third set tiebreak - you can't walk up to the line scared. You have to be arrogant. Patty went up and hit a service winner. So you have to have arrogance."

Beverly Schaeffer (Photographer): "Back in the 90's in Philadelphia indoors. I just started working with a Swedish magazine as a photographer. That's when Rios started working with Peter Lundgren as a coach. Swedish magazine wanted me to get photos of Rios with Lundgren at a practice. The story is about Lundgren. I go to the practice center. It's February, indoors, at the University of Pennsylvania, one of their buildings that's like a hundred years old. First thing in the morning, really dim lights. I'm there to do the pictures with Lundgren and Rios wouldn't cooperate. At all. At all. I would ask him something - this is not during the practice session - I'm not interrupting. I just want to do a quick shot of him and Lundgren together for the same picture, that's all. Just stand here for two seconds. And when I spoke to him, he wouldn't even look at me. As if I was an insect talking to him. And I never did get that picture! He wouldn't cooperate. He wouldn't even stand there to let me take a picture with the coach. I had to explain that to my editor."

"Another memory was back when Edberg, Graf and Rios were all with adidas. And it was the day before the French Open started, over at adidas hospitality. It's a press conference with three players up on a stage, sitting up in high, tall chairs, almost like the old Dating Game (TV show). Three of them lined up there. They've got the press there. The adidas guy asks each to say what they respect in each other's game. And what parts of each other's game you would wish to emulate? Edberg said, Steffi's forehand. Steffi said how it was wonderful how Edberg could charge to the net and be so comfortable around the net. And then it comes to Rios, the young kid, the young whippersnapper, with Stefan Edberg and Steffi Graf. And he comes out and says, 'No, there's nothing in their games that I would want.' And it was like a train screeching to a halt. Everybody in the press just stopped and looked at him. And Edberg and Graf had just been taken aback, they had been so kind and generous. You could never say a bad word about Edberg and Graf, who were so magnanimous. And Rios hadn't proven anything at this point and - 'No, there's nothing in their games that I would like to emulate.'"

Daniel Orsanic (ATP Player): "I was a lot older. I played him in doubles in his Challenger period. He was always in his own world, I would say. He would carry himself like he was better than all of the other players. A bit arrogant, a bit cocky. Standing on the court playing a doubles match without moving a centimeter, like, this is too easy for me. But then he would practice a lot during those weeks and of course he was winning in Challenger events, coming up the ranking. I remember that he was a guy that he liked to play. He liked to practice, even though he would show a lazy attitude. I always felt like he liked to play tennis. He would make excellent footwork on the court when he was young. He was much better than the other young boys, very naturally light on the feet. I played him in doubles in Santiago. Massu and him against Lucas Arnold and I. And I remember he had to play a night session match and we were also due to play doubles. He said to the tournament director, 'Don't worry, I can play the doubles before my singles,' at four in the afternoon. And then he was playing at eight at night in his singles match. Not many of the guys would do that. That day we beat him. He played it like a warm-up to relax for his singles match. He was playing very relaxed and that day we won 6-4 in the third."

"Not a good or bad relationship but I could not say we were friends. The closest I was with him was when he worked with Luis Lobo. I'm good friends with him. We shared a couple of dinners or conversations."

Vince Spadea Sr. (Coach): "I remember Rios. The Italian/Portugal clay swing. We actually got along with Marcelo. 'Hey Vince, you want to practice?' Back then, nobody wanted to practice with him and we didn't have anybody, so we would practice with him quite a bit. Back then Rios was coached by Red Ayme and the Spaniards and Argentines didn't like to practice with Rios because they like to practice hard, work hard. And back then Rios would get into arguments with Ayme. After five minutes Ayme would want him to do something a certain way and Marcelo would say, 'Don't talk to me like that.' And they'd argue and Rios would pack up his bags and leave the court. This happened many times, so no one wanted to practice with him. But we would practice with him."

Roger Smith (Coach and Former ATP Player): "I played him in doubles in Davis Cup when he was young, like 16 or 17. It was in Chile. We won the match against him and Gabriel Silberstein. He was so young. Mark Knowles and myself were good doubles players. We could see he was going to be a very good singles player. A few returns he took the ball really early. His serve at the time was mediocre, his volleys were okay. But his returns were very good, especially the two-hand return. Three years after that Davis Cup match I played him in the last round of the doubles qualies at the U.S. Open. We actually beat him and Leonardo Lavalle of Mexico. The crowd was kind of for us and Rios hit a ball right in the direction of what happened to be my brother-in-law at the time. But it was no point-penalty because it was off of a serve. A return - crazy. Nuts, man. He just went nuts. We beat them. But he was losing his mind a little bit. Very talented player, good hands, very confident. He had a good feel for the ball. He hit a good, clean ball."

Nicolas Lapentti (ATP Player): "I know Marcelo since we were 12 or 14. We played the final of the tournament in Bolivia, 15 or 16. Then we played again in Chile, so we go a long way back. Marcelo was very difficult with a lot of people. But I had a pretty good relationship with him especially because we used to play golf together a lot. So I guess when he was off the tennis courts he was a bit more relaxed. And when we went on the golf course we'd talk about anything but tennis. So I got to know him a bit better. Of course he did some bad things with the press and maybe with the fans. But in a way, it's not easy to be a top player. I think nowadays, we have two great examples - I mean Federer and Nadal being top players and also great with fans. I guess Marcelo was different and people just have to accept it that way. And people in Chile - it was kind of a love/hate relationship. Like sometimes a lot of people hated him but at the same time those were the first people to go and buy tickets to watch him play."

"I think he was special and of course a great player and really did a lot for tennis. We played a lot of times and he was also very competitive on the golf course. He had a great swing. He played golf since he was a kid. Very easy swing. He was very good, probably a seven or eight handicap."

"I'm sure he has some things that he never shared with the media or the world. He was very shy, always introverted. He never really spoke a lot about his personal things and I never really asked. (Keep in touch with him?) I think the last time I saw him was maybe three years ago in Barcelona, he was playing a Senior event. (How did you fare against him on court?) I think he won most of our matches in juniors - or even all of them. Then as pros, we probably played six or seven times, he won four or five. I just beat him twice in the pros. He was so talented. Great mover, great athlete and his anticipation - the way he read a point was amazing. He was always on top of every shot. He was a lefty that had an advantage. He had a great backhand. Very good forehand. His serve - nobody really talk about his serve. His serve was very tough to return. It wasn't a huge serve but it had good location. I think his hand-eye coordination was one of the best things he had. I think Marcelo was very talented. I think, what happened to him when he came up to big matches, he made people feel or believe that he was not trying enough but sometimes maybe he didn't want to face those big moments. Like the final in Australia, it was like he was never on the court. So he had some opportunities. Of course, when he played to be #1, he played a great match in Miami. I think with his talent he could have won at least three or four Grand Slams. I mean, he was a great player. (Consider him a friend?) Yes I do. I do."

Adrian Escarate (College Player): "I play at an NAIA school called St. Thomas University as a junior majoring in Communications Arts and #1 player on the tennis team here. I was born in Santiago, Chile but raised since age four in Miami, FL, U.S. I find it very nice and actually flattering as a fellow Chilean that you are writing a book on Marcelo Rios. He was definitely my favorite player growing up as a Chilean tennis player living in Miami, FL, along with Michael Chang, but since Rios is a compatriot he had an edge on Chang. There were a few experiences I shared alongside Rios, I can say that he was a nice guy. First time I met him was at the IMG Bollettieri Tennis Academy. I was probably eight or nine-years-old, walking around the grounds with my dad, mom, and older brother when we run into him getting out of the gym. My parents had warned us already of his character and reputation that he had with the public, but my brother and I still approached him and asked for autographs and a picture. To our surprise, he signed our tennis balls AND took the photograph! I thought to myself, This guy isn't as mean as everyone else says. The funny part of the situation was that we were also staying in the same hotel as Rios that weekend, so the next morning we see him at the continental breakfast area, too. This time we stayed our distance because then we probably would have been shoved off if he saw the same two little kids annoying him again. Also, the few times that I ran into him at the Sony Ericsson he was always nice to my brother and me. We were never denied an autograph which is very hard to say as a Marcelo Rios fan. I remember he might have even tossed his towel at my brother one time after a match. Also, some years after that photograph was taken, we were able to give the picture to a good friend of Marcelo at the time, a Chilean tennis player named Robinson Gamonal, who my family knows very well. He took the picture to Rios and got him to sign it for my brother and I with our names and a dedicatory message on the back. So, in retrospect, Marcelo Rios might have been - and probably was - one of the most hated tennis players on the ATP tour, having controversial relationships with the press, the public, and the rest of the players in the locker room, but I never had a problem with him. He was always nice, respectful, and courteous with me which molded my thoughts about him both as a tennis player and as a person in a very good way. I still believe he is one of the most talented players to ever play the game along with the likes of Roger Federer, Marat Safin, and John McEnroe. Actually, now that I think about it, I have two pictures with Marcelo Rios! Only a handful of fans can say that."

Chapter 6
The Bollettieri Perspective

"What a man thinks of himself, this is which determines, or rather indicates, his fate." -Henry David Thoreau

Nick Bollettieri (Coach): "My first memory of Rios is, Who is this guy? He came here with a Chilean group when he was about 14. He wasn't big in stature. But he had an air on the tennis court - that he could do anything with the ball. And that air is difficult to teach. And the ironic thing is, he could do anything with it. Even at that age he just had the ability to do those things. And then being a lefty - it was much more interesting to me because lefties are peculiar in ways. They do things you don't think anybody can do and sometimes they do things off the chart. They think different, they react differently. And they really cannot be stymied early in their career. Because if you stymie them, you never know what that boy and girl can do. And lefties are far different than righties. He wasn't too jovial on the tennis court, he didn't mess around. He wasn't joking. That's my first memory of Marcelo."

Question: Who did he like to practice with here?

Nick Bollettieri: "Marcelo would actually practice with anyone. He never thought anyone was too young or too poor. If you say to hit, he'd go out and hit. That was very good. I think Jimmy Arias said it better than anybody. Because he'd play with ding dongs, ping pongs, choppers, chippers. Because you never know when you might run into somebody that way. He would never say, Oh they're not good enough, or something like that. But he was very serious when he practiced. He was serious. And he worked like hell on the court. He would never say, I'm tired, I had enough. He would run for every ball. And he was the same way in the gym. He worked his ass off. He never complained."

Question: He loved the sport?

Nick Bollettieri: "He seemed to love it. However, he didn't show too many signs of satisfaction. So you never knew what was going through his mind. You didn't know whether he was self-conscious, over-conscious, stuck up. You didn't know. He trained with the very best - can't get any better than Larry Stefanki did a helluva job with him. And then I had him. I was a little taken aback because I began to see a little bit of a different trait of Marcelo. I don't know if he really appreciated the sport or what he could get out of the sport - it was very difficult for him to say thank you to all the people that helped him. It was very difficult for him to talk to young children, when they waited for autographs and things like that. And I was a little surprised. And he wasn't overly generous. And he was very tight with his money. I remember he'd come down from the eighth floor down to the third floor at two o'clock in the morning when the water was free. He'd go all the way down there. That was in Germany, we were playing the Grand Slam Cup in Munich and he won (d. Agassi in five sets). In fact, I had Williams then and we won the doubleheader. And so when we won, I tipped the stringer and I tipped the ballboys. And then when I presented them, he said, 'What did you do that for?' And then he even questioned whether or not I should get paid because that wasn't on the regular Tour [smiles]."

"I believe that Marcelo had as much talent - feet, movement, anticipation, hands, his eyes - of any player that's played the game. He wasn't afraid to work. But tough for him to communicate. And perhaps, to understand how devastating it was to a youngster that would wait two or three hours for autographs and then not do that. And of all the students I've had, I believe that he didn't get to a point where he was capable of doing. I think he could have been top dog, man, top dog."

Question: How has Marcelo changed and matured?

Nick Bollettieri:"He was divorced and he's married now - he's very, very, very polite. Extremely, extremely polite. He came here to watch his daughter (in 2009) - by the way, his daughter (Constanza) is excellent, excellent. No, she's better than excellent. She moves well. Good groundstrokes. Great foundation. She can volley. She can do a lot of things. She could be a very good player. And Marcelo is very happy to see that. And he was very appreciative, (saying) Thank you, he was very warm. And I said to myself, I think having the children that he has now, helped him change. But did he fulfill his career? No. No sir. He was one out of a million. What he had, you can't teach."

Question: He was the only guy I ever saw who could toy with Agassi on the court. Your comment?

Nick Bollettieri: "He could toy with anybody. Fast as anything. He created shots that most people don't even think they could do. But he was #1 for a week or so. Never won a Grand Slam. He probably fell short of the mark he could have made on tennis."

Question: What was missing in his makeup?

Nick Bollettieri: "Himself. You have to understand that life is a multitude of things. It's being humble. It's sharing. It's knowing that when a little kid waits hours - so excited - that it's your obligation - this is your profession - to give that child time. I think now he seems to be much more subdued. But he was never lazy. Never lazy. Never. He worked like an animal."

Question: When did you see the change in his personality?

Nick Bollettieri: "When he came here (in 2009), to see his daughter in the fall time he was here. He came, he watched, he said hello. He was very, very nice. So many people fall short of what they can do in life. And so few people do not accept the responsibility to give back. And to know the impact on little children and that you can have on them when they're so excited. That could effect them for the rest of their life. I think Marcelo, having children like that, it has made him feel different. He was never rude to me, never sarcastic. Of course I didn't take any shit from him. But Larry Stefanki did a helluva job. Helluva job."

Question: Lasting image, lasting memory of Rios that stays with you?

Nick Bollettieri: "When I saw him right there (points to entrance corner of indoor court). With his wife and baby. Right over there. And he introduced me and, I thought that was...I saw a different person within. Tough to read people within themselves. But he was very proud and it was nice to see him."

• • •

David "Red" Ayme (Coach at Bollettieri): "During the time Marcelo was here, Nick was able too keep him so focused on his tennis. It was little things. We're not talking major technical changes with these guys. But just to keep Marcelo right into the next tournaments, keep him going. Marcelo loved tennis. Maybe that's a misconception about him, he just loved to play. That's one of the things I respect about him - he just loved to play. We still get along great, even today. We knew, no matter what he said to the press, or Nick talking about that little arrogance or rudeness, he loved to play. The few people that had the chance to work with him I think will tell you he really loved to play."

"The first thing I remember about him was when he came here, he was about 13 or 14. He was the little guy who was losing to everybody on the court. But he played unbelievable. He'd be playing with 18-year-olds. We do that here. He was little, just getting beat up by the bigger guys. But you could just see how good this guy was gonna be. I saw him later when he had gotten older and had already gotten ATP points, breaking through, so to speak. He had the combination of unbelievable eyes, hand, feet. As a coach, when you look at those three elements - then he had the other part, the competitive spirit. You combine those three on the court - and the other one about competing - man! That's what you saw early with Marcelo. He had those three capabilities - the eyes, the hands, the feet, all at once. And then he competed well."

"In the time I spent with him on the road, when he was about 17 - this is when he played the qualies in New Haven, The Open. Then I went over to Europe with him and actually, we didn't have great success. Then in South America the two months after. It was a combination of things. He just had really tough draws. That was the time Alberto Berasategui was playing ridiculously good, right after the French Open. And Marcelo drew him three out of four tournaments. He lost in three sets each time. He also lost to Franco Davin."

"At U.S. Open qualies, I remember he was just destroying people. And then he played Jared Palmer in the first round. At that time, Jared Palmer was a top 50 player, very experienced. He beat Palmer then he lost to Wayne Ferreira. That was his first U.S. Open. The way Marcelo handled pace, he was able to re-direct pace, then all of a sudden generate pace. Still, to this day, I think coaches look at his backhand and wonder how did he hit that cross-court, at that height, how hard with that bottom angle. I still think, to this day, there is a little bit of genius with him. How he knew how to accelerate and re-direct pace into the court. Genius. Especially with his backhand. He could flick and create these cross-court angles with pace. I don't know if you can teach that out of a textbook. I go to the seminars of coaching, been coaching with Nick for 20 years, and sometimes he hit shots that you would say, That's not the right shot. But it worked. And it worked for him. So you would have to allow him to have that kind of freedom."

"Jimmy Arias and Rios used to practice together. They would wager. Jimmy's a character. They'd play a dollar a point. Then it would turn into...I really feel like, I've seen guys on the circuit like Marcelo and Jimmy play harder in practice with $20 on the line than they do with first round prize money in an ATP tournament - because it's theirs. I'll stand by that comment [smiles]."

"Those practices at the time with Jimmy, Malisse, Max, Haas, Philippoussis. But Jimmy's a talker. Jimmy and Marcelo would direct it at each other. It was really good [smiles]. Really good stuff to watch. Some of the best of his career. Marcelo would let go some of that that he wouldn't in a tournament match. He had that freedom then, to do that."

Question: Lasting memory of Rios?

Red Ayme: "Genius on the court. Just you could see the genius in him, in all areas, all spaces, all spots, all tournaments, all surfaces. He proved over the years he could play on any surface. If anything needs to be remembered, I think Marcelo was a genius on the court. How he was able to use pace, take pace, manufacture these angles. I think from a tennis standpoint, strictly talking as a tennis player, he definitely needs to be looked at about how he took space from an opponent, how he took the ball early, how he hit the overhead for a guy his size, generated incredible power but never overhit it. A combination of factors: the eyes - to see the ball, the hands - to be able to generate or re-direct pace, the feet - to be in the right position and balance. And be so fluent, so it looks like he's not doing anything. For a tennis player, what more can you ask? He competed hard and loved to play. Which was an underlying factor that a lot of people didn't know."

"He started the running jump shot backhand. He'd jump off the right leg and hit it in the air. Not only did he start the shot, it was an effective shot. Because it's taken so early. And with his timing, he'd actually generate a lot of pace. The first time I saw it, Whooaa. I didn't over-react. Whoa. He made a great shot. He missed it very little. Inside the court is where he used it. He would hit the jumping backhand from on the baseline or inside. Nick, to his credit, was smart enough not to discourage it but say that's the right time to do it. And that's underestimated. You can get into battles with theory in tennis and you can over-coach in tennis. Or over-analyze. And with great players sometimes it's best to backup and say, With your style it actually works. Nick didn't take that creativity away, he encouraged it."

"I remember once he got stung by a bee in the mouth right before the U.S. Open. On a clay court tournament. I wasn't there, I remember hearing the story. He was drinking out of a Coke can on the changeover and a bee stung his lip. Late in the third set. His lip swells up. He still goes on to win the match. You look at the little things. The fact of the matter is the guy loved to play, he loved to compete. Loved it."

• • •

Rios vs. Tim Henman in Rome 1998: Match Study

#3 Rios was unable to defend in Monte Carlo because of injury and lost his first match in Hamburg. His record on the year is a marvelous 26 wins, just four defeats, three titles won and over a million dollars in earnings already this year. Henman, ATP #17, is 19-13 on the year. Eurosport commentary: "This match, as always, is being televised live in Chile. I was talking to the Chilean commentator who said, 'If Rios was playing in Timbuktu, we'd show it live.'"

"All three opening games have gone to deuce."

"Oh dear, snatched at that one. And Rios has the break, 2-1."

"Oh, that's beautiful play from Rios. Another good-looking shot (low forehand volley) made to look easy."

"I remember Greg Rusedski had a lot of success against Rios in Indian Wells with the slice backhand. Henman needs to be more patient."

"Oooh dear, a Wild Bill Hickock of a serve by Henman, his second double fault."

"Rios, the smallest man to be ranked #1 in the world. And the first South American to be #1 and of course, the first from Chile. He only played one match as the #1 player - in Davis Cup. I have a sneaking suspicion he'll get to play two or three more."

"At the moment Rios is winning 90% of his points behind the first serve."

Henman serves at 3-5. "That's wonderful attacking the Henman second serve, then following it up with a wonderful drive volley."

"Oh wow, that's unanswerable. That's #1 in the world type play those two points. Henman backhand long. Three set points. Henman ends the first set as he started it, with a double fault."

Second set:

"I think Henman is trying to force too much. I think he's got to tell himself to play two or three shots more until Rios will offer him the short ball."

"Rios wins the set with no aces or double faults. Almost a serene set by Rios."

3-1 Rios.

"Rios is a very fair man on the court. If he describes a mark you know that's the mark."

"First ace of the match for Rios who's galloping away with it now. The #3 seed leading by a set and 4-1."

"Love-40. This is almost getting embarrassing. It's the stage Sampras got into with Santoro in Monte Carlo. It can happen to the very best as well."

"Like taking candy from a baby."

"Rios, unhurried, like a forehand jab on the slide. 5-1." To pass Henman at the net.

Rios serves for the match.

Rios nets a drop shot.

"You might think Rios would take pity on his doubles partner from last week and let him win a few points."

Rios wins next point.

"Any thoughts quickly dismissed."

"It's been a demolition job. Tim Henman has been given a real lesson out here. Tremendous performance from Rios. Henman completely outclassed."

"He knows now what it takes to take on the best on clay and Rios is right up there among the very best."

Rios wins the match, then signs about five autographs, without looking he tosses the pen for the fan to catch, quickly loads his Yonex racquets into a black Nike bag and in an apparent haste, exits the Foro Italico court.

Chapter 7
The King Of Tennis

"A Champion owes everybody something. He can never pay back for all the help he got, for making him an idol." - Jack Dempsey, former World Heavyweight champion

"In everyone's life, at some time, our inner fire goes out. It is then burst into flame by an encounter with another human being. We should all be thankful for those people who rekindle the inner spirit." -Albert Schweitzer

Guy Forget (ATP Player): "He was a very talented player, a lefty. He did great things. He could have done great things, even better. Too bad he didn't play longer. I like his game. He was strange as a person – he didn't get along with all the guys. He definitely had a temper [laughs]. That's just the way he was. The way he played was just incredible. So different. You can't get along with everyone, I guess. I hope now that he's stopped playing, he's enjoying life a little more. When we get older, you have a kid and a family, life on the Tour - it doesn't stabilize you with stability. Tennis wasn't real life. And people think that's the way you live when you're a tennis player. You think it's normal but it's not. I think he had children. And I'm sure now he's doing better, more than when he was playing. I didn't know him well, so I can't tell you much more than that."

Teddy Blackburn (Photographer): "I almost got fired, because I was supposed to shoot a match but I was watching Rios instead. He was like Muhammad Ali - when Rios plays, you have to go watch Rios. These guys out there are like contenders. Rios is champ. Whether he's in shape or out of shape, you have to watch him. He had fun on the court. A lot of these guys are stone-faced, been hitting the ball for 15-20 years. Rios, win or lose, you gotta watch him. He put on a show. I remember the quote he gave the media in Monte Carlo. As he kept winning, going further in the draw, the more it kept him out of the casinos, gambling and drinking [smiles]. Any kid here, or first-time fan, you don't go to watch Roddick or Isner - go watch Rios. He had personality, he had fun out there. You watch these top guys, Nadal, Murray, Federer, they don't have fun. They kill. Like programmed machines. But Rios had fun. He played ping pong out there, he played a different game. You can't name another player who played like Rios."

Magnus Norman (ATP Player): "A very talented player. I actually like him a lot. He was a good guy on the court. I had no problems with him. He was one of the best players and the first South American to be the top one. We had a lot of good memories. I remember the one year we played in Shanghai. He had the match point. And I was able to win the match and I was able to win the title. That's one of my favorite players for sure. We were friendly. We don't have any contact right now, for the moment. He was playing in doubles a lot with Enqvist, so we were hanging out a lot. He was a little erratic. He was not like everybody else. I had no problems. He was a nice kid to me."

Jonas Bjorkman (ATP Player): "Super talented. Was able to do more or less, what no one else can do. I have only positive memories. We practice quite a lot, he was always good to practice with. Very focused on the practice. We had some singles matches - I can't remember, there were so many [smiles]. We have a few doubles. I won a few, he's probably ahead of me on the record. Probably the most talented player to have not won a Grand Slam I would say. He can't quite put it together but he had a super game, super talent. His career was a little too short I think."

(Magnus Norman just told me Rios got along with the Swedes but very few others. Why?) "I don't know. I think we respected him and he respected us. Maybe we have, more or less, the same mentalities. We're quite easy to deal with and he appreciated that. Magnus and Enqvist as well - we all were practicing quite a lot with him. We never had any problems or issues, he was always nice to us. And we tried to be nice to him as well. (Go to dinner ever?) Never went to dinner actually. But every time we saw him at the courts and during the tournaments, we chatted a bit. If we have a chance to practice, we tried. Because we both said it was a good practice for both of us."

Thomas Enqvist (ATP Player): "He's a wizard with a racquet."

Indianapolis Ballkid: "I was a ballkid for Marcelo Rios at the RCA Championships in Indianapolis. I could understand a lot of Spanish and the things he said were not appropriate to say to a minor. Every year I would get as many players as possible to autograph my event T-shirt. I don't have a Rios autograph because I didn't want it."

Derrick Applegate (Yonex USA, National Sales Manager): "I met Rios at the U.S. Open a few times. He usually picked up some equipment from us at our Yonex retail booth there on-site by court 10. Pretty much just said, 'Hi.' Our player services staff were usually there to take care of him. I never really had a conversation with him since he just picked up some equipment and left right away because the fans would start to gather."

Alexander Dolgopolov (ATP Player): "Well, my favorite player to watch - it used to be Marcelo Rios. He was really fun to watch. He was really improvising on the court. Now, I don't know, tennis has gotten more monotone and everything. Running and physical. Because everyone is hitting so fast, you can't really play that style. I mean, Roger's got some of that still in him. He still does that playing style – volleys and drop shots, slices. I like to watch his game the most probably. (Did you meet Rios?) I met him when I was small. Not really in person, that I remember. The second time my father was coaching Andrei Medvedev was in 1998, that time when Rios won in a row Indian Wells and Miami. I was at the tournaments and I was always killing my parents to go to the matches. He was always playing night matches and I was (saying), 'Let's go watch him. Let's go watch him [smiles].' I really like to watch his matches. I was crazy about him that time. The style of his game was incredible. He could pull out any of the shots in any moment. It was really fun. You don't know what the guy can do. He wasn't playing the same game all the time. He was really variative, tough to play, I think."

Pete Sampras (after defeating Rios 7-6, 7-6, 6-4 at 1994 Roland Garros): "I think you have to give him a lot of credit because he didn't let the situation really make him nervous or intimidated, he came out and just played another tennis match and he's got a pretty good game. Obviously, he made me work extremely hard today and he has a pretty good first serve, backs it up with a really good backhand. And obviously I didn't play him before so I didn't know what to expect. It took me a while to get used to his game."

Patrick Rafter (ATP Player): "He was rude, he was arrogant."

Dan Markowitz (Journalist): "A friend of mine who attends the Newcombe annual camp said that one year at the U. S. Open, Rios came back to the locker room after a victory and Roy Emerson congratulated him. Rios said, 'Who the fuck are you?' and Patrick Rafter went nuts on Rios and made him apologize to Emerson."

Cindy Schmerler (Journalist): "Marcelo Rios seemed to do everything he could to make people hate him."

Rios vs. Andre Agassi in Miami 1998: Match Study

Rios aiming to win second Super Nine final of year against Agassi and attain ATP #1 ranking. Court conditions are perfect. It's the first meeting between the two icons who both have equal 24-3 records on the season. 8 million are expected to tune in on television in Chile.

Agassi said in the press conference: "The key is going to be who is going to control the points."

Eurosport commentator: "I think it's going to be a macho first set. I believe Agassi has the edge. The first set is so important to Rios in this first matchup with Agassi, to prove he can stay with the American. Agassi was practicing this morning with Brad Gilbert and looked in prime form. He was working on his cross-court forehands."

"Rios is controlling the early points. Agassi said, Prove it to me. Rios is proving it early on."

Rios pops a string on the fourth point of the match.

"Rios is an enigma, really. Hard to work out. Slightly more charming than a year ago. His press conferences have been noticably longer. Better than before when he was so hard to work out. Now there's an occasional sympathy (for the media)."

"It's an absolute sellout here, 14,000 people. 1-love Rios."

Agassi opens with a double fault.

"Agassi's looking a little ill at ease, he's looking nervous to me."

Rios strikes first blood with an early break on an inside out forehand winner. "Lovely shot. The key is how relaxed he is on the preparation. It's a very impressive beginning for Rios."

Agassi missed a forehand down the line and then, in a show of disgust, blows two snot rockets on the court.

"Rios is pouring sweat, it's very hot here, I think the temperature is 86, 87, with the breeze."

Three-love Rios. "There's no sense of the unease Rios started and then ended the Australian Open final. The anxiety seems to be with Agassi at the moment. Plenty for Agassi to ponder as he sits down."

"That's a better game for Agassi. A love game should settle him down."

"Rios counters a love game from Agassi with one of his own. 4-1, Rios."

"Agassi this year hasn't lost to a lefthander, he's beaten Tarango and Siemerink."

"Rios doesn't exactly endear himself to the Miami media. But Rios doesn't much care what people think."

"Rios is giving Agassi nothing to feed on, no short balls."

Rios misses a backhand long and Agassi gets the break back. "Agassi gives the fist to his supporters, to say he's back in it." 4-3 Rios.

Rios hits a forehand long, "He knows now he's in a contest. Billie Jean King watching on."

"Rios has to prove, particularly with his serve, so he can dictate like he did earlier on."

"5-4 Rios. Very important game for Marcelo Rios. Three games in a row for Agassi countered there."

"Agassi is still a little careful with the backhand down the line."

6-5 Rios. "It's a carnival atmopshere here. The bottom two tiers support Agassi, the top two are for Rios."

"Agassi backhand long. There's been so few short balls in the first set."

Rios forehand volley winner. "Wonderful rally from Rios. Rios taking control - one of the few volleys we've seen."

At 30-all Rios snaps a backhand return winner on second serve cross court. "Uh! Unbelievable shot!"

Agassi double faults on fourth the set point, 7-5 Rios.

Second set:

"Wonderful play by Rios. Again, Agassi giving absolutely everything he has."

Agassi nets a forehand to go down a break, 1-3.

"Rios looks unstoppable right now. If there's anyone with the weapons to change it around, it's Agassi."

"Uh! What a volley, that's unbelievable! I thought that Rios was toying with Agassi in the last game with his volleys. That one was just outrageous."

"Really disappointing rally for Agassi. He tried to control, but Rios, with that anticipation, with that quickness."

"Three set points for Rios." Agassi nets a forehand return of a second serve.

"A befitting set by a player who looks now like the next world #1. Rios with 16 winners and two errors the whole set. 6-3."

Third set:

"Rios is undefeated this year after winning the first set."

"That's Rod Laver in the dark shades."

"Larry Stefanki said, interestingly, earlier this week, that Rios hasn't been playing that well, what he has been doing is playing that consistently. I think Stefanki is underrating what consistency does for a player."

"He's won the rally and he broke a string about three shots ago. Relied on his touch. Another bad sign for the American." Agassi cracked a backhand cross court wide by inches.

"3-2. There's a feeling of inevitability about it at the moment."

"A virtuoso performance by Rios. He's thoroughly enjoying himself down there."

"On the line. Fantastic return by Rios. Now he's just a few moments from being on the top of the pile."

"Rios playing phenomenal tennis, 4-3, third set.

"There's no doubt that he will be a worthy #1."

"Agassi hasn't played badly, just a little subdued. Rios has commanded him. Always in command."

"Agassi outgunned. I thought it would be the opposite of this."

Match point, on a second serve, Agassi backhands the return long.

"A fantastic performance. Undoubtedly the best performance of any tennis player this year, even better than Petr Korda in Australia. We thought the anxiety might torment Rios but far from it. It seemed to have made him stronger."

"I've rarely seen a better performance from any player, any match, from my time in watching tennis. This performance by Rios stands up to any match. 7-5 6-3 6-4, Rios is the world #1."

Gilad Bloom is having lunch in the U.S. Open player's lounge. I remember reading that he had beaten Rios in one of the Champions Series events by a very decisive score. I am fascinated and curious to hear what happened in that match. Bloom invites me to sit down with him and spares no detail of the match which was played in Brazil...

Gilad Bloom (ATP Player): "My time with Marcelo Rios was very short and brief - and glorious for me. I was playing

1983 to 1995. When I quit, Marcelo Rios was right in the beginning. I think I remember him coming to the scene when I was winding down my career. Our paths never crossed until 2009 when I got a phone call out of the blue one day when I was walking my son to school. I get a phone call from the tournament director asking me to play the veteran's tour in Sao Paulo, Brazil. I haven't played a tournament in five years. The tournament was played at a Jewish club in Sao Paulo and the owner of the club told the ATP, 'We will sponsor the tournament but we want one player from Israel in the draw.' They call me because I live in New York, the tournament director knew me. He called me and said, 'We want you down there in five weeks.' They gave me a nice chunk of money for a guy like me, $10,000 for three days."

"And I started to practice. I hadn't played in five years. I called my friend Johnny Mac - John McEnroe, who actually lives 20 blocks from me. We hit sometimes, when he needs a hit. I said, 'John, I'm back on the Tour for one week.' So I practice with Johnny Mac for five weeks. We played on Sunday, once a week. He helped me prepare. And the first match I played was with Marcelo Rios. Having not played for five years, I had no expectations. In my group were Marcelo, Henri Leconte and Fernando Meligeni - all lefthanders. I'm a lefty too. I played a whole month with Johnny Mac. So intense. His serve is so good. I got used to a lefty serve on a very high level. And John is still so intense. His serve is so hard to read. He takes every ball on the rise and comes in. If he misses a ball, he throws the racquet. So intense."

"When I go into Sao Paulo, I didn't know who I was going to play. And my first match against Rios is live on TV. And as I walk out of the plane, I see all the posters and billboards of Rios around town and on buses, on buildings promoting the tournament. Oh, shit! Then as I went in there, Jewish club, so out of the crowd, 80% are Jewish. And they're all rooting for me. I met Rios in the morning at the swimming pool, I went to the swimming pool with Haarhuis and Enqvist. We were just reading books at the pool, drink Coke, whatever. He came in with his wife and met him for a few minutes. Hi, how are you? He had the goatee, with a very short haircut. Bulked up like a frikkin' boxer! And I was like, Shit, I'm in trouble. I'm 42 at the time, he was 33. I never play. And he plays every week. I teach - I have an academy in New York. They brought me out of the grave. Now I'm facing frikkin' Rios."

"My plan was to not give him one rally. The whole match just play a different point. One shot, I came in behind a second serve. One time I chipped and charged on his second serve. The next time I drop-shotted and came in. The next time I played moonballs, then I played serve and volley. And I just hit dropshots, top spin. I didn't want to give him any rhythm."

"But here's the thing: his serve is so much easier to return than Johnny Mac's. So after returning Johnny Mac, returning Rios was a joke. He leans back and kicks it - it seemed like I had five seconds to hit the return, compared to Mac. I'm up 6-0 1-0, the crowd starts booing him. They want to see a show. Who wants to see somebody get killed? He picked up his game a little bit, 3-all. I break him at 4-3 - 5-3. And the next thing I know - cameras and microphones and press conferences. And McEnroe is texting me from the French Open, 'What the fuck?' He was following it on the internet. He's a freak. He texted me one hour after the match, 'You cannot be serious?!'

"When he heard my group he said, 'You can handle Leconte and Meligeni but Rios, he's too tough. I never beat him.' Because McEnroe never beat Rios. And McEnroe has a lot of respect for him and he told me Rios is too tough, too young, But the other two you can handle. In reality, I beat Rios and killed him and I lost to the other two. But thanks to Rios, he has a very special place in my heart. I had my 15 minutes of fame again. And went back to the grave again. And I got my best win against Rios when I was 42."

(How did Rios accept this defeat?) "Let's put it this way. First, what happened was, I think he never heard of me. This guy's just a filler. Never really highly ranked. He even skipped the warm-up - I was warming up for 30-40 minutes - he showed up like five minutes before the match, warms up for barely five-six minutes. Didn't move his feet much, kind of lethargic. That's how he was. He probably thought I was going to hand it to him. When this obviously happened, he started to try really hard, because, you know, his pride came in. He tried harder. We actually had a few deuce games. But he was whipped. He couldn't really turn it around. So I think it was one of those matches - he played better the next two matches. He was much more competitive. I caught him the first match. The next day I saw him at breakfast and he said, 'How you doing?' He said his back operation - that he never really recovered from that back operation. That (on) that day his back was more stiff than usual, whatever. He was nice. I've seen what you call, the 'new' Rios, trying to be a little more civilized. He came to the party, trying to mingle. He wasn't living up to his old repuation. By that time, he showed up with a baby, his wife. Actually, we were all partying. And he was the only one who came with a wife [smiles]. And we were just there, middle of Sao Paulo, beers every night, and Leconte smoking cigars at the party - and Rios was hangin' out with his wife and baby. That's what I remember. That's my contact with the guy."

Anonymous: "Did you hear about the car accident? I don't remember where exactly it was but they give you a car for the tournament, so you can drive your own car, don't need taxis or drivers to pick you up. He took a car one night, got drunk and crashed the car, totaled the car, with some girl. And the ATP covered up the whole story. It never got out."

Dan C. Weil (Journalist): "I was staying at the Sonesta Hotel on Key Biscayne during the tournament in '97 or '98. One morning, I was working out in the gym and Rios walked in, gave a friendly smile and hello and he was nothing but polite. He may have even asked me if it was okay to use the equipment. I couldn't believe he was so nice and polite after all the bad things everyone said about him. I guess Rios is very complicated – just like the rest of us."

Neil Harmon (Journalist, The Times Of London): "Rios came back on the Champions Tour in London and they had their usual roundtable. Everyone's invited to speak to anyone they would like to. And he cut quite a lonely figure. Nobody was at his table. So I went back in my mind thinking how he was fantastic to watch and interesting because he never showed much, you never quite knew what was going on in his head. So I went over and had a chat and found him to be disconcertingly pleasant. He wasn't one of the greatest interviews of all time nor did it last long. It wasn't negative, it was okay. It was okay. He used to be such a hard sell in terms of media - he just didn't give you anything. So when he walked into the media interview rooms, it wasn't a place that he wanted to be. In this sport, the #1 player in the sport has to give quite a lot of himself. I suppose we've come to the ridiculously sublime in Federer and Nadal who are so brilliant. And you think it was nothing like Rios, who was a total nightmare. But I actually think, deep down, he's just terribly shy. He didn't want to speak in a language that wasn't his own. And that made it very difficult - for the sport to sell the guy. Impossible."

Al Bello (Photographer): "He was nasty. He never smiled. One year he won Miami. We were supposed to do a shoot with him on the beach, with his trophy. And he made us wait two hours. Before the sun went down. And then he came out. And the light had already gone.

And he didn't smile. And he stood there for like three seconds. And then he left. And I just thought, Wow, what a scumbag. And that was it...He was a good lefty. I remember he was lefty. Like a comet, came and went quick. Never won a major. Got to #1 for like a week, then he was gone. I haven't really thought about him till just now, till you just said something. Not a nice guy. Always mad, always scowling, never smiled."

Excerpts from newspaper report of highlights of Rios' 6-3 6-2 1993 Eddie Herr 18's final win: "...Two points from the match, Rios broke into a wide grin after drilling his favorite shot, a scorching backhand down the line, and patted his stomach as if to mock others who get nervous before closing out a victory... Up 3-0 in the second set, Rios smiled at a courtside photographer long enough for him to get the picture. The photographer walked away shaking his head...At triple match point, Rios let a high ball bounce, then swatted it long. Then he shrugged and, on the next point, nailed a backhand cross-court to win...In the match's most critical moment, at 4-3 and deuce in the first set with (Lior) Mor rallying, Rios nonchalantly walked up to mid-court and missed a drop shot. No matter. He still won that game, and seven of the next nine...Serving for the match, Rios looked to his coach, as if to say, 'Watch this.' He then hit his first serve insensibly hard – and straight into the net. He got the next serve in, but whaled the next forehand into the net...'This is my style,' said Rios, who was already playing for his country's Davis Cup team at 16 and who was dogged by cameras from two Chilean TV stations during the Eddie Herr tournament. 'Always when I play, I want to have fun. I can't change. I've always been that way. I have a lot of what you say – confidence. I never think I will lose a game, a set...Now that I'm going out of the juniors, I'll have to be more serious.'"

Allen Fox PHD (Former Pro Player): "Rios was a different breed of cat and probably has an interesting back story. I had no personal interaction with him. I first saw him play at the Orange Bowl, where he was small, quick, and with a good set of hands. His becoming the #1 player in the world would not have been predicted. I hear that as a person he was a bit of an asshole and very difficult. Stefanki did a hell of a job with him. I never heard why he fell so far so fast afterward. The personal and psychological aspects of that fall would be interesting."

Pete Sampras (From his book 'A Champion's Mind' with Peter Bodo): "Rios was an odd one, a surly, strange sort of guy who had a lot of talent but seemed a misfit and an outsider on the Tour. It's hard to enjoy life and survive that way...He was like a left-handed Andre Agassi. He was a great striker of the ball and could take it early but he didn't serve as big as Andre and his game lacked the heft that made you feel like you were really in trouble. I always felt like Rios had nothing that could hurt me. Still, Rios was very creative and 'handsy' - he could change direction and pace on his shots with ease and he just had a nice feel for the ball and the game in general...Rios held the #1 ranking briefly. He made my life truly miserable in 1998 when I was trying to lock up that record sixth-straight year-end #1 ranking."

Jon Wertheim (Journalist and Author): "You know the Orange Bowl final story right? Maybe you can get a contemporary like Roddick or Gimelstob to confirm the story...I gather that in the Orange Bowl, Rios had a running feud with and opponent. On match point, he hits a drop shot. The opponent scrambles to retrieve it and pops up a lob but then trips and is sprawled on the gound. Rather than putting away the easy sitter, Rios drills the opponent with the shot - and wins the match by virtue of the ball-can't-hit-your-body-on-the-fly rule."

Justin Gimelstob (ATP Player): "I can't confirm that story, but Rios was a rough dude. Unfriendly, contentious, disrespectful, and, sadly, a waste of serious talent."

Jena (Tennis Fan): "I became a fan of Marcelo Rios in late 1996. I had access to cable TV and the Eurosport TV channel – and I remember watching Marcelo for the first time. I can't remember whom he was playing, but he played really badly, and the commentators were talking about him as the 'South American Agassi'. So awful was he, I remember thinking 'you must be crazy!' Agassi was never a favorite of mine. I didn't like his brashness, and his image, but admired his game. I couldn't believe this awful Chilean was being compared to him. In those days I didn't have access to the Internet, so relied on Eurosport to find out what was happening in tennis. For some reason, Rios always seemed to be on, and the more I saw of him, the more I realized he was the most talented player I'd ever seen. I loved his footwork – he moved so effortlessly, always seeming to bounce on his feet. He read the game so well, went for improbable shots and wasn't afraid to come to the net. He made it all look so easy."

"The British press didn't really discuss him, so I only heard the commentators, who always praised his game but complained about his surliness. And in those days, Eurosport would occasionally have interviews after matches, and I got to see the surliness – but it didn't put me off. After one match, in a live interview, asked about his press image, Rios replied, 'Oh, the press, they get pissed if I don't give an interview.' I liked Marcelo's honesty – he never tried to 'fake' an image. His surliness never bothered me – Rios is a tennis player first and foremost – if he chooses not to speak to the press or sign an autograph, that's his choice – he's not selling an album or film. I like the fact he is what he is. Anyway, I prefer to let Rios' tennis do the talking, so to speak. Of course, all this is easy for me to say, because I've got his autograph many, many times, actually nine times, and he's never been rude or unpleasant when I've seen him on the practice courts or spoken to him at meet and greets."

"Watching Marcelo at the 1997 French Open, I was by then completely hooked, and it suddenly occurred to me that I could actually go to Roland Garros. I'd been to Wimbledon in the late 1980's, early 90's, braving the queues and the weather, until I was tired of doing it. Marcelo's magical performance encouraged me to plan a trip in 1998, which I did. The excitement of seeing him play live was awesome. By now Marcelo had been #1 in the world. This inspired me to finally get online. And I discovered a thriving Rios community on CNN tennis message boards. What was immediately noticeable was that Marcelo has an international following – fans from Australia, Singapore, the USA, France, Germany, the UK, as well as fans from East Europe. We'd meet-up online to follow Marcelo's matches wherever he played. Through following Marcelo, I got to meet up with many of these fans and attend tournaments around the world – Roland Garros, Monte Carlo, the U.S. Open, the Miami and Cincinnati Masters events, meeting fellow Rios fans and getting to see Marcelo play many times."

"There was always a great atmosphere watching the matches, especially if any Chilean fans were there. I got to watch him practice many times as well – and I can honestly say, I've never seen him be rude or impolite to anybody. He has refused autographs – saying 'not now' – but this is always before a practice session, which is never a good time to ask any players, because time is precious for them."

"Rios was probably at his most relaxed at the Monte Carlo Masters event. Most of the players seemed to be, because Monaco is such a small place and the players don't get hassled. One year, 2000, Marcelo was coming back from injury yet again, and lost a tight first-round match to Felix Mantilla. I decided to check the practice courts before heading back to my hotel, and saw Marcelo out practicing. It must have been about 6 pm, and having just lost, I thought that would be the last thing he'd want to do. But no, there he was – and he was in a very playful mood. He was hitting with his then coach Luis Lobo, and began to hit some trick shots. Lobo encouraged him by a mixture of mockery and praise. A crowd began to form, and even some players came out to watch and applaud him – Carlos Moya, Alberto Costa and Fernando Vicente. His touch was unbelievable. He really put on a show. At the time, Marcelo's former coach Larry Stefanki was coaching Kafelnikov, and he lost as Marcelo was practicing. One of the player's friends shouted out the result – and Marcelo just shrugged his shoulders. Despite his loss and the lateness, Marcelo seemed to be enjoying himself."

"I actually got to see Marcelo's last Grand Slam match, at Roland Garros. It was quite sad that they'd scheduled him for court 17 – behind the practice courts. Chile had just won the World Team Cup, and I didn't think I'd see Marcelo on the practice courts the next day, but there he was, hitting with Nicolas Massu. Massu was grunting really loudly, and Marcelo was teasing him by doing louder and longer grunts. The next day, he played Ancic in the first round and from the start, his arm was bothering him. He really struggled with his serve, and when he called for the trainer, he was told he'd have to wait a while – probably because he was on an outside court. Marcelo didn't want to wait, so he played another two games instead of waiting for the trainer. He was given treatment, including painkillers, but he just seemed to have no strength in his arm – his serve was awful. At 6-1, Marcelo retired from the match."

"I saw Marcelo on the Senior Tour. As much as I was excited about seeing Marcelo play again, he was too young and way too good for the Senior Tour. I went with friends to Portugal, and he just annihilated players. The Portuguese tournament is very family orientated and attracts holidaying tourists. Marcelo was presented to the press and the crowd in a big ceremony, and looked a bit like a deer caught in headlights. He had to do two meet and greets at the event, and I managed to tell him how much I admired his game and wished him well. He obliged with a half-smile and a thank you. The children at the tournament really warmed to him – the other players seemingly 'too old' to interest them. Marcelo joked with the crowd and played some brilliant shots – but it was all way too easy for him. His first match hadn't taxed him that much – he went to the gym to work out afterwards! It was about midnight."

"In the final with McEnroe, he joked with the crowd who had bet on him and his odds. The tournament has the players' restaurant changing rooms overlooking the court. Marcelo was the only player who sat and watched all the other players' matches. He might not have been playing until 10 pm, but he was there for the first match at 6 pm. When he played the final, a lot of the catering staff from the restaurant came out to watch him and applauded him when he won."

"He returned the following year with his new wife Paula Pavic, and the tournament and reaction was the same. He seemed very relaxed at this tournament. I watched a 'hit with the players' session, in which Marcelo made a huge fuss of a child whose father he hit against. The little boy sat in the umpire's chair and Marcelo teased him about calling the score. Even though it was meant to be fun and relaxed, Marcelo hit some spectacular shots, all the while puffing on a cigarette – not a great example for the child. This tournament was when he would play Guillermo Vilas. Marcelo had arrived at the clubhouse before Vilas, and we watched eagerly to see who would acknowledge the other first. In the end it was Vilas who made his way over to Marcelo to say hello. Can't say I was surprised. When he gave a press conference at the end, he thanked the organizers, the resort, the staff etc., before adding with a big smile, 'You know, all the usual shit.' At the end of event party, Marcelo was the only player not to attend."

"The last time he played Portugal was really disappointing. He clearly hadn't been practicing and was just awful – and he knew it. When he served, the ball couldn't even make it over the net. I felt bad for the kids who had come to see him again. I heard adults say how he didn't seem the same player as previous years. He never stayed to watch other players' matches. In his first match, he constantly checked his hand, and when I asked him at a 'meet and greet' if he had a problem, he showed me a huge blister on his hand, smiled and shrugged. I asked Meligeni if he knew what was up with Rios, and he told me, 'He's just not been playing.' It was such a shame. At the final night of the tournament, Marcelo played a truly awful doubles match with Leconte. He then went up to the clubhouse to wait until after the final to be presented on court with all the other players. He was laughing and joking with some of the other players, having a few drinks and smoking – I later found out he had just announced his wife was expecting again. He may not have been enjoying his tennis, but he seemed really happy in himself."

"Another memory I have of him is in Monte Carlo one year, one of my friends stayed at the players' hotel, Le Meridien, and when we went to visit her, Rios was chatting with Safin - the difference in size was hilarious - and he actually stood aside to let us use the elevator, now, how polite is that? Luis Lobo was coaching him at the time, and we saw him heading out with some of the other Argentine players in the early evening - and Marcelo sat on his own in the hotel restaurant. He didn't seem bothered that he was on his own, or that Lobo was heading out."

Chapter 8
The Prince of Darkness

"The most beautiful thing we can experience is the mysterious. It is the source of all true art and science." -Albert Einstein

"The highest level of human experience or expression would be creating art. Art is the highest level of human achievement, whatever the art is." -LeRoy Neiman

Luis Miles (Former Chilean Junior Player): "My first memory of Marcelo Rios was of him warming up during a junior tournament in Santiago, Chile in 1990. I was barely 14, I was warming up for my own match with my tennis buddy and best friend Marcelo Pagani, and my dreams of professional tennis were still very much alive in my mind. Close by, unbeknownst to me, was Marcelo Rios, sliding up and down the court with the grace of a swan, covering the entire area with feet that seemed to fly, hitting balls from and to any angle, applying the kind of topspin that defied gravity bringing the yellow sphere down just inches away from the baseline, every single time. I momentarily stopped and asked my friend, 'Who on earth is this guy that makes tennis look like the easiest sport in the world? If there are people who can play tennis like that, then I have no chance of making it.'"

"'That's El Chino Rios,'" said my friend. I immediately stopped playing - leaving my friend baffled on the court, forgotten just as the nerves from my upcoming match, and got a bit closer to watch the warm up routine. With Marcelo Rios, you only needed two seconds to realize that what you were seeing was not entirely of this world. Marcelo was barely three months older than me, but we had never met because given his level of play he would always compete in the higher categories. At 14, he was already competing against 16 and 18-year olds. I had heard stories about 'El Chino' but never got to see him until that day."

Question: Did you ever see him smile or laugh on the court?

Luis Miles: "Yes, but only as he grew older, in his twenties, he began to accept some of the praise and recognition from audiences around the world. During his younger days, I do not remember seeing him smile or laugh, it was all business and all seriousness."

Question: Why do you think people misunderstood him as a person and player?

Luis Miles: "People did not quite understand that, when they were watching Marcelo play, they were watching a corporate machine. When Marcelo stepped onto the court, so did Prince, Yonex, Nike, adidas and the myriad of sponsors that supported him at one point or another in his career. The problem was that, while most players started grabbing the attention of one or two sponsors during the early teen years, everyone wanted to jump on the Chino train. At such young age, I believe this took some of the 'fun' out of the sport for him. This, consequently, made him very angry."

"While he had plenty of time to develop as a tennis player, he had no time to develop as a human being, aka social skills, and this problem was exacerbated by his early successes, and the adulation he received by doing something what came so naturally for him."

• • •

At the 2010 U.S. Open I attempt to get an interview with the chair umpire Tony Nimmons, who defaulted Rios out of the ATP Los Angeles event. Nimmons is here working as I spot his name on the daily match schedule, so I put in a request to the officiating supervisor Rich Kauffman. Mr. Kauffman politely declines my request to speak with Nimmons because of policy but he is kind enough to share his own memories of Rios...

Rich Kauffman (Former ATP Umpire): "I did a number of his matches. I never had any issues. He was kind of a quiet guy anyway. I do recall when I was referee at the Davis Cup in Calgary, they were playing on that lightning fast court. And I remember the Chilean players - both Rios and Fernando Gonzalez - comment to me about how fast the court was. It was pretty quick, like playing on an ice rink. Fernando couldn't even keep the ball in the court because he hit the ball so hard. Rios played a very good match against Daniel Nestor but I think Nestor beat him in that match. It was five sets and I think Rios was hurt. His knee was bothering him. As I recall, it was a pretty gutsy performance and he hung in there."

"The funny thing about those teams meeting - whenever they met, one would move up, one would move down. The Chileans could never beat the Canadians in the fast, lightning court in Calgary. So it was a vicious cycle in the Group, trying to move up to World Group, always running into each other."

"Rios was a feisty player, we all knew he had a lot of energy, a lot of emotion. I never had a problem with him. Boy, he played some great tennis. I saw him the year he was #1, even before, when he was moving up. He won some great matches. I remember umpiring some matches with him where he just wasn't missing. Lefty, all over the place, you couldn't even compare him to anybody. He was sort of a unique player. He wasn't just a clay courter. He could play on a fast court, slow court, medium court. He could adjust his game. Just great natural talent. We were all impressed with him even when we saw him coming up in juniors. One of the best players I ever saw, that's for sure. He was a shy, quiet guy, that was just his demeanor. A little misunderstood."

"Rios was competitive. We, as officials, once th[at]
starts, the fire just burns in some of those g[uys],
that doesn't bother us. We're just dealing with him
professionally and on court, pre-match or after match.
None of us ever put him in the category of a player that
was difficult. He just was feisty and emotional. If he
believed something, he was gonna let you know. We,
as officials, respect those kinds of guys, where some
people question their behavior, we're ready to deal
with the emotions of a player like that. And there's been
a number of players like that over the years, obviously.
But when he was focused, he was a tough player for
the opponent. He returned well, he pressured your
serve every time, he could come in and he could stay
back. Great topspin, he had a great backhand. He could
swing that serve out being a lefty. Really had a natural
talent for the game. It almost looked like it flowed from
him. Didn't have to think too much about it. He just
played his confident level and knew what he could do."

"I enjoyed watching Rios play. I started as an official
just to watch great players play tennis. I always got a
thrill out of watching real talented players, whoever it
was. Even if they're getting in my face, it didn't bother
me. I still enjoyed watching those kind of guys play.
Just a natural talent, there weren't many players that
were like him, that could play on that level. The kind
of game he played, he might have been the best at it.
He wasn't a very big guy. Compact, strong as a bull and
fiery. But the umpires, in a funny sort of way, umpires
like fiery players. It brings about more energy. Keeps us
a little more focused. Keeps our concentration. Instead

of getting lulled in just some matches. It keeps us on our toes. It keeps our concentration going."

Down at Delray Beach at the International Tennis Center, Mats Wilander is playing doubles with two local players and his Wilander On Wheels partner Cameron Lickle. After the friendly sets, Wilander takes photos, chats and signs some autographs. It's not the best time to ask a tennis legend and former world #1 like Mats Wilander, out of the blue what he thinks of Marcelo Rios, but I ask anyway, as this is the only chance there will be. Surprisingly, Mats is quite friendly and seems interested to discuss Rios. Before some more photos and small talk he tells me to wait, that he wants to share some thoughts. Little did I expect to receive about five minutes of gold on my recorder...

Mats Wilander (Hall of Famer): "I never played him. What was his years? (1993-2004.) There you go, exactly. I stopped in '91. I started playing again in '93. And I remember seeing him around the locker room. And to be 100% honest - I thought he was a ball kid. Because he looks so young. He looked really young when he was younger. And he was pretty small. Obviously, he still had the long hair and it made him look really young. And I kept thinking, Who is this guy? And he was around. And he was around. And then he won. And then he was around. And it was like, What? Who? And I just could never put the name to the face. But I realized that he was still around, like, so he must be winning. So he's a good player because he's around. And then, eventually, a couple years later, I'm like, Wow, that's just him. And then of course he looked the same way his whole life. He still looks the same."

"But hey, what can I say, maybe the most talented player of all...not of all-time but pretty much, pretty close? Great understanding of the game - great understanding of the game is a broad answer - great understanding of pace versus no pace, where you step in, hit really clean, play really flat. But also had this ability to recognize that, Okay, let me throw one in - let me play one deep, let me soften the thing up and then start attacking again. So he was one of those guys when he was playing well, he was hard to beat. And when he played bad, he got in his own way. He got a little too crazy."

"The fact that he didn't win a Grand Slam and he didn't do better in Grand Slams - sometimes that has to do with the mindset. Three out of five sets, two weeks, you're not there to win the tournament really. You're there to put in eight hours of work every day. And then at the end of it, there's one winner. And I think, if you don't get into the majors early enough in your life, you never really learn how to play majors. Because it's a long haul. And I don't think, for me, that he really got it. I really don't. And some players don't get it. They don't get it, as in they didn't have this freebie. I had a freebie in the majors because I won when I was 17. So it was like, Oh, okay, that's what it's about. And after that, it was, I know I'm here, I must be here for 2 1/2 weeks or potentially. And I think, for some guys, early on, if they don't succeed, it's a long way. It's two weeks.

No, it's more, it's 2 1/2, three weeks, the same hotel, the same restaurants, same clubs, three out of five sets, the grind, grind, grind. And every day. And I don't think he got that. Unfortunately, because he was a big match player."

"But again, he was missed. When he stopped, it was like, Back to the guys that don't have the flair kind of thing. It was hard. It was really hard to see him go I have to say. Don't know how old he was when he went."

"I talked to him. Not much. I mean, obviously, I met him. Again, we were just - I was just sort of one of those guys that was around. I would think, if he ever thought of me or saw me, I would think that I was one of those guys that he would walk into the locker room and say, What the hell is he still doing playing? He played, didn't he? What's he doing here? He won seven majors? Get out of here. Just when you're coming in young with that much talent and you're somebody that is ten years older with not as much talent - and I play a completely different game - it's very easy to think, Are you kidding me? Like, What is he doing here? And so I think we were in that way quite different. Or really different. Obviously, I was talented in my own way and he's talented and working hard in his way. And I work hard in another way. We were different. But anyway, yeah, he was missed. He was really missed. He was fun. He was fun. Not irresponsible...but irregular. Like, you didn't know what is gonna happen? No idea. Erratic. Play well. But who knows. Where's he going? Is he playing well today? Is he showing up?"

Florent Serra (ATP Player): "The one time I played Rios was in Mexico (in a Challenger which was the final professional tournament of Rios' career). He was a nice player. I remember, I look and play. I didn't play [laughs]. I was watching him to play. He was a #1, a very nice player, nice game. (Did you talk with Rios?) No."

Random fan comments about Rios:

"Yes, when Rios was it his best he was a genius at work. As was mentioned his thrashing of Agassi in the final of Miami in 1998 was an awesome sight to behold. Also, he played a fanatstic match against Guga in Rome that year and beat him 7-5,6-0. Guga was the then defending Roland Garros champ!"

• • •

"Marcelo, (I) loved watching him at his best, such wonderful shots. Such a pity what happened to him, never the same after the groin injuries/surgeries."

• • •

"Wonder what would happen if the '98 world #1 Rios played Federer today...now that would have been a rivalry for the tennis faithfuls!"

• • •

"I never know how to take Marcelo. But as a person who hopes to be a freelance journalist at some point, I know that I would want to interivew either a player like Marat who gives great quotes (and Andy Roddick too at times) or someone like Marcelo, who with his non-responses gives an amusing interview. 99% of the guys on the Tour give pat, bland answers. Fans blame the journalists (and yes they do ask stupid questions sometimes), but they don't have much to work with - these guys are taught early how to reveal nothing. As one of our guest lecturers said in my sports reporting class - tennis players more than any other professional athlete live in a sheltered bubble."

• • •

"Rios was by far my favorite player to watch, ever. More than Federer, more than Sampras. He was like a combination of McEnroe and Federer, with the attitude of Safin. He definitely had a bad attitude, but who cares, his tennis was amazing. There was an article on him in Sports Illustrated a long while back called, 'Blame it on Rios' that has some really nasty stuff about him, like how he treated fans, tournament directors, etc."

• • •

"The thing that I remember about Rios was that he watched other players. I recall being at the Indian Wells Tournament in '96 or '97 and looking up in the stands and Rios was there, actually watching other matches going on, you don't see that too often. On the negative side, I recall that he dumped Stefanki after he became #1 and told him, 'I want to go in a different direction," and Stefanki replied, 'The only direction you can go from here is down.'"

. . .

"If you think that Rios press conference interview was rude and awkward, you should have been in the official ATP online real-time chat with Rios several years ago! It's like he did the chat with the purpose of insulting and ignoring fans. He hardly answered any fan questions. He told fans to shut up and worse. Many fans got riled up and expressed their disgusted feelings toward Rios. One fan was kicked off the chat. That chatroom was a madhouse by the time the whole event was mercifully over!"

. . .

"I do believe that was the chat where he was asked if he prefered tennis or sex and replied, 'Depends on what type of sex it is.' What a gem of a question, eh?"

. . .

"No one knows his 'real personality' anyway. But no one is 100% 'nice/bad'. We're all a combination."

. . .

"I'm from and live in Wales, part of Britain. I have to say, part of the appeal of Marcelo is his 'bad boy' persona. My friends and I like the fact that he's his own person, even if he can be a bit of a horror. One name we had for him was 'The Prince of Darkness.' I have met many tennis/Rios fans via the internet and there are still four of us in regular touch. I have seen Marcelo play a number of times - meeting up with these fans - including on the Seniors Tour. I got to see him play at Roland Garros, Monte Carlo, the U.S. Open and Portugal, and have had an excellent success rate in asking for his autograph - yes really - six out of six times. One of our group has translated the two bios of Marcelo published in Chile into English - luckily, her job was translating. In the first bio, I found it very interesting that as a child, Marcelo was prescribed ritalin - the drug for ADHD - and that his parents discontinued the medication because they didn't like the change in his personality. For me, that speaks volumes about him and his family. I'm not surprised Stefanki doesn't like to speak now, publicly, about Rios. I'm sure he's still holding out for a coaching job. I will say this though - Larry Stefanki did not make Marcelo Rios #1 - Marcelo Rios did."

· · ·

"Definitely a gifted player, wasted talent maybe. Social misfit, very likely. He was great to watch play tennis. I suppose that he didn't/couldn't win a Grand Slam says a lot – for that you need a combination of hard work, talent, discipline and a bit of luck as well. Being likeable helps too."

· · ·

"I was a big Rios fan, but I can't overlook his tanking like so many of his fans are willing to do. I don't mind his surly behavior with fans and the media - except the fact that he wouldn't give autographs to children, that's pretty messed up. But I was disgusted how often he just 'gave up.' That is unacceptable in any sport, his genius doesn't make it okay. I remember a '96 match vs. Woodbridge at the Toronto Masters Series, in which he was so blatantly tanking, the commentator advised viewers to change the channel."

• • •

"As for Rios' personality - if you read the bio of Marcelo, that gives an insight. Unlike a lot of players, he didn't pick up a racquet until he was ten, and his parents never dreamed he could make a career out of it. He had no interest in watching tennis as a child, and his parents didn't realise how good he was. In fact, they tried to curb his tennis playing. He had difficulties in school - was even put on ritalin for ADHD at one point (not really a surprise, eh?) and his mother stopped him taking it because it altered his personality. He was allowed to play tennis because that was his only interest - but his parents took steps to try and stop him playing - not the usual tennis parents story, eh? He only took up tennis partly as a way of getting out of school when he was 14. His family were amazed he could make a living out of it - so naive that they got badly ripped off by the Chilean Tennis Federation - the family took their case to court and won. One of the guys from the Federation had a brother who was on a national Chilean newspaper and made sure Rios got plenty of bad press. In my opinion, not having pushy parents who were naive, and being the first big Chilean player for a long time, made Marcelo unprepared for life on the Tour. He likes to keep himself to himself - if he could play tennis as he wished and not participate in off-court activities, he would have been much happier. A pyschology report states that Marcelo's attitude was similar to an artist - if he didn't like what he was doing, i.e., when playing a match, he'd lose and just think he could begin again - an artist spoils a painting he's not happy with and just starts again. Of course, this attitude wasn't going to get him anywhere on the Tour."

. . .

"I love the fact that he was never seeking acceptance from the media or fans, it doesn't really matter what they think. Is it going to help him win any more matches than he actually did if the media thinks he's this great guy or other players like him? Actually, his mentality worked to his advantage because he 'psyched out' other players, his erratic behavior, accompanied by his erratic play (one match he paints a masterpiece and the next match he's urinating on the canvas) – does this remind you of anyone? Perhaps Marat? Fact of the matter is, great guy, great mentality and, most of all, straight-forward and to the point. Don't waste your time. Also for being vertically challenged, this guy proved that size really doesn't matter. Sad to see him come up short, he is truly one of the only players I've come to appreciate of South American descent, aside from Gustavo Kuerten, who played a beautiful game when at his peak."

. . .

"Of course Marcelo was misunderstood – most geniuses are! I miss you Marcelo Rios! Now HE was an exciting, unpredictable player!"

. . .

"The only time I ever saw Rios was in around 2000 at the Australian Open. He played an absolutely brilliant match and then a few hours later I was walking around the practice courts and he was sitting down watching someone else practice and he had bags of ice all over him. A bag taped to his knee, one strapped to his shoulder and one on his groin. I think his body just wasn't strong enough for him to produce his best tennis every day. Seemed like he paid a price for being able to hit all those outrageous shots."

• • •

"There was just something about Rios that was captivating, that goes beyond the tennis court. Perhaps it was what he stood for or what his game stood for. It was almost as if he challenged all our conventions of what good tennis is or what a good tennis player should be like. Talented beyond doubts yet predominantly a baseliner who relies not on brute strength or stamina but on craft and subtlety, it was this contradiction that attracted me. One of the most damning arguments against Rios was the fact that he reached world #1 status without ever winning a Grand Slam. Without doubt, his best chance was in the Australian Open final against Petr Korda and while there is no proof, I somehow feel that the doping scandal or allegations against the Czech must have played some part in his "convincing" or "crushing" victory against Rios. Had Korda been "clean" would Rios have won? That is a question that will forever bug me. Is that also why Rios reacted so strongly against Agassi's own drug admissions, I wonder."

• • •

"I wish I could play like Rios. After seeing him play in Washington DC in 2001, I went to the courts with my best friend and hit a few shots that had some Rios in them – best shots I ever hit in my life. For Rios, they would have been two unmemorable seconds of his tennis career."

The Weller Evans Interview

Weller Evans worked on the ATP Tour for 25 years as a Communications manager and Vice President.

Weller Evans: "As far as making the sport interesting, Rios did that. Every sport needs a villain to make things interesting, someone that is universally hated. Obviously, Marcelo Rios clearly went out of his way to, as Sports Illustrated portrayed him, become the most hated man in tennis."

"Probably the biggest mistake I made in my 25 years at the ATP was not letting Marcelo Rios go to jail in 1995 in Cincinnati. At the ATP event in Cincinnati, every player gets a car to use during the week of the tournament. I think in '95 he was 19. He needed to be 21 to be able to take the car for the week and Marcelo wasn't old enough at the time. His coach signed the papers and said he would be the guy to drive the car. That agreement didn't last. Rios got behind the wheel of the car and peeled out of the parking lot at 50 miles an hour - and almost ran down a police officer. The police went after him and brought him back to the tournament and were going to arrest him."

"I made the mistake of speaking to the police and diffusing the situation, telling them that it would not happen again and that we would take responsibility for Marcelo Rios the rest of the week. So they relented and didn't take him to downtown Mason. I would say that is probably my biggest mistake because maybe one night in jail (and perhaps meeting a guy named 'Bubba') might have been the best thing for Marcelo's personal development."

"That was a watershed moment. But unfortunately, I let the opportunity pass." (Rios lost 6-3 6-3 in the first round at Cincinnati to Brett Steven.)

Question: Did Rios show any kind of gratitude for you helping him get out of that situation?

Weller Evans: "I don't think he could spell the word gratitude. A couple of weeks later he wanted to play the Long Island tournament, a US Open warm-up event. Although I think he was top 50 in 1995, he needed a wildcard. He wanted to play the week before, maybe he felt he needed some match play. Jeff Schwartz, his agent, asked if I would have a word with the tournament director, which, again, I did. Having put in a good word, Marcelo received the wildcard. Just to show how grateful he was to be in the tournament, after he lost a game of pool in the players' lounge to one of his buddies, he went ahead and broke one of the two pool cues. (He eventually lost in the Hamlet Cup 1-6 5-7 to Mal Washington in R16)."

"I don't know how you say 'I don't care' in Spanish but that is probably something that should be etched on his tombstone."

Question: It seemed he was a spoiled, immature kid who did not sufficiently develop his social skills to the same level of his tennis abilities.

Weller Evans: "That's quite honestly the air that he gave off throughout his career: a spoiled kid who was immature and who just didn't care. Mark Woodforde, a pretty astute individual and student of the game, predicted that, even at the height of Rios' career, that he wouldn't win a Grand Slam because he didn't have the heart and fortitude. Mark Woodforde was astute enough to realize that Rios didn't have what it takes. He came close in Australia. I was there. I think he was very, very tight. Korda just took him apart, 2, 2 and 2. I think he was very nervous. Sometimes the bravado that an individual displays, like Marcelo, can be a mask, a facade, for insecurities. In that big moment, Marcelo's insecurity rose to the top. He was very, very tight, very nervous."

Question: Were you in the dressing room before the match? Could you sense this?

Weller Evans: "I was in the locker room. The locker room before a Grand Slam final is a pretty quiet place.

There's not a lot of hustle and bustle like the first week. It's pretty subdued. I felt that Marcelo, once I saw him on the court, was overcome by the moment. He just seemed a little uptight, nervous. Not as free-flowing as he normally was."

Question: What is a lasting image you have of Rios?

Weller Evans: "I think if you were going to call central casting and ask them to send over a drug-dealing terrorist, they'd probably send over a guy who looked like Marcelo Rios."

Question: Was he ever out of character? Did you ever see him where you said to yourself, Whoa, I didn't know he had that in him?

Weller Evans: "Honestly...no. No. I also remember being in Gstaad in 1995 as well. The players have to walk a fair distance from the players' lounge to the stadium. I think Marcelo was playing Jacob Hlasek in the quarterfinal. Jacob walked to the stadium from the players' lounge. I can't tell you the number of people... fans, tournament staff, other players, you name it, that applauded Jacob on that short walk, that implored him just to give Rios a beatdown. Now granted, we're in Switzerland and Jacob is Swiss. Obviously national pride had something to do with that wave of support. But clearly, from my perspective, there was a little extra show of support for Jacob there because of who his opponent was in the quarterfinal. (Hlasek won the match 6-2 in the third set.)

"I always find it fascinating that you have these guys - and Rios is not alone, Marat Safin falls in this category as well, guys who complain about life on the circuit and the conditions of the pro tour. Then they retire and they are finally free from this nightmare life on the circuit. Then guess who's back playing senior tournaments? The same guys who complained how miserable they were on the professional tennis tour! You saw it with Rios and you saw it with Safin - within months he was back playing an exhibition in Atlantic City, New Jersey!"

"Talented athletes like Mike Tyson and Marcelo Rios have to work very hard in order to get people to despise them, the way they ultimately did. Why would sports fans not want to embrace such supremely talented athletes as Mike Tyson and Marcelo Rios? We want to appreciate them and embrace them. I got into pro tennis events for free for 25 years and, as I told you earlier, I would pay to watch Marcelo Rios play. Sports fans like us want to embrace the supremely talented athletes like Mike Tyson and Marcelo Rios, not despise them."

Question: Did you ever have a normal conversation with Rios?

Weller Evans: "No."

Question: Were there any other players that you never had a conversation with, who were as anti-social as Rios?

Weller Evans: "No. Even the ones that you might be tempted to throw in that "difficult" category - and I won't name any names - there isn't one with whom I didn't have a more substantive series of conversations. Marcelo is the only one with whom I never had any meaningful conversation. I don't think we can completely blame our different languages."

Question: Did Rios have any friends on the Tour?

Weller Evans: "I'm sure he did. I think Luis Lobo, who was playing primarily doubles when Rios was playing. My recollection is that Luis Lobo, who is a great guy, a terrific guy, had a rapport with Rios that so many of us missed out on. I would think that Luis would be about the only one who could portray a different side of Rios."

Question: Don't know about that. I still remember when I approached Lobo one afternoon at the US Open a few years ago around the outer courts and told him I was doing a story on Rios and if he could share a memory of Rios, the reaction he gave me was a rolling of his eyes while he muttered something like, Oh gosh. But then he gave a political answer. One last thing. The laundry incident in Scottsdale.

Weller Evans: "Marcelo lost a pretty tough match 7-6 in the third, to Byron Black in Scottsdale in 1997. He left the tournament rather abruptly, headed off to Indian Wells. At the end of the week I'm headed to Indian Wells as well. The volunteers in the player's lounge said they still had Marcelo Rios' laundry. They asked every player if they would be so kind to take Marcelo's laundry to Indian Wells. They "surprisingly" had no takers. So I told the volunteers I would take the laundry with me. When I got to Indian Wells I found him and told him that I had it. Then we got into a discussion about common courtesy because he seemed to want the laundry more urgently and faster than I could deliver it. And he was not prepared to say please or thank you, for me going out of my way to get his laundry, which none of his fellow players were willing to do."

"I got a call that evening from his agent Jeff Schwartz. He said, I understand you and Marcelo had a bit of an altercation. This was not the first time I had a conversation with Jeff about his personal development. I told Jeff I think Marcelo should show some common courtesy when people do him a favor. I didn't want an apology. Maybe he could say, Hey, I was having a bad day, thanks for looking out for me. I'm fine with that."

"Jeff called back and said I don't think Marcelo is prepared to say anything right now. This was when he was wearing adidas apparel. So he didn't need the clothes. I'm pretty sure there was an adidas representative there in Indian Wells at the tournament site. However, Jeff said, he really needed his underwear."

"The next morning I was playing basketball early in the morning with some of the other tournament staff, coaches and trainers. I got to the locker room at 7:30, knowing how important it was for Marcelo to get his laundry and, most importantly, his underwear. I then left to play basketball. When the game was over at nine, I went into the locker room and was horrified to see Marcelo's underwear was now swirling around the jacuzzi. Somebody had gotten into the locker room and vandalized his laundry. One of his pairs of underwear was even in the water fountain. It was my responsibility to deal with this incident, I reported the incident to the tournament director Steve Simon and he agreed we couldn't tolerate a player's property being vandalized like this, in a sanctuary like the players' locker room. In his characteristic fashion, Steve Simon got on the case right away and we did not have another issue the rest of the week. Who did it? It's one of those unsolved mysteries. Nobody ever stepped forward and either admitted doing it or even saw the perpetrator."

(Rios lost his first match at Indian Wells that year to Magnus Larsson, 3-6 7-5 6-7.)

Marcelo Rios Dateline

1975 - Born on December 26 in Santiago, Chile.

1985 - Rios family moves to a new home next to a country club.

1986-1987 - Starts to play tennis at Sports Frances Golf Club.

1992 - Leaves home to pursue tennis full-time at age 16.

February 1993 - Plays first ATP Challenger in Vina Del Mar but loses in first round to Spain's Federico Sanchez 0-6, 2-6.

1993 - Finishes season as #1 ranked junior, winning U.S. Open juniors and reaching SF at Roland Garros and Italian Open juniors. Turns Pro after winning U.S. Open juniors.

1995 - Wins first ATP title in Bologna. Wins additional singles titles in Amsterdam and Kuala Lumpur.

April 1997 - Wins first Master Series title in Monte Carlo.

1997 - Says grass was for "cows and soccer" and unsuited for tennis.

1998 - Achieves ATP #1 ranking on March 3, 1998.

1998 - Fined $10,000 for speeding during Stuttgart event.

July 2000 - Diqualified from Los Angeles ATP event and fined $5,000 for saying "Fuck you," to the chair umpire Tony Nimmons.

December 2000 - Marries Giuliana Sotela, 17, of Costa Rica, who he met at the Bollettieri Academy when she was 15 and he was 23.

2001 - Arrested in Rome after punching taxi driver and fighting with the arresting police officer.

June 2001 - First child daughter Constanza is born.

2001 - Wins final two ATP singles titles in Doha and Hong Kong.

July 2003 - Plays final Davis Cup singles matches, losing to Jose De Armas and Kepler Orellana of Veneuzuela. Chile won the tie though, 3-2. Final Davis Cup record is 28-17.

2003 - Arrested after being involved in a brawl in a Santiago restaurant.

March 2004 - Splits with first wife Sotela.

April 2004 - Plays final pro tournament in San Luis Potosi, Mexico, defeats Florent Serra 7-5, 6-3 in R32 then retires in R16 to Mariano Delfino after splitting sets 7-5, 3-6.

2005 - Second marriage to Maria Larrain, lasts five months.

2007 - Meets Paula Pavic.

2008 - Tells 'Animal Nocturno' - "I am sure that, after so long, I found the person that fills me."

December 2008 - Second daughter Isidora is born.

May 2009 - Third marriage to Paula Pavic.

2010 - Daughter Colomba is born.

Rios Head-to-Head stats:

Rios vs Sampras 0-2

Rios vs Roddick 0-2

Rios vs Chang 1-6

Rios vs Muster 1-3

Rios vs Kafelnikov 2-6

Rios vs Becker 2-3

Rios vs Hewitt 2-3

Rios vs Safin 1-3

Rios vs Rafter 1-2

Rios vs Kuerten 2-2

Rios vs Agassi 2-1

Rios vs Courier 3-0

Rios vs Moya 5-2

Rios vs Ferriera 5-3

Some random Rios quotes over the years:

Rios stated that he thinks the ATP protects high-profile Americans of doping: "I know that if nandrolone were found on Agassi, they would not disclose it. He is a very prominent, very popular player and if he were to fall, the world of tennis would fall with him. The ATP would not say it. They are such a large dependent organization that it would be a problem if Agassi or Sampras tested positive. [We] the South Americans have discussed it repeatedly. It is a complicated subject. I do not have problem in saying it: we always said, (we asked ourselves) who publicly certifies the doping tests of Agassi or Sampras?"

"I would love to be able to see and certify Agassi's doping tests because now I currently have no idea who is doing the test, and who decides who gets it and who doesn't."

"I know that if they were to find nandrolone on Agassi, they wouldn't say it to anybody. It would taint his reputation and bring tennis down dramatically. ATP would not say it. It is such a large organization that it would be a problem if Agassi tested positive."

Rios on Roger Federer: "When I was retiring from the ATP circuit (2003) he was only playing serve and volley. He didn't play that well from the baseline back then. Now he just won his fifth Wimbledon from the baseline and that shows that he is a really complete player. I think Federer is the best player and he is going to be the best player ever and hopefully he will."

Rios after winning 1999 Hamburg Masters Series final in five sets over Mariano Zabaleta, saving a match point in four hours, seven minutes - the longest final of 1999: "To win this match at this tournament in front of these people makes me feel like a double champion. It really does feel good to win the title in five sets."

"I am at my best when it is just me against the world."

"The papers invent too many things about me. They always look for the bad in my life and try to put me down."

"Unfortunately, anybody can be a tennis journalist. They are not really smart people."

In November 1998 Rios suggested moving the ATP Tour World Championships to South America and play it on a different surface because the indoor surface in Hannover, Germany favors fast-court players: "It's not fair for clay-court players like me. The court is made for Sampras, Becker. That's one of the reasons Sampras wins every year, because the surface is too fast indoors. Right now the Tour is not fair for everybody."

Chapter 9
"The Van Gogh Of Tennis"

"Painting is freedom. If you jump, you might fall on the wrong side of the rope. But if you're not willing to take the risk of breaking your neck, what good is it? You don't jump at all. You have to wake people up. To revolutionize their way of identifying things. You've got to create images they won't accept. Force them to understand that they're living in a pretty queer world. A world that's not reassuring, a world that's not what they think it is." - Pablo Picasso

Anonymous: "I was with Rios in a bar in Indian Wells one year and he picked up three girls. We all went back to his hotel suite. He went into his room with one of the girls and they weren't in there for more than five minutes when I heard her scream. She came out and all three girls started to run out of the suite. The girl who had gone into the room with him had tried to steal one of his racquets, I guess as a souvenir, and he grabbed it from her. I asked him what had happened but he wouldn't tell me."

Jeff Tarango (ATP Player): "The best match I ever played was when I beat Rios in the Grandstand at the U.S. Open. That's where I felt everything was perfect that night. I just felt like any shot I tried to make, I made. And it was just a great feeling. And to be able to play someone who was #1 in the world and beat him, felt really good. Because everyone knew how the rankings worked and everyone knew he was going to be #1 some day real soon. So it was a lot of fun to win that...I was actually down in the match. I won a set and it was one set all and I think I was down 4-1 in the second set, serving down a break point. And I said to myself, There's no way I'm going to win this match unless I start hitting some second serve aces. And I went for it right then and there. Started going in. And I said, If these things keep going in, I'm gonna win. And they did [laughs]. (Tarango won 64 46 76 62 at 1996 U.S. Open - but Rios won their four future matches, all in straight sets.) And that's why I said it was the best feeling to be able to go for two first serve aces on every point and one of the two would go in. Rios just sort of faded off into the sunset didn't he? He was a great player."

Question: What else do you remember from that match?

Tarango: "I remember I had to take on the Chileans - they were really into that match. As far as Marcelo is concerned, I remember him telling me afterward, 'That was one of the best matches. I didn't want to lose.' So I think he respected the fact I fought hard and gave it back to them. It ended up being a good bonding experience for Rios and me. Rios didn't have too many good friends on the Tour at that time and that was one of those matches where you're both bulldogs in the ring and you both play so hard at the end you come off calm and with respect for each other. So Marcelo and I actually became friends because of that match. It's funny how tennis can bring people together that way."

Filip Dewulf (ATP Player and current journalist): "What I remember about Rios is that he was too good [laughs]. I didn't stand a chance. I played him once in Ljubljana, Slovenia on clay (1995) - I lost 62 61. Then I played him in the Challenger in Indian Wells on hard court ('95) - lost 61 62. So pretty clear [laughs]. He was an unbelievable player. Maybe the best player I ever played."

Question: Did you play Agassi and Sampras?

Dewulf: "I practiced with Sampras a few times. Never played Agassi. I played Lendl, Muster, played Corretja, Kafelnikov. So, talent-wise, maybe he was the best player I ever played. He took the ball so early. He was way ahead of me (Note: DeWulf made the French Open semis in 1997). I didn't have a chance. It was terrible to play him [smiles]. He was taking the ball so fast. You didn't know where he was gonna put the ball. You didn't see anything. It was, yeah, ridiculous."

Question: Ever talk with Rios?

Dewulf: "No, not really. You probably know how he was [smiles]. Outside the court, not really a pleasant figure. He hardly said hi to anybody else. He spoke a little to the South American guys. So I didn't talk with him at all actually."

Question: Why do you think he didn't win a major, or two, or three?

Dewulf: "Because he got injured. I think, mentally, maybe he did not have that urge to push him to go all the way. And he was playing in the era when you had Sampras, Agassi, good players. He just didn't physically have enough to go all the way. I think, talent-wise, he had it all. Maybe, I don't know, it was a mental thing. You should ask him [smiles]. Tennis-wise, he was really a good player."

Question: More talented than Sampras?

Dewulf: "If you mean talent in his hands, touch, I think he had more talent than Sampras, yeah. But Sampras had mentally and physically - and his serve was unbelievable. He had more of the whole, complete package of a champion. Where Rios was like, sometimes he felt like he didn't need to work that hard, or he didn't have the right mentality to go all the way in the big tournaments. So that was the difference with Sampras."

Question: Any inside stories of Rios?

Dewulf: "I just remember him walking through the corridors of the locker room of Roland Garros. And not saying hi to anyone. With his face, like, how do you say it, stone-faced. And, like, minding his own business. And looking a little bored [laughs]. That's my rememberance of Marcelo Rios."

Luke Jensen (ATP Player): "The first thought that comes into my mind - a beautiful genius. Marcelo Rios was a genius on and off the court. And he was just a lightning rod, a polarizing figure in the game, because you either liked him or hated him. He didn't care either way. This is how he's gonna play his cards. I think he was before his time. I don't even think his time has come up yet, to be honest. He did things on the court - hit shots without power, thought through situations. He played in a time with big servers. He wasn't even a big guy. But he was dominant with the way he played. He intimidated just the way he stalked around the court."

• • •

Dean Goldfine (ATP and WTA Coach): "So talented. When the guy was playing well he was one of those guys that was unbeatable."

At the 1998 U.S. Open Rios was playing a second round night match on Louis Armstrong Stadium against the Italian qualifier Giorgio Galimberti, who was ranked #320. It was a perfect late summer night in New York and Rios, then ranked #2 in the world, won the first set 6-2, but then seemed to lose interest in the match and lost a second set tiebreak. Early in the third set, Donald Trump and his girlfriend Melania Knauss arrived to the court to watch Rios play, rather than the WTA blowout which was happening on the main Arthur Ashe Stadium court.

Trump's entrance into the open-air arena during a changeover caused a buzz in the crowd which was quite surprised to see the millionaire celebrity walking in a fast-footed hurry to a seat behind the far baseline to watch Rios attempt to get out of trouble against the feisty Galimberti.

The unexpected guest to his match did not escape the attention of Rios, who decided it was time to awaken from his slumber. Rios switched gears to a different intensity level, and in no time he was playing his A game at full speed and fury. After one Galimberti shot sailed long, a sneering Rios defiantly waved his tongue out at it, like a dragon obscenely mocking his helpless victim. Rios gave his audience what it wanted, some colorful, crowd-pleasing tennis, dominating the journeyman in the third and fourth sets by 6-2 and 6-2.

Next, Rios would lose his following match in the third round to Magnus Larsson of Sweden, 2-6 in the fifth set.

· · ·

Corinne Dubreuil (France-based Photographer): "Rios did the middle finger on the court. But here (Key Biscayne), people like him a lot. He had a lot of support here. It was very difficult to talk with him, to try to do something with him. He was not an easy guy, no. I liked to shoot him because of the hair. When you were shooting him, the ponytail and the sweat and the hair was very nice. It was nice to shoot him. It was like, flying. I remember that I like to shoot him."

Peter De Voecht (Belgium-based Photographer): "I saw Rios play at the French Open. I have a really nice picture of him. A picture with the sun going down, and it has a big reflection going on the court. And it's just the game of flight and shadow. It's a very nice picture. That's why I remember Rios."

Galo Blanco (ATP Player): "I play him a few times, never beat him. We spend a lot of time on the Tour. A good guy. For me, he was one of the most talented players in the history. He played unbelievable, he got to #1, and he was a great player. He's a shy guy, he was really closed. He had his friends. For me, he's a great guy."

Chris Rogers (Florida-based Photographer): "I was here the year Marcelo Rios won the title here (Key Biscayne). The most impressive thing was how supportive the Chileans fans were in the final, with all the flags and the fans chanting: Chi Chi Chi - Le Le Le and all that going on. I had never seen that level of support, maybe for the Australian players when Rafter and Hewitt were at their peaks. Rios got more support than American players. Something about the Latin American players here during the tournament, they really get the crowd going. Rios was a moody guy, sometimes he was in a good mood, sometimes he wasn't, he could have a real temper on the court. I remember there wasn't a seat to be found in the stadium when he won the final against Agassi. It was a great match."

Former Wimbledon official: "One of the worst experiences I've had in tennis was with Rios. It happened here actually (Key Biscayne). But I'd rather not repeat it."

Steve Ulrich (Umpire): "One of my favorite matches was Rios against Philippoussis in Singapore. The big guy against the smaller guy. They were both playing great tennis back and forth."

Francisco Clavet (ATP Player): "I played him many times (five). I remember he was one of the most talented players that I played and also that I've seen in my life. He was a really, really good player. And a pity that he retired because he was young when he retired. I think he could achieve more things than he did. I remember him as a very good player and one of the best I ever played in my life. For sure. Not as many titles as Agassi or Sampras but yes, as a player, talented player for me. He didn't play for long. Sometimes his character wasn't good for him. It was one of the worst things for him, his character."

Question: You beat Rios. What was your strategy?

Clavet: "Run a lot [laughs]. And keep on fighting every time. I knew that he was better than me. But also he has a lot of up and downs. And sometimes he wasn't very steady. Just try to keep him out of his game, out of mine also, this is the way I could beat him twice (actually once, 1-4 lifetime, with the win coming at 1998 Wimbledon in five sets)."

Question: Did you talk with Rios?

Clavet: "I didn't have close relations with him. He was a particular player, always alone with his team. He didn't talk so much with the other players. I had good relation with him, very correct, very polite with him. But not very close, not very friendly. He was a little bit strange guy, especially at the beginning. He was always alone. No relation with other players. After the years he became more sociable, he start to talk with the others. But he had a different character, that also reflect on his tennis. Waste of talent for sure. If he could continue his career, can better manage his personality and character, right now we will be talking about one of the greatest players in the history of tennis."

• • •

Rios vs. Marzio Martelli in Rome 1998: Match Study

ATP #3 vs. #140. Rios is broken in first game but breaks back, 1-1.

Eurosport commentary: "Not a big crowd, two-three thousand. It's live in Chile, 3 o'clock in the afternoon, where Rios is, by far, the #1 sportsman. And that's why his audience against Agassi in the final of Miami was 7,000,000 out of 13,000,000 on television. 61% of the population watched the Rios-Agassi match on a Sunday morning. When he returned to Santiago, 40,000 people were there to welcome him. When asked if he wanted to say anything to the people, he said, 'Not really [chuckles].' His tennis does his talking."

In a baseline rally with Martelli in the first set Rios hits a forehand just barely long. The commentator states: "Rios long on the baseline. Maybe there's a few people who don't understand him off the court but on the court he's the genuine article: Sportsmanlike, fair and honest."

Rios begins to take command of the match with Martelli, taking a 4-2 lead. "Wonderful, pinpoint precision. Rios really rising to the occasion."

"Just a little extra in that doublehander."

"Another desperate shot from Martelli. He seems to have him by the throat now after dropping the early break, 5-2 Rios. 5-2 for the former #1 in the world, he's beginning to play like it. Of course, he only had the one match as #1 in the world, in the Davis Cup match against Argentina, Hernan Gumy. That's when the elbow went really badly. It had been creeping up on him. After that he decided it was time to stop."

"Rios beginning to exude confidence in everything he does - even his pickups from the baseline."

"Rios showing again what a good sportsman he is. He didn't complain when the double fault wasn't called."

"Glorious hands."

"Three set points for the man from Chile. Teasing him a little bit (Rios hit two overheads at less than full power into each corner). Rios, 6-3, in 35 minutes."

In the second set, Rios hits a backhand dropshot winner after popping a string. "Broken string and all [chuckles]. The way he's playing, he could win the match with no strings. It's not often you see a player with a broken string win a point."

"A set and a break for Rios. Things getting serious now for Marzio Martelli."

"He doesn't serve a lot of aces but he has hurtful first serves. Such variety. Yes, it's an economical serve, it doesn't take a lot out of Rios."

"Ten points in a row for Rios. He's a winner, he knows how to win matches. 3-love, Rios."

"He's slowly but surely dismantling Martelli. It's not the match he anticipated, perhaps the one he feared. You can almost sense Rios enjoying himself now."

Rios defeats Martelli 6-3 6-0.

Tennis Fans Discuss Rios...

"I manage to watch live tennis at tournaments two, three, four times per year, when I travel every year around Florida pro tournaments. I've been doing so since 1994. Rios had the best feel of the ball that I've seen out of any player! And you can imagine I've seen tons of players since 1994. That's how good he was."

• • •

"I was very fortunate to watch Rios live when he came to Singapore in the 90's to play the then Heineken Cup. He was up against some of the young, up and coming players including a very young Lleyton Hewitt and Paradorn Srichiphan. Rios was superb in every sense of the word. He had such amazing court craft and balance and never seemed to allow his opponent to control any of the rallies. He was adept at maneuvering his opponent around the court, often causing him to be wrong-footed completely. Or he would suddenly pop up at the net to kill off the points with ease. Rios just seemed so relaxed and natural on the tennis court, it's a joy to watch. It's really too bad that injuries put an early end to his ATP career, otherwise he would have been a worthy challenger to many of the best players around."

• • •

"Marcelo Rios was possibly the best player I've ever seen. I saw him practice, and he hit shots I'll never see again - like a left-handed Federer of sorts. I saw him practice twice in Washington D.C., and it was just sick what he could do – in terms of talent, it was unreal. I asked a coach who said he would not overcome some injury in his ankles. I got the sense he didn't like tennis. I told him in Washington that he was my favorite player of all time, but he didnt care much! That's the thing. He enjoyed killing players in practice, and possibly even on the Tour. But he didnt seem to like tennis very much. I've seen so many players. The most talented have to be Rios, Federer, Nadal, and Kuerten – with Sampras and Agassi not far behind. But of all of them, Rios just did stuff I'll never see repeated on a court, ever."

• • •

"Rios was one of the greatest ball artists of all time. His best quality was disguising his shots, making opponents continuously guess where his next shot was going to land. Sadly, he was mentally weak and completely failed to achieve the great career he was probably pre-destined to. Another explanation might be that his touch and finesse game could not really stand up against the power game that started to come up. Actually when he got to the #1 spot I felt he had renounced to some creativity to the benefit of power. I enjoyed watching him most in the period before he really became famous. He was a pleasure to watch. I remember seeing him for the first time at Roland Garros against Sampras. He made Sampras look bad but typically lost the match."

• • •

"A single, great overwhelming shot is a 'talent' too in my book. You don't necessarily have to be balanced to win, it's about whose strengths win the most matches overall consistently that counts in the end."

"Rios' primary strength and talent to me was that you couldn't read his shot direction AT ALL. Santoro has all kind of tricks up his sleeve, every bit as much touch as Rios, if not more, the difference is that Rios' disguise is unparalleled. His 'trick' in making players look so dumbfounded at his best was that with the same simple, non-descript takeback off BOTH wings, he could place it on a dime, ANYWHERE...on the court. And THAT is what left players looking dead on their feet against him."

"Yet, if I were to individually break down each of his shots, I wouldn't say he had THE greatest touch of all time (say McEnroe, Santoro, Mecir types), or THE greatest topsin of all time (say Bruguera, Borg, Nadal, Muster types), or THE greatest precision of all time (say a guy like Wilander or even Connors as a flat power baseliner), or THE greatest power of all time (say a Gonzalez type), or THE greatest volleys of all time (say an Edberg), or THE greatest serve of all time (say a Sampras), or THE greatest return of all time (say an Agassi or Connors or peak Hewitt), or THE greatest wheels of all time (say guys like Borg, Coria, Chang, Hewitt, Nadal), etc."

"So then what do you have? You have a remarkably well-rounded player whose greatest strength was in his chameleon-like quality out there. He was a shape-shifter, materializer-dematerializer Star Trek 'beam me up' style. He was Bruce Lee's definition of water, and so on and so forth."

"Rios' great and overwhelming talent in other words was his inherent transparency."

"A great talent? Yes, undoubtedly. But also if you look at it realistcally, a VERY difficult kind of talent to uphold and maintain for any signifcant stretch of time. Rios couldn't overwhelm you with one single brazen in your face superpower the way guys like Sampras and Becker could with say just their serves alone, or the way Courier and Berasategui could with their forehands alone, etc. As such, Rios really did need to be ALL there mentally and physically to put together his Houdini act out there."

"Yes, he was often injured and often mentally not all there, but even if he was, I still find it hard to believe that his style of play, being illusive and transparent, and winning could be consistently maintained over the long haul. To me, it's simply not realistic as it never really allows for any coasting. One of the great secrets of Sampras' longevity in my opinion was that he could coast on just his serve when need be."

"Actually, I look at Rios more as dirty, threesome hybrid of a knuckle baller like Santoro, a 'feel' baseliner like Mecir/Kucera/Murray, and a baseline enforcer like Agassi."

"That really is his game to me. Agassi relied very little on the offspeed stuff. Agassi was a pretty straight forward, I'm going to punish you kind of guy, and why he was nicknamed The Punisher. Rios was much more illusive, and reminds me more of the black caped magician shrouded in mystery who pulls rabbits out of his hats and scarves out of his sleeves. With Rios at his best, you never knew what shots he'd pull out of from any position in the court. Agassi played more to strict patterns, it's just that he did it REALLY well and was RELENTLESS with it. He was basically a guy who for the second half of his career tried to pound you into submission, while in the first half of his career, he would go for the one-punch knockouts. Either way you look at it, Agassi's way of playing was far more predictable than Rios. Rios is by his very nature unpredictable, he's like a SADISTIC cold-blooded psychopath out there. You can see the Hannibal Lecter operating within him. He actually CALCULATES throwing every kind of pitch in the book at you to keep you guessing, and when he does throw his occasional fastball it's very effective, like a dart, but not necessarily because his fast ball is THAT fast but rather because he SETS IT UP so well that you don't see it coming. Rios is more like a pitcher who spot mixes it up beautifully and has a reasonable fastball of say low 90-92, but isn't a 95-plus guy who leaves guys in the dust with just the fastball alone."

"Put it this way, you can be effective in baseball as a dominating hurler and also a Greg Maddux or Dennis Eckersley type who throw people's timing all out of whack."

"If Agassi is The Punisher then Rios is a black alley cat with a wry smile and chipped tooth. Trust me, you don't want to be messing with Rios in a back alley when he's feeling good about himself and looking for a feast. Why? 'Cause while you may survive, you ain't gonna be comin' out looking pretty."

• • •

"I'm in bathroom stall at Indian Wells circa 2001 or so, and in comes the li'l genius and ponies up RIGHT next to me in next stall. He took a bathroom break from his match - ATP official right behind him - so we are doing our business, I see he has the same black/orange old Nike Air Court Motion Internationals as I have on. I say to him, 'Nice shoes Marcelo, must be nice to get them free!' He says, 'That's only why I wear them.'

"Another story, I'm watching the Chilean Puma cat practice at night at Indian Wells circa 1997 at the old location, the Hyatt Grand Champions. His coach then was Larry Stefanki and they got in this minor argument because Larry Stefanki invited Marcelo to a barbeque with his family and some sponsors and Marcelo wanted nothin to do with it. Impression I got is that he is a somewhat angry, chip-on-shoulder, very shy loner. I'VE SEEN EM ALL UP CLOSE LIVE MANY TIMES, AND I MEAN ALL, GOING BACK TO BORG/CONNORS/ MAC AND THIS DUDE WAS SPECIAL, A GIFTED FREAKIN' GENIUS, ONE OF THE FEW I WOULD BE MESMERIZED JUST WATCHIN PRACTICE FOR HOURS. EFFORTLESS POWER, BALANCE AND SUPERB BALL STRIKING.....WITH A GOD LIKE HAUGHTINESS/CONFINDENCE..... BUT TROUBLED..... THE VAN GOGH OF TENNIS."

• • •

"Marion Jones had to forfeit all her Olympic medals as well as all her prize money when it was discovered that she was using banned substances. Why should it be any different for tennis? Korda (allegedly) cheated his way to his Australian Open title and he should be stripped of it (Korda tested positive later that year and had to surrender ranking points and prize money). It should also be rewarded to Marcelo Rios, just like all the silver medalists that lost to Jones were awarded gold medals and so on."

• • •

"Everyone has a moment of weakness and lets the tongue slip and may say disrespectful things. Rios' damage to the sport is deeper than that. He was a bad sportsman at every level and he did not play the game with the integrity that the great champions did. This is why his failure to win a Grand Slam was justice. He remains at a crest below the games' greats, where he does belong."

• • •

"I think that getting angry at Rios for performing super poorly merely hours after playing unthinkable tennis is really missing the point of the man. Tennis players like that don't come around everyday...so rare. And when they produce you must simply enjoy it, because with most genius there must be a flaw...a flipside. The counterbalance. And that you must accept too, which, if you think about it, is easy with Rios because according to him he never asked you to buy the ticket, nor is he telling you to watch your TV."

• • •

Andrew Miller (Tennis Fan): "2001, the Legg Mason Classic tournament in Washington DC. I attended the qualifier round and practice sessions the Saturday and Sunday before the tournament in Rock Creek Park, which straddles the DC and Maryland borders. After seeing some players hit around – among them a cursing Alex Corretja and a cursing Justin Gimelstob - who mangled a racquet during his practice session, as well as the ubiquitous Bryan brothers – ubiquitous because they seem everywhere at once, I had the privilege of seeing Marcelo Rios practice against Ramon Delgado, of Paraguay, who I remember because a fellow fan in the stands said, 'He's different from the other Delgado on tour – Jamie, who's from the U.K.' Marcelo Rios needed no such distinction. Apart from the pony tail, his style of play separated him from anyone on the planet that day. He simply hit the tennis ball to parts of the tennis court that his opponent did not know existed. I have never seen a player with as much grace or knowledge of the sport – in terms of how it can be played – exploit opportunities on the tennis court like Rios did. For a player of his diminutive size, he hit his serve as hard as someone 6-foot-5, somewhere in the 120 range flat to any part of the service box. The sound of the ball coming off his strings, somehow, SOUNDED cleaner than anyone in the park that day or any day that week - those who passed through included Agassi, a day later, who hit the same court a day later for a workout session. Rios would take mid-court balls in the air for swinging volley winners, place the ball in spots that had his opponent nearly break their ankles to move to after seeing that they did not anticipate the correct direction of the ball. His disguise on shots at times left Delgado guessing: would Rios go to the right or left, only for Rios to hit a drop shot winner from the baseline. He hit every imaginable shot during that practice session, which was only thirty minutes or so, including topspin lobs, aces, crushing forehands, nasty passing shots. He hit flat balls, junk balls, balls with ripping spin. The best I can say about him: he could play blindfolded and still steal a set off an opponent. He also showed a lot of disgust: he destroyed one of his Yonex racquets by putting it under his foot and snapping it, execution style, after a point that did not go his way. Ramon Delgado, after the session, seemed to thank Rios for practicing with him, and congratulated him on every winner that made my head shake as if to say: 'How did he do that?' When I saw Federer play two years later, in a doubles match with Max Mirnyi in Key Biscayne, my little sister would say that Federer was smooth and he would go on and become one of the greats. After seeing him several more times in Miami, I thought back to the practice session with Marcelo Rios and felt that Federer wouldn't have all the shots, nor Nadal, they were lacking Rios' example of someone that used a superior knowledge of the tennis court to break an opponent's spirit. Anyhow, I looked up a lot of quotes on Rios from opponents that played him: he is the best tennis player to never win a major. His style, if a player comes along and replicates it after Federer and Nadal, in the right hands, will translate into Grand Slam victories. The guy was that good. Federer and Nadal and Sampras may be the best players to ever swing a racquet and certainly several of the greatest champions the sport will ever see, but Marcelo Rios was the most talented player ever to have a racquet put in his hands. I'm not exaggerating, it was just an extraordinary display of skills that Rios possessed."

Chapter 10
"Now we win."

"Beauty is a short-lived reign." -Socrates

Michael Joyce (Former ATP Player and Coach): "We trained together in Palm Springs. We're both around the same age, we were coming up around the same time. The first time I saw him was in Palm Springs. I was working with Jose Higueras and he was with Larry Stefanki, he just started with Stefanki. At first we practiced and I thought he was one of the biggest jackasses I ever met in tennis. I thought, What a jerk. But then I liked him. We played doubles qualifying in Kuala Lumpur, we lost in the last round. He ended up winning the singles there, his first pro tournament win (d. Philippoussis 76 62 in October '95). His ranking took off from there."

"I played him in Australia, the French Open - which wasn't too fun. He was a character. I remember a story in New Haven. I tell this story a lot. I'll never forget it. We were playing doubles together against Wayne Black and Kevin Ullyet. We both won our singles matches earlier that day so we weren't playing 100%. He was

237

going through the motions. Sometimes he could play unbelievable tennis, sometimes he played like he didn't want to be out there. We were down a set and 4-5 in the second. He was serving down love-40. Triple match point. He wasn't even telling me where he was going to serve. His first serve was a fault. Then all of the sudden, he hits the second serve as hard as he can and it's an ace. I walk back to the service line, then he says, 'Now we win.' I swear to God, the guy hit like a winner on every ball. He held serve and we won the tiebreak 7-1, then we won the third set 6-0. It was so funny, he said, 'Now we win.'

"Another story. In Kuala Lumpur. He didn't talk like tons. So I rememeber when he would talk about some things, it stuck with me. Earlier that year I played Agassi somewhere. He beat me. And Rios played Sampras at the French Open. We were at practice, driving back on the bus. He goes, 'Hey, you played Agassi, is he good?' Meanwhile, Agassi and Sampras are like #1 and #2 in the world at the time. I said, 'Yeah, he's good.' He asked, 'What does he do?' Similar to me, he just does everything better. I said I lost 2 and 2 but after the match I felt like I played five sets. Then I decided to turn the tables on him, I asked how is Sampras? Is he good? 'No, he's shit, man.' I can't even make this stuff up, man [laughs]. He said Sampras was shit. I said, 'Well, he beat you.' Rios said, 'Yeah, I thought he was gonna be much better. He has no backhand and all these things wrong with his game. 'Next time I kill him.' I'm thinking, 'He's a nut.' Lo and behold, Rios goes on and wins the tournament and makes top 10 in the world the next year."

"I remember I played him at the French Open in '96. I used to play the green clay tournaments in the U.S. then went over there just to basically collect the money at the French Open. I remember one year he was like the hottest player going into the French Open, he won like four tournaments going in. I played him in the first round, on Court One. I swear to God, the guy drop-shotted me about fifty times. I'd run after his drop shots and he was standing there at the net laughing at me. It was so ridiculous. The first set was close - it was a tiebreak which he won. The second set he killed me 6-1. He kept drop-shotting me. Drop shot, drop shot, angles. He was toying with me. Then he must have lost concentration a little bit and I almost won the third set. That match I must have changed my shirt ten times because they kept getting dirty, I fell on the clay so many times."

"It's funny that you contacted me about this, I tell these stories to people all the time. People don't really remember Rios that well. They say he never won a major or that he was an underachiever. But playing with him - he was a magician. I played with Agassi, Sampras two or three times each. But I always tell people that Rios was the best tennis player that I ever played. If he had the same mental as Agassi, I mean...he was tougher than Agassi to play. The things he could do on the tennis court were amazing."

"For a while, I thought I was the only guy he'd talk to. He had the reputation - a lot of guys thought he was a jerk. I ended up really liking the guy. He was real straight-forward as a person, as a competitor, I respected him as a straight-shooter. He's not fake, especially in this business where there's so many fake people. I respected how he did his job, how hard he worked. He obviously worked very hard to be that good."

"Maria (Sharapova) and I went down to Chile last year for an exhibition. I hoped to run into him there. Somebody there told me he played Sampras and just kicked his ass. The organizers wanted it to be a close match but Rios killed him. Then he told me Rios played in another exhibition after with Andy Roddick and Roddick beat Rios like 2 and 3. Roddick said he played Rios when he was just starting out on the ATP Tour and he said Rios wasn't very nice to him so he wanted to kick his butt. Maria knows (Rios') first wife (Giuliana Sotela) from when she was playing at the Bollettieri Academy. "

"Another memory I have of Rios is when we were playing a practice set in Palm Springs, it was on the center court. And we were cheating each other and fighting on the court. It was a disaster. The guy that ran the place had to come out and tell us to tone it down. I remember that night thinking this guy Rios is the biggest asshole. That night I was driving between the hotel and the restaurant and I saw him walking down the street by himself. I think, What the heck, I drove up to him. Just at that time I had got this new car, a Mitsubishi 3000. He asked about the car and we became friends. Went out for dinner, we didn't talk much. We became friends little by little. We spent a lot of time together those years. He was definitely very interesting."

"Rios is Maria's dad's favorite player. Yuri always asked me about when I played him. He loved to watch him practice at Bollettieri. He always asked me questions about him. He would say, 'Oh, he's a magician!' Maria actually hit with him a few times. Maria's dad is the type of guy who will talk to anybody, he probably arranged it."

"I played in a Challenger in Aruba in 1995, the second week of the U.S. Open. I went there as a vacation, more or less. The tournament was trying to get players to go there, they paid us to play there. When I got there, it was so windy, hot. I really didn't feel like playing. I remember seeing Rios there (after Rios lost the fifth set tiebreak to Thomas Enqvist in the first round at the U.S. Open), he was practicing like seven hours. He didn't have a coach then. He hit with me, then another guy. I thought, What's wrong with this guy? He had just lost in the first round at the U.S. Open 7-6 in the fifth set. He went down there and was practicing like a crazy man. It was impressive. He was there by himself, practicing by the hour."

"When people ask me who the best player I played against, I always say him. I played him in Australia, the French Open and at the end of my career I played him in Washington. He won like 6-2 6-2. I never beat him. He was always on top of his game. But it was a pleasure to play him. I had trouble with his serve. My return was my strength but I had problems with his lefty serve. He got a lot out of his serve. Being lefty, I thought he got out of a lot of trouble with his serve. It would have been interesting if he was still in his prime when Federer was. With his lefty serve and his game he could have given Federer a lot of trouble (Federer defeated Rios in their two ATP matches both in 2002 - 67 76 63 in Sydney and 64 62 in Madrid)."

"The way tennis is today, tennis needs a character like Marcelo Rios. Though he had the reputation as a bad guy, I think he was misunderstood. It was partially his own fault. I think he kind of laid it on too because the press made him out to be such a bad guy. So maybe he knew they were gonna do it anyway, why even try to make people like him? So he laid it on. You gotta respect the way he was. It wasn't an act. He was a fighter. Some people may think he was a tanker who didn't always try his best. But he was a fighter to get to #1, to get to where he got to. He acted the same way at a Challenger as he did at a big tournament. It goes back to him being who he was. Another thing - he acted like he didn't like to play on grass. But I think he actually could have done well on grass with his lefty serve. It surprised me that he didn't play better on grass. He was definitely an interesting character. Probably the most talented player I've ever seen. Like a Leconte. If you talk to him, tell him I say hello."

Horacio Morales (Chilean Tennis Supporter): "I don't remember the exact date, but by mid-spring 1994 Rios was already a big deal in Chile, let alone in Santiago.

It was then when my whole class jumped over the window to take a close look at the rising star himself, chewing gum and slightly uncomfortable at having a bunch of about five or six pimple-faced 13-year-old kids chit-chatting about him. A few months before he had made Pistol Pete Sampras, quite literally, eat some of the Roland Garros red dust - well, actually just a little - and now he was in this insignificantly mundane situation of picking his girlfriend up from school. In fact, this was the last time I saw Rios as a human being and in the process he made me realize how far away I was, at least in terms of age and merits, from captivating any of the lovely girls from the class above."

"To understand what a pivotal point that match against Sampras was, it's necessary to give a little background on how tennis was perceived as a popular sport in Chile at the time. Or more accurately, what tennis meant to an average middle class family. As everywhere in the world, tennis at its essence was an elite sport back in the late 1980's - golf only kicked-in during the 90's as a snobbish consequence of the country's economic surge, or upper middle-class, I should say. Not even in that social circle did tennis make you feel or look like the popular kid at school or whatsoever."

"In South American society, that's a place only granted for the good soccer players, which was what we all wanted to become until our parents silently but relentlessly decided we did not stand much of a chance and preferred we focus all the efforts on a future law or engineering career. But tennis, perhaps as the individual activity it is, gave many fathers the possibility to teach their son a sport which involved discipline and work on the kid's innate talents but at the same time immerse them into a so-called gentlemen sport. You did not have to witness your little lad coming back full of bruises and covered in dust after ten hours on the street playing ball and climbing trees, you could actually dress him up in neat white on a Sunday morning and, more importantly, be part of the learning activity. So that's what dad did with my elder brother. He was tall and strong enough to deserve the investment in private lessons, racquet and all the necessary tennis gear. From my end, I happily accepted my support role hitting the ball against the wall and getting a few minutes each session to figure out how to correctly grab the grip. And I guess that's quite an accurate picture of how many of us learned the game."

"But again, you did not wander around, pretending to be a big tennis fan unless you were surrounded by tennis-loving people. The same way you wouldn't do it if you were a cricket follower. There was this classmate friend who was not the 'Tom Cruise' of the school in terms of popularity but anyway, step by step, he was building this mysterious aura of being a really, really good tennis player. But the timing was not right. We did not have any idols at all whom to aspire to become. Midway between seriousness and jest we only had the good-old Sergio 'Checho' Cortes as a household name. Cortez, quite surrealistically, made it to the third round of the 1993 U.S. Open, but only to be mercifully and undeservedly trashed by the society for, as far as I remember, being the only professional player never to approach the net for a volley, let alone, in Davis Cup."

"However, that 1993 U.S. Open also brought to scene a more significant story. Marcelo Rios was already widely known by the so-called 'Tennis Family' but he became well known for the rest of us after winning the boys singles in New York (d. Steven Downs of New Zealand, 7-6 6-3). Once Rios became a pro in 1994, he smoothly played Sampras and even beat 'Checho' Cortes twice that year. A country with such a lack of idols or more honestly, talented sportsmen, joyously welcomed her new star. If only Rios felt the same way."

"In all fairness, it was by late 1995 and 1996 the time when we all officially went mad with Rios. His rise in the rankings seemed unstoppable. When he started to face the big names of the Tour, it was hard to believe because most of them, those animals, just a few years back seemed to be from a different galaxy. Sampras, Agassi, Chang, Edberg, Becker. It felt as if only weeks before my dad was telling me, 'I'm glad he killed that hippie' when Sampras won the 1990 U.S. Open against Agassi. And now they were just a game away from facing our very own Chilean folk. I personally recall when he faced Chang in the Indian Wells semis. That could not be true, I mean, it was like, 'What the hell is he doing up there?'"

"A whole generation of teenagers started to drink booze as Rios ascended. We realized how much we loved the sport when no matter how bad the hangover, we did not hesitate to wake up at 7 am to watch him play the last rounds of the tournaments. Whenever he played important matches during school time, we managed to sneakily listen in the matches on a radio, in pairs of friends, writing comments about the game on pieces of paper. Recreating in our minds the rallies and the winning shots. It was a big thing, you could only hear three sounds on the radio - the feet sliding on clay, the shouts when they hit the ball, and the crowd. The teachers hopelessly continued the classes though once in a while we could not hide our emotions. Vamos mierda! ('C'mon goddammit!') when Chino won an important point. Puta madre! ('Oh fuck it!') when Chino lost an important point."

"Nothing was more intense than when he was fighting to get into the Top 10 in those weeks before Roland Garros. If I remember correctly, he was two or three tournaments, just one win away from making it, until he beat Wayne Ferreira in Hamburg. Smart kids, we generated this euphoric atmosphere which inevitably led us to spend a couple of hours free of classes drawing on the yard, singing the national anthem and even mimicking some of Marcelo's shots, in particular the mid-flight backhand."

"Watching those matches on TV, it made you go play tennis right then. From then on tennis became cool and popular. We started challenging my classmate, the mysterious, really, really good tennis player, only to lose categorically 6-0 6-0. But it did not matter. Now, all those who had not grabbed a racquet in years allegedly had been in tennis lessons when they were kids or have been genuine closet players. To illustrate what was the feeling like in those days, I will quote what a friend from Antofagasta, a city 700 miles north of Santiago, told me: 'Look Horacio, I used to go every Sunday to play soccer at the university pitch and on the way to the pitch there were some five tennis courts. Before Chino, there were always two courts occupied with people in perfect white tennis gear. Shorts and T-shirt, Prince racquet. During Chino's heyday everything changed. The five courts were full with people awaiting outside, no longer in perfect white tennis gear but folks in knee-cut jeans, scruffy T-shirts and old school tennis racquets.' As one of those folks in knee-cut jeans and scruffy T-shirts, I remember my dad coming to watch us play with my brother and jumping on the court for a couple of rallies, dressed smart in a suit and a tie. 'Ok son! Let's do it! 150 forehands,' he shouted. 'Hundred backhands! This is the only way you will improve your game!'

"It's an irony that many of the slackers who started playing tennis thanks to Rios' style and talent were the first at getting pissed off whenever he acted like a slacker himself on the court. An important Argentinean commentator, Guillermo Salatino, used to introduce his TV matches, more or less, like this: 'Good evening our Fox Sports friends, tonight we'll see Marcelo Rios, who wins when he wants to...' We just hated when he dropped the matches. For every magic moment, we had the same number of upsets. And I am not even mentioning here his off-court behaviour which was usually idiotic. But that was his own business, so he could do whatever he wanted without caring what the press said."

"As an example, in a 2002 semifinal, although already painfully struggling with injuries, he was outplaying the up-to-that-moment, mostly unknown Paradorn Srichaphan of Thailand. Note: I have a theory. If there is such a ranking or statistic that measures the boost of a player such as Srichaphan, Arazi or Hrbaty after they upset a champion like Rios, Rios would be the player who helped launch many players to future successes. First set 6-3 easy, beautiful shots barely moving his feet. I went for lunch, came back and Rios was trailing something like 5-2 in the third. It was like when you had the same old argument with your girlfriend and its time to give it a break…that's how I felt. Complete realization that Rios had lost the comeback boost of the first part of the season, the interest, and the energy to continue fighting against his fitness."

"However, nothing compares to the frustration and angst we felt when Rios was actually trying but being unable to change the fate of the game. 1997 U.S. Open quarterfinal against Chang was a harsh one. 2002 Australia quarterfinal against Haas was upsetting too. Although the most difficult for us to swallow was definitely Roland Garros quarterfinal in '98 and '99. They still hurt when I watch the videos or read about it. After he lost to Hrbaty - I hated Hrbaty forever after that - Rios said, 'I think he played better than me today.

Losing is always sad. I'll try again next year.' And he was never the same after that."

"I think during the six or seven years he was on the elite, especially the ones at his best, we as a society were living in this unreal situation where we pretended that having a sportsman like Rios was the norm. But he was one of a kind and he was the best, no matter for how long. Think of tennis as an art form, music, for example. You can argue that Muse or Coldplay are the best bands ever because they are on the way to win several Grammy awards and fill arenas over and over again, year after year - the two main parameters of success. However, no music expert would ever, impossible, state that those bands are more relevant to the music history than particular albums like 'London Calling' of 'The Clash', 'The Velvet Underground' and 'Nico' or 'The Queen is Dead' of 'The Smiths'. Those single moments of greatness and creativity…There have been many consistent tennis players like Muse and Coldplay, some of them with Grand Slams under their belts. But what Rios did was enough to expand the boundaries of what could be done inside a tennis court. Utterly unique moments of magic and most important of all, everything done with authenticity."

· · ·

An interview with Peter Lundgren, the former coach of Rios

Question: How did you first start to work with Marcelo Rios?

Peter Lundgren: "I was an IMG client and he was as well. Then, he was looking for a coach. So I went over to the States and practiced with him. He liked me and I liked him, so, that's how we started."

Question: What was your initial reaction working with him?

Peter Lundgren: "Well, obviously he was a really talented player, amazing guy, and how he played, with what he could do with the ball. He was kind of shy, quiet. It wasn't easy to get to know him at first. But after a few months he got better and better."

Question: You did get to know him?

Peter Lundgren: "Yes and no [smiles]. I mean, he was not very open but I got to know him pretty close. Yes."

Question: How long were you together and what changes and enhancements did you make to his game?

Peter Lundgren: "I was with him eight months. I changed - we worked on everything actually. He already had a good base. He already was top 20. He was a good player, we worked on the volleys, a little bit on the serve and how to play and what to do. Basically everything. He was already formed."

Question: What was one of the best moments working with him in 1996?

Peter Lundgren: "I think it was Indian Wells. That was one of the first tournaments together. He made semifinals, he beat some good players, lost to Michael Chang. That was a good start. And then he had lost Barcelona final against Muster. And semifinal in Monte Carlo (lost to A. Costa) and Hamburg (lost to Corretja). So we had a lot of times success."

Question: And the worst moment?

Peter Lundgren: "I would say, would be Gstaad, Stuttgart. The last four tournaments we worked, because he was not in a good mood."

Question: What happened?

Peter Lundgren: "Well, he came back from Chile a little bit out of shape and not really into it, and not really focused. And he was tanking in some matches, which is not fun to watch. Yeah, that's why I said it's better for us not to continue. Because if it's like this, why have a coach?"

Question: Were you surprised he was able to achieve what he did?

Peter Lundgren: "No, I'm not surprised. I thought he was a great player. He just needed to calm down with himself. I think he was fighting himself more than fighting the opponent."

Question: What do you mean - fighting himself?

Peter Lundgren: "Well, he started to lose matches with himself. One of the fights is tanking. Didn't want to be there sometimes. And motivation - sometimes he didn't want to practice. But I think, in general, he achieved a lot as a player."

Question: And last, what is a lasting memory, a lasting anecdote for you of Marcelo Rios?

Peter Lundgren: "I met him actually - a good memory was a few years later while I was working with Federer, he came to me and said, 'I'm sorry. I thought you were a great coach and I'm really sorry I was like that.' Yeah, it was really nice, you know. And I appreciate that a lot. That was my best memory I think."

Question: Where was that?

Peter Lundgren: "In Miami. He came to me. We met outside somewhere. He just came and we sat and talked for a little bit. And it was nice of him to say that."

Nori Shimojo (Yonex Sales Representative & International Tennis Player Service): "Marcelo use his pro career with Yonex, he started from 1994. Before he use Prince. The first Yonex racquet that Marcelo played with was the RD-7. He liked it so much since that racquet is one of the champions' racquets also used by Richard Krajicek, Sergi Bruguera, and Arantxa Sanchez-Vicario. He then switched to RD Power 10 Long, then when he stopped playing, he used RDTi50. He was very, very picky on racquet specs. All the racquets need to be in his specs specifically, which he must have thanked for since he used Yonex products. To deal with him, very calm with little talk. But inside very passionate. Wild appearance but very delicate inside. To me he is one of very few talented players in history. And can bring people's attention, and people always want to see him on and off court. He is a charismatic person. His precise racquet specs are not known since the racquets were customized by one of the racquet engineers. I guess the complete racquet was about 350g and balance 325mm. And he loves Yonex and he still uses Yonex."

Andre Sa (ATP Player): "I remember Marcelo Rios a long time ago, when I was starting on the Tour, my second year is I think when he got to #1 in 1998. I mean, he's got a strong personality, even on the court. Such a great talent. I've never seen a guy play like him at his height. Not a big guy and he's just moving the ball around so much. Kinda made you look silly sometimes. How good of ball control he had with his racquet. It's one thing when you have power, but it's another when it's all speed and talent. The way he was on the court, moving his feet, you couldn't even hear it when he was moving his feet. He was everywhere every time. Tough to compete against. Just an unbelievable talent. He was a tough guy to get along, he was not well-liked in the locker room. Not because he was a bad guy. The way he was. I knew him since juniors, he was always the same. People came up and ask for autographs, he would say no. Even when he was 16 or 17. And he was pretty much the same when he was a pro. He was not very popular but you gotta respect the way he is."

Question: Why do you think Rios was like that? Do you think it helped his tennis career - having the 'me against the world' attitude?

Andre Sa: "Kind of. I guess so. Because tennis, like it or not, is an individual sport. You have to be out there fighting for every inch of the court. You have to be fighting for every point. You don't really have to care about how your opponent is feeling or how he's doing. So I guess it helps. But it's also not so good to be like that off the court. I wouldn't recommend anybody to be like that. You just have to be natural. You have to come naturally."

Question: Did you ever see the other side of his personality? The laughter, enjoying the tennis life?

Andre Sa: "Oh, of course, of course. He used to hang around in the player lounge in the South American circuit, even in Santiago, Brazil, or Argentina, he was around. I think he was further away from the North American and Europeans. He had some - I wouldn't say good friends - guys that he got along with, especially from South America. I've seen him many times playing cards with us, hangin' around the players area."

Question: What is your very first memory of Rios?

Andre Sa: "I was playing COSAT event back when we were juniors. And everybody was talking about that guy from Chile, lefty. So talented. And the first memory I have is I was 14 - he was probably 15 or 16. And he came to play on the court dressed all black which was very unusual [laughs]. But I mean, for a guy that good to be dressed like that, everybody says, That's unbelievable, wow, I wish I could be like this guy. That's the very first memory I have. He walked on the court dressed all black, even black socks and black shoes, and everybody's like, What's going on? Nobody had ever seen that before. That was a pretty good memory."

Olivier Rochus (ATP Player): "We played one set. Paris indoors, Bercy. Then he retired. I won the set but he was not playing 100%. He was injured, I think it was shoulder. He was a great player. One of the most talented in the game I think. It was just sometimes he did not want to play. But when he was playing he was one of the best. He won back to back Masters Series."

Mike Nakajima (Nike Tennis Sports Marketing): "He was one of my all-time favorite athletes that we had. Part of it was his personality, the way he was, we could fight fire with fire. I think there was a mutual respect there. There are some things I'd love to tell you but out of respect for him I won't. As you know, he was one of the guys on the Tour that wasn't well-liked. He was the kind of guy that was very focused and kept to himself. A lot of times when you keep to yourself, people see that as conceited. One of the first things I remember is we got him under contract in July 1997. For us at the time, there was a question whether Agassi was going to be able to finish in 1997 or play much longer. He had the wrist injury and those could be fatal for a tennis player."

"If Agassi was going to be finished, when one of your star endorsers ends his career, you have to plan for that. You can't bank on all the top athletes playing at the same level every year. We felt like Rios was the guy. He was already endorsed by adidas, but he was the guy. When we consider an athlete, we're not looking at guys who are vanilla, just plain. We're always looking for guys with attitude, of course, who can, at the end of the day, win Grand Slams. I love Tim Henman and Todd Martin but they weren't the kind of athletes that we went after. Rios was. He fit our mold."

"He started wearing our product the middle weekend of Wimbledon 1997. Rios vowed to change in the middle of the tournament. He was playing Boris Becker and we knew he was probably going to lose to Becker because he didn't have the patience. The match kept getting delayed by rain. Rain delay after rain delay. He started the match wearing adidas, after the rain delays, sure enough, he walked on the court wearing Nike. Head to toe Nike. He lost that match. But that was a huge moment for us. Nobody does something like that. No tennis player changes his shoes and clothing in the middle of a tournament, let alone, Wimbledon. Tennis players are so careful and superstitious about what they eat, how they eat, how they prepare, where they sit. He wanted out of his adidas attire and it was just an unbelievable moment for us. Then he got to the Australian Open final and lost to Korda in 1998. Then he won Indian Wells, Miami back to back to become #1 in the world in Miami."

"I remember in Australia after losing the final, he was in the same party after the match. Nike had a party for Korda, who wore our Nike shoes, the Air Ace Lows. Korda won a slam in our shoes. It was an unofficial party, Rios came, he just wanted to hang out. You don't see that. You just don't see that. You don't see Roger coming to Rafa's French Open winning party."

"The guy was loose. I enjoyed his company. He is one of the guys, you can get to know him well if you understand him. That was how we started out."

Question: A unique character?

Mike Nakajima: "Oh for sure. His agent Jeff Schwartz once told me, when sitting next to him at a match. And Rios missed a shot. If he'd miss a shot, he'd sometimes hit a ball high in the air with a lot of spin, so the ball would bounce away from the ballkid. Jeff said, Every time he does something stupid like that I wish I could have a buzzer and zap him. He'd be toying with an opponent and Jeff would say, I wish I could zap this guy. He was a guy who just lived his life and did what he wanted to do. He could care less what people thought. If you understood where he was and he understood where you were, you'd get along great. I heard a story of where adidas would entertain people and they'd bring in Rios to talk about their product and he would just bang on the shoe. I know he had problems with adidas. He'd speak his mind. At a function, he'd tell people, These shoes are awful. That's just the kind of person he is."

Question: What is the first time you remember meeting him?

Mike Nakajima: "It was at the French Open in 1997. Following Wimbledon he was going to wear our product. He was very quick, very fast, he had amazing feet. We created a shoe called Air Anticipate. That was a shoe made specially for him, based on his style of play. It was sort of like a running shoe. The idea was he just wanted to get to the ball faster."

Question: That was the shoe he became #1 in and wore for most of 1998. He seemed to like that shoe.

Mike Nakajima: "Oh yeah, he still wears our stuff now."

Question: What's a lasting memory you have of Rios?

Mike Nakajima: "1998 when he became #1 in Key Biscayne. I'm going out to have dinner with a group of people, with him, to a steakhouse in Miami. I was sitting with Chris Chandler, the Atlanta Falcons quarterback - I believe Larry Stefanki's sister is Chris Chandler's wife. We're on one end, playing 80's one hit wonder songs. In the middle of the table was Rios with his group. One guy was there at the restaurant, draped with a Chilean flag. Every ten minutes the guy would stand up and would chant that, Chile-Chile-Chile! Okay, we know you're from Chile. In the middle of the dinner, Rios gets up to go to use the bathroom. And the guy gets up and follows him. Then Rios comes back to our table. And says to Chris, You gotta help. I punched this guy. He cold-cocked him. We go into the bathroom and the guy is out cold. Chris Chandler said, You don't need my help [smiles]."

"Another memory is he was supposed to do an appearance in Miami. I think I called him every day, Chino, you gonna be there? Yeah, yeah. But I knew his girlfriend was coming in. The day of the event, he doesn't take my calls. Uh oh. So I have to make a backup plan. Monica Seles agreed to come. I was so pissed that he didn't come. Or even take my calls, to tell me that he wasn't coming."

"Jeff Schwartz said, Just get back at him. At the French Open he came to the Nike house to pick up his clothes. CBS Topspin was there and they wanted to do a five-minute interview with him. Rios wanted to talk about something, he wanted to have lunch but I couldn't because I had to leave. But I tell him, I'll come back and do lunch with him the following noon. The next day he shows up at the house. And I'm not there. Chino is calling. He's pissed. I don't show up. Later I went to the house and people are telling me Marcelo Rios was here, he was so pissed. He said you had a meeting with him. So I go back to the courts and the first guy I see is Rios. Rios makes a bee-line, 'Where the fuck were you?' I said, 'Remember that appearance in Miami - and you didn't show up?' Then he looked at me and said, 'Okay, we're even.' He knew what it felt like to be stood up. He understood. We were fine after that. Like I said, he was one of my all-time favorites."

"Chino is a special guy. He didn't win a Slam but everything else, he did it his way. I think he's happy with that."

Marcelo Rios ATP Record (W-L): 391-192

Prize Money: $9,713,771

Marcelo Rios ATP Results - singles

1993

Bronx, NY, U.S.A.; 16.08.1993; CH; Outdoor: Hard; Draw: 32

Round	Opponent	Ranking	Score
R32	Doug Flach (USA)	142	L 6-4, 4-6, 6-7

This Event Points: 1, South African Airways ATP Ranking: 396, Prize Money: $520

Santiago, Chile; 12.04.1993; CH; Outdoor: Clay; Draw: 32

Round	Opponent	Ranking	Score
R32	Fernando Meligeni (BRA)	182	W 6-0, 7-5
R16	Nelson Aerts (BRA)	372	W 7-6, 6-3
Q	Mark Knowles (BAH)	241	W 7-6, 7-6
S	Jose-Luis Noriega (PER)	458	L

This Event Points: 26, South African Airways ATP Ranking: 494, Prize Money: $1,255

CAN V CHI AZPO, Chile; 26.03.1993; DC; Outdoor: Clay; Draw: 4

Round	Opponent	Ranking	Score
RR	Andrew Sznajder (CAN)	N/A	L 6-4, 4-6, 4-6, 4-6

This Event Points: , South African Airways ATP Ranking: , Prize Money: $

Vina Del Mar, Chile; 22.02.1993; CH; Outdoor: Clay; Draw: 32

Round	Opponent	Ranking	Score
R32	Federico Sanchez (ESP)	181	L 0-6, 2-6

This Event Points: 1, South African Airways ATP Ranking: 489, Prize Money: $260

1994

Napoli, FL, U.S.A.; 05.12.1994; CH; Outdoor: Clay; Draw: 32

Round	Opponent	Ranking	Score
R32	Kris Goossens (BEL)	N/A	W 7-5, 6-4

R16   Brian Dunn (USA)   N/A   L 6-4, 4-6, 2-6
This Event Points: 9, South African Airways ATP Ranking: , Prize
Money: $860

Guadalajara, Mexico; 21.11.1994; CH; Outdoor: Clay; Draw: 32
Round   Opponent   Ranking Score
R32   Shuzo Matsuoka (JPN)   125   L 6-4, 3-6, 4-6
This Event Points: 1, South African Airways ATP Ranking: 107, Prize
Money: $1,040

Buenos Aires, Argentina; 07.11.1994; GP; Outdoor: Clay; Draw: 32
Round   Opponent   Ranking Score
R32   Jordi Arrese (ESP)   75   L 6-3, 2-6, 4-6
This Event Points: 1, South African Airways ATP Ranking: 106, Prize
Money: $3,000

Montevideo, Uruguay; 31.10.1994; GP; Outdoor: Clay; Draw: 32
Round   Opponent   Ranking Score
R32   Juan Gisbert Jr (ESP)   276   W 6-2, 6-0
R16   Gilbert Schaller (AUT)   44   L 6-3, 1-6, 2-6
This Event Points: 14, South African Airways ATP Ranking: 109,
Prize Money: $3,270

Santiago, Chile; 24.10.1994; GP; Outdoor: Clay; Draw: 32
Round   Opponent   Ranking Score
R32   Alberto Berasategui (ESP)   9   L 4-6, 6-3, 1-6
This Event Points: 1, South African Airways ATP Ranking: 111, Prize
Money: $1,950

Lima, Peru; 10.10.1994; CH; Outdoor: Clay; Draw: 32
Round   Opponent   Ranking Score
R32   Xavier Daufresne (BEL)   187   W 6-2, 6-2
R16   Sjeng Schalken (NED)   242   W 6-1, 4-6, 6-4
Q   Gerard Solves (FRA)   142   L 4-6, 4-6
This Event Points: 16, South African Airways ATP Ranking: 111,
Prize Money: $1,465

Athens, Greece; 03.10.1994; GP; Outdoor: Clay; Draw: 32
Round   Opponent   Ranking Score

R32   Pantelis Moschoutis (GRE) 856   W 7-6(4), 6-2
R16   Alberto Berasategui (ESP) 8   L 2-6, 7-6(4), 3-6
This Event Points: 14, South African Airways ATP Ranking: 112,
Prize Money: $3,270

Palermo, Italy; 26.09.1994; GP; Outdoor: Clay; Draw: 32
Round   Opponent   Ranking Score
R32   Franco Davin (ARG)   62   L 1-6, 6-4, 4-6
This Event Points: 1, South African Airways ATP Ranking: 113, Prize
Money: $3,000

US Open, NY, U.S.A.; 29.08.1994; GS; Outdoor: Hard; Draw: 128
Round   Opponent   Ranking Score
R128   Jared Palmer (USA)   52   W 6-2, 7-6(1), 6-2
R64   Wayne Ferreira (RSA)   13   L 4-6, 2-6, 4-6
This Event Points: 23, South African Airways ATP Ranking: 123,
Prize Money: $13,750

New Haven, CT, U.S.A.; 15.08.1994; GP; Outdoor: Hard; Draw: 56
Round   Opponent   Ranking Score
R64   David Nainkin (RSA)   203   W 6-4, 3-6, 6-1
R32   Michael Stich (GER)   5   L 3-6, 5-7
This Event Points: 15, South African Airways ATP Ranking: 121,
Prize Money: $6,180

Hilversum, The Netherlands; 25.07.1994; GP; Outdoor: Clay; Draw:
32
Round   Opponent   Ranking Score
R32   Hendrik Jan Davids (NED) 209   W 6-2, 6-3
R16   Javier Sanchez (ESP)   28   W 6-4, 0-6, 6-1
Q   Guy Forget (FRA) 114   W 6-3, 6-3
S   Karel Novacek (CZE)   76   L 6-3, 3-6, 4-6
This Event Points: 80, South African Airways ATP Ranking: 145,
Prize Money: $13,750

Scheveningen, The Netherlands; 18.07.1994; CH; Outdoor: Clay;
Draw: 32
Round   Opponent   Ranking Score
R32   Martin Blackman (USA)   164   W 6-4, 6-2

R16	Mark Koevermans (NED)	600	W 6-4, 6-3
Q	Sergio Cortes (CHI)	140	W 6-4, 6-2
S	Karol Kucera (SVK)	98	L 1-6, 3-6

This Event Points: 38, South African Airways ATP Ranking: 163, Prize Money: $3,750

Neu Ulm, Germany; 11.07.1994; CH; Outdoor: Clay; Draw: 32

Round	Opponent	Ranking	Score
R32	Alejo Mancisidor (ESP)	210	W 4-6, 6-3, 6-3
R16	Sergio Cortes (CHI)	142	W 6-1, 7-6
Q	Oscar Martinez (ESP)	159	L 6-4, 4-6, 1-6

This Event Points: 17, South African Airways ATP Ranking: 174, Prize Money: $1,465

Gstaad, Switzerland; 04.07.1994; GP; Outdoor: Clay; Draw: 32

Round	Opponent	Ranking	Score
R32	Amos Mansdorf (ISR)	45	W 6-4, 6-4
R16	Alberto Berasategui (ESP)	14	W 4-6, 6-3, 7-6(1)
Q	Andrea Gaudenzi (ITA)	31	L 4-6, 6-3, 3-6

This Event Points: 74, South African Airways ATP Ranking: 238, Prize Money: $13,185

Porto, Portugal; 27.06.1994; CH; Outdoor: Clay; Draw: 32

Round	Opponent	Ranking	Score
R32	Gerard Solves (FRA)	N/A	W 6-4, 6-0
R16	Gilbert Schaller (AUT)	N/A	L 4-6, 3-6

This Event Points: 14, South African Airways ATP Ranking: , Prize Money: $2,150

Roland Garros, France; 23.05.1994; GS; Outdoor: Clay; Draw: 128

Round	Opponent	Ranking	Score
R128	Joshua Eagle (AUS)	239	W 6-2, 6-3, 6-2
R64	Pete Sampras (USA)	1	L 6-7(5), 6-7(4), 4-6

This Event Points: 17, South African Airways ATP Ranking: 283, Prize Money: $13,193

Budapest, Hungary; 16.05.1994; CH; Outdoor: Clay; Draw: 32

Round	Opponent	Ranking	Score
R32	Davide Sanguinetti (ITA)	163	L 6-7, 6-1, 1-6

This Event Points: 1, South African Airways ATP Ranking: 286, Prize Money: $260

Dresden, Germany; 09.05.1994; CH; Outdoor: Clay; Draw: 32

Round	Opponent	Ranking	Score
R32	Pietro Pennisi (ITA)	218	W 6-1, 6-0
R16	Dimitri Poliakov (UKR)	124	W 6-1, 6-2
Q	Christian Ruud (NOR)	138	W 6-1, 6-1
S	Patricio Arnold (ARG)	139	W 6-4, 6-3
W	Oliver Gross (GER)	157	W 5-7, 6-3, 6-3

This Event Points: 77, South African Airways ATP Ranking: 541, Prize Money: $7,200

Monte Carlo, Monaco; 11.04.1994; CH; Outdoor: Clay; Draw: 32

Round	Opponent	Ranking	Score
R32	Jean-Philippe Fleurian (FRA)	79	L 3-6, 2-6

This Event Points: 1, South African Airways ATP Ranking: 413, Prize Money: $520

Barcelona, Spain; 04.04.1994; GP; Outdoor: Clay; Draw: 56

Round	Opponent	Ranking	Score
R64	Marian Vajda (SVK)	272	W 6-3, 6-2
R32	Roberto Carretero (ESP)	424	W 7-6(1), 7-6(5)
R16	Andrea Gaudenzi (ITA)	60	L 1-6, 1-6

This Event Points: 28, South African Airways ATP Ranking: 559, Prize Money: $10,000

1995

Buenos Aires, Argentina; 06.11.1995; GP; Outdoor: Clay; Draw: 32

Round	Opponent	Ranking	Score
R32	Franco Davin (ARG)	253	W 6-7(6), 6-4, 6-4
R16	Alex Corretja (ESP)	47	L 6-3, 2-6, 3-6

This Event Points: 17, South African Airways ATP Ranking: 24, Prize Money: $5,100

Montevideo, Uruguay; 30.10.1995; GP; Outdoor: Clay; Draw: 32

Round	Opponent	Ranking	Score
R32	Jiri Novak (CZE)	65	L 4-6, 6-4, 2-6

This Event Points: 1, South African Airways ATP Ranking: 25, Prize Money: $2,080

Santiago, Chile; 23.10.1995; GP; Outdoor: Clay; Draw: 32

Round	Opponent	Ranking	Score
R32	Jordi Burillo (ESP)	67	W 7-6(2), 7-5
R16	Karim Alami (MAR)	71	W 6-1, 6-2
Q	David Rikl (CZE)	88	W 6-2, 4-6, 6-4
S	Hernan Gumy (ARG)	77	W 3-6, 6-4, 6-2
F	Slava Dosedel (CZE)	70	L 6-7(3), 3-6

This Event Points: 111, South African Airways ATP Ranking: 26, Prize Money: $17,000

Tokyo Indoor, Japan; 09.10.1995; GP; Indoor: Carpet; Draw: 48

Round	Opponent	Ranking	Score
R64	Bye	N/A	W
R32	Jonathan Stark (USA)	92	L 7-6(6), 4-6, 4-6

This Event Points: 1, South African Airways ATP Ranking: 27, Prize Money: $6,200

Kuala Lumpur, Malaysia; 02.10.1995; GP; Indoor: Carpet; Draw: 32

Round	Opponent	Ranking	Score
R32	Sandon Stolle (AUS)	186	W 7-6(6), 4-6, 7-6(2)
R16	Hendrik Dreekmann (GER)	112	W 3-6, 6-2, 6-2
Q	Jacco Eltingh (NED)	28	W 7-5, 6-4
S	Cristiano Caratti (ITA)	161	W 6-4, 6-1
W	Mark Philippoussis (AUS)	90	W 7-6(6), 6-2

This Event Points: 185, South African Airways ATP Ranking: 32, Prize Money: $55,000

Bogota, Colombia; 11.09.1995; GP; Outdoor: Clay; Draw: 32

Round	Opponent	Ranking	Score
R32	Alex Lopez Moron (ESP)	119	W 6-4, 6-2
R16	Gaston Etlis (ARG)	129	W 6-4, 3-6, 6-3
Q	Nicolas Lapentti (ECU)	258	L 3-6, 4-6

This Event Points: 37, South African Airways ATP Ranking: 38, Prize Money: $8,800

Aruba, Aruba; 04.09.1995; CH; Outdoor: Hard; Draw: 32

Round	Opponent	Ranking	Score
R32	Fernon Wibier (NED)	N/A	L 1-6, 2-6

This Event Points: 1, South African Airways ATP Ranking: , Prize Money: $1,300

US Open, NY, U.S.A.; 28.08.1995; GS; Outdoor: Hard; Draw: 128

Round	Opponent	Ranking	Score
R128	Thomas Enqvist (SWE)	9	L 6-2, 2-6, 6-4, 3-6, 6-7(7)

This Event Points: 1, South African Airways ATP Ranking: 34, Prize Money: $8,500

Long Island, NY, U.S.A.; 21.08.1995; GP; Outdoor: Hard; Draw: 32

Round	Opponent	Ranking	Score
R32	Daniel Vacek (CZE)	68	W 7-5, 6-4
R16	MaliVai Washington (USA)	49	L 1-6, 5-7

This Event Points: 23, South African Airways ATP Ranking: 34, Prize Money: $5,100

New Haven, CT, U.S.A.; 14.08.1995; GP; Outdoor: Hard; Draw: 56

Round	Opponent	Ranking	Score
R64	Leander Paes (IND)	133	W 1-6, 6-1, 6-4
R32	Daniele Musa (ITA)	148	W 6-2, 6-4
R16	Yevgeny Kafelnikov (RUS)	6	L 3-6, 6-7(2)

This Event Points: 33, South African Airways ATP Ranking: 38, Prize Money: $11,500

ATP Masters Series Cincinnati, OH, U.S.A.; 07.08.1995; SU; Outdoor: Hard; Draw: 56

Round	Opponent	Ranking	Score
R64	Brett Steven (NZL)	39	L 3-6, 3-6

This Event Points: 1, South African Airways ATP Ranking: 38, Prize Money: $5,400

Amsterdam, The Netherlands; 24.07.1995; GP; Outdoor: Clay; Draw: 32

Round	Opponent	Ranking	Score

R32	Renzo Furlan (ITA)	48	W 6-3, 7-6(2)
Stats			
R16	Alex Corretja (ESP)	21	W 7-6(3), 6-4
Q	Bernd Karbacher (GER)	44	W 5-7, 7-6(2), 7-5
S	Carlos Costa (ESP)	47	W 7-6(1), 6-0
W	Jan Siemerink (NED)	51	W 6-4, 7-5, 6-4

This Event Points: 230, South African Airways ATP Ranking: 57, Prize Money: $66,400

Stuttgart Outdoor, Germany; 17.07.1995; GP; Outdoor: Clay; Draw: 48

Round	Opponent	Ranking	Score
R64	Javier Sanchez (ESP)	62	W 6-2, 6-2
R32	Thomas Muster (AUT)	4	L 2-6, 4-6

This Event Points: 21, South African Airways ATP Ranking: 53, Prize Money: $6,300

Gstaad, Switzerland; 10.07.1995; GP; Outdoor: Clay; Draw: 32

Round	Opponent	Ranking	Score
R32	Patrick Mohr (SUI)	277	W 6-4, 6-4
R16	Guy Forget (FRA) 33		W 6-2, 6-3
Q	Jakob Hlasek (SUI)	124	L 6-7(5), 6-3, 2-6

This Event Points: 52, South African Airways ATP Ranking: 55, Prize Money: $15,000

Wimbledon, England; 26.06.1995; GS; Outdoor: Grass; Draw: 128

| Round | Opponent | Ranking | Score |
| R128 | Mark Knowles (BAH) | 204 | L 6-4, 3-6, 4-6, 6-7(4) |

This Event Points: 1, South African Airways ATP Ranking: 49, Prize Money: $8,238

Nottingham, England; 19.06.1995; GP; Outdoor: Grass; Draw: 32

Round	Opponent	Ranking	Score
R32	Cedric Pioline (FRA)	55	W 6-2, 7-5
R16	Tommy Ho (USA) 88		L 4-6, 0-6

This Event Points: 23, South African Airways ATP Ranking: 46, Prize Money: $5,100

Roland Garros, France; 29.05.1995; GS; Outdoor: Clay; Draw: 128

Round	Opponent	Ranking	Score
R128	Vincent Spadea (USA)	59	W 6-4, 6-4, 6-7(8), 6-3
R64	Alberto Berasategui (ESP)	11	L 4-6, 5-7, 7-6(3), 6-3, 1-6

This Event Points: 24, South African Airways ATP Ranking: 48, Prize Money: $15,930

Bologna, Italy; 22.05.1995; GP; Outdoor: Clay; Draw: 32

Round	Opponent	Ranking	Score
R32	Byron Black (ZIM)	65	W 5-7, 6-3, 6-0
R16	Renzo Furlan (ITA)	59	W 6-4, 7-6(6)
Q	Gilbert Schaller (AUT)	24	W 6-1, 3-6, 6-2
S	Mark Philippoussis (AUS)	131	W 6-4, 7-6(6)
W	Marcelo Filippini (URU)	63	W 6-2, 6-4

This Event Points: 188, South African Airways ATP Ranking: 69, Prize Money: $43,000

ATP Masters Series Rome, Italy; 15.05.1995; SU; Outdoor: Clay; Draw: 64

Round	Opponent	Ranking	Score
R64	Emilio Benfele Alvarez (ESP)	173	W 7-5, 6-2
R32	Stefan Edberg (SWE)	17	L 3-6, 3-6

This Event Points: 21, South African Airways ATP Ranking: 67, Prize Money: $11,210

Ljubljana, Slovenia; 08.05.1995; CH; Outdoor: Clay; Draw: 32

Round	Opponent	Ranking	Score
R32	Sandor Noszaly (HUN)	122	W 4-6, 6-1, 6-3
R16	Carsten Arriens (GER)	131	W 7-5, 6-1
Q	Filip Dewulf (BEL)	117	W 6-2, 6-1
S	Adrian Voinea (ROU)	147	L 1-6, 1-6

This Event Points: 51, South African Airways ATP Ranking: 62, Prize Money: $6,275

Monte Carlo, Monaco; 17.04.1995; CH; Outdoor: Clay; Draw: 32

Round	Opponent	Ranking	Score
R32	Chris Wilkinson (GBR)	147	W 7-6, 6-3
R16	Alex Lopez Moron (ESP)	140	W 6-1, 1-6, 6-1
Q	Marcos Aurelio Gorriz (ESP)	295	W 6-1, 6-2

S   Frederik Fetterlein (DEN)   105   L 5-7, 6-7
This Event Points: 34, South African Airways ATP Ranking: 67, Prize
Money: $2,500

Barcelona, Spain; 10.04.1995; GP; Outdoor: Clay; Draw: 56

Round	Opponent	Ranking	Score
R64	Marcelo Filippini (URU)	60	W 6-2, 6-0
R32	Bernd Karbacher (GER)	23	W 6-3, 6-3
R16	Yevgeny Kafelnikov (RUS)	5	L 4-6, 3-6

This Event Points: 52, South African Airways ATP Ranking: 74, Prize
Money: $9,800

URU V CHI AZPO, Chile; 31.03.1995; DC; Outdoor: Clay; Draw: 4

Round	Opponent	Ranking	Score
RR	Diego Perez (URU)	N/A	W 6-0, 6-1, 6-1
RR	Victor Caldarelli (URU)	N/A	W 7-6, 6-3

This Event Points: , South African Airways ATP Ranking: , Prize
Money: $

ATP Masters Series Miami, FL, U.S.A.; 13.03.1995; SU; Outdoor:
Hard; Draw: 96

Round	Opponent	Ranking	Score
R128	Lars Jonsson (SWE)	124	W 6-3, 3-6, 7-6(7)
R64	Petr Korda (CZE)	32	W 6-3, 7-6(5)
R32	Todd Woodbridge (AUS)	93	L 5-7, 3-6

This Event Points: 36, South African Airways ATP Ranking: 81, Prize
Money: $13,400

ATP Masters Series Indian Wells, CA, U.S.A.; 06.03.1995; SU;
Outdoor: Hard; Draw: 56

Round	Opponent	Ranking	Score
R64	Renzo Furlan (ITA)	48	W 6-1, 7-6(5)
R32	Andrea Gaudenzi (ITA)	19	W 6-3, 6-0
R16	Boris Becker (GER)	3	L 3-6, 2-3 RET

This Event Points: 73, South African Airways ATP Ranking: 100,
Prize Money: $19,500

Indian Wells, CA, U.S.A.; 27.02.1995; CH; Outdoor: Hard; Draw: 32

Round	Opponent	Ranking	Score

| R32 | Filip Dewulf (BEL) | 116 | W 6-1, 6-2 |
| R16 | Leander Paes (IND) | 129 | L 7-5, 3-6, 4-6 |

This Event Points: 10, South African Airways ATP Ranking: 97, Prize Money: $860

Memphis, TN, U.S.A.; 13.02.1995; GP; Indoor: Hard; Draw: 48

Round	Opponent	Ranking	Score
R64	Andrew Sznajder (CAN)	343	W 6-1, 7-5
R32	Marcelo Filippini (URU)	58	L 4-6, 1-6

This Event Points: 14, South African Airways ATP Ranking: 98, Prize Money: $4,700

San Jose, CA, U.S.A.; 06.02.1995; GP; Indoor: Hard; Draw: 32

Round	Opponent	Ranking	Score
R32	Michael Chang (USA)	6	L 4-6, 5-7

This Event Points: 1, South African Airways ATP Ranking: 99, Prize Money: $3,100

CHI V ARG AZ1, Argentina; 03.02.1995; DC; Outdoor: Clay; Draw: 4

Round	Opponent	Ranking	Score
RR	Javier Frana (ARG)	N/A	L 6-3, 2-6, 2-6, 6-4, 5-7
RR	Franco Davin (ARG)	N/A	W 7-5, 6-3, 6-2

This Event Points: , South African Airways ATP Ranking: , Prize Money: $

1996

Santiago, Chile; 04.11.1996; GP; Outdoor: Clay; Draw: 32

Round	Opponent	Ranking	Score
R32	Alex Lopez Moron (ESP)	564	W 6-2, 6-3
R16	Mariano Zabaleta (ARG)	105	W 6-3, 7-6(3)
Q	Fernando Meligeni (BRA)	104	W 6-3, 6-2
S	Alberto Berasategui (ESP)	21	W 6-2, 6-4
F	Hernan Gumy (ARG)	58	L 4-6, 5-7

This Event Points: 115, South African Airways ATP Ranking: 11, Prize Money: $17,000

ATP Masters Series Paris, France; 28.10.1996; SU; Indoor: Carpet; Draw: 48

Round	Opponent	Ranking	Score
R64	Bye	N/A	W
R32	Petr Korda (CZE)	37	L 3-6, 4-6

This Event Points: 1, South African Airways ATP Ranking: 10, Prize Money: $15,880

ATP Masters Series Stuttgart, Germany; 21.10.1996; SU; Indoor: Carpet; Draw: 48

Round	Opponent	Ranking	Score
R64	Bye	N/A	W
R32	Sebastien Lareau (CAN)	121	W 6-7(4), 7-6(4), 6-4
R16	Richard Krajicek (NED)	7	W 6-4, 6-4
Q	Michael Chang (USA)	2	L 4-6, 3-6

This Event Points: 118, South African Airways ATP Ranking: 10, Prize Money: $48,600

Toulouse, France; 14.10.1996; GP; Indoor: Hard; Draw: 32

Round	Opponent	Ranking	Score
R32	Frederic Vitoux (FRA)	298	W 5-2 RET
R16	Lionel Roux (FRA)	101	W 6-2, 6-2
Q	Orlin Stanoytchev (BUL)	122	W 7-6(7), 6-3
S	Magnus Larsson (SWE)	54	L 4-6, 4-6

This Event Points: 74, South African Airways ATP Ranking: 10, Prize Money: $18,400

Vienna, Austria; 07.10.1996; GP; Indoor: Carpet; Draw: 32

Round	Opponent	Ranking	Score
R32	Arnaud Boetsch (FRA)	23	L 2-6, 4-6

This Event Points: 1, South African Airways ATP Ranking: 10, Prize Money: $5,100

Lyon, France; 30.09.1996; GP; Indoor: Carpet; Draw: 32

Round	Opponent	Ranking	Score
R32	Alex Radulescu (GER)	61	W 4-6, 6-4, 7-6(5)
R16	Mikael Tillstrom (SWE)	40	W 6-3, 6-1
Q	Thomas Enqvist (SWE)	13	L 3-6, 6-2, 5-7

This Event Points: 63, South African Airways ATP Ranking: 10, Prize Money: $20,730

PER V CHI AZG1, Chile; 20.09.1996; DC; Outdoor: Clay; Draw: 4

Round	Opponent	Ranking	Score
RR	Americo Tupi Venero (PER)	N/A	W 7-5, 6-2, 6-4
RR	Alejandro Aramburu (PER)	N/A	W 6-2, 6-3

This Event Points: , South African Airways ATP Ranking: , Prize Money: $

US Open, NY, U.S.A.; 26.08.1996; GS; Outdoor: Hard; Draw: 128

Round	Opponent	Ranking	Score
R128	Andrei Pavel (ROU)	198	W 4-6, 6-1, 6-4, 6-2
R64	Jeff Tarango (USA)	104	L 4-6, 6-4, 6-7(5), 2-6

This Event Points: 22, South African Airways ATP Ranking: 11, Prize Money: $15,000

ATP Masters Series Canada, Toronto, Canada; 19.08.1996; SU; Outdoor: Hard; Draw: 56

Round	Opponent	Ranking	Score
R64	Bye	N/A	W
R32	Kenneth Carlsen (DEN)	65	W 6-3, 6-2
R16	Daniel Vacek (CZE)	34	W 6-4, 6-3
Q	Patrick Rafter (AUS)	70	W 0-6, 7-6(4), 6-1
S	Todd Woodbridge (AUS)	43	L 0-6, 3-6

This Event Points: 184, South African Airways ATP Ranking: 11, Prize Money: $80,090

New Haven, CT, U.S.A.; 12.08.1996; GP; Outdoor: Hard; Draw: 56

Round	Opponent	Ranking	Score
R64	Bye	N/A	W
R32	Leander Paes (IND)	149	W 6-0, 6-2
R16	Daniel Vacek (CZE)	34	L 1-6, 1-6

This Event Points: 31, South African Airways ATP Ranking: 11, Prize Money: $11,500

Amsterdam, The Netherlands; 29.07.1996; GP; Outdoor: Clay; Draw: 32

Round	Opponent	Ranking	Score
R32	Sandor Noszaly (HUN)	111	W 7-5, 6-2
R16	Adrian Voinea (ROU)	75	L 0-6, 5-7

This Event Points: 21, South African Airways ATP Ranking: 12, Prize Money: $8,000

Kitzbuhel, Austria; 22.07.1996; GP; Outdoor: Clay; Draw: 48

Round	Opponent	Ranking	Score
R64	Bye	N/A	W
R32	Markus Hipfl (AUT)	550	W 7-5, 6-7(5), 6-1
R16	Juan Albert Viloca-Puig (ESP)	163	L 1-6, 6-7(4)

This Event Points: 18, South African Airways ATP Ranking: 12, Prize Money: $6,000

Stuttgart Outdoor, Germany; 15.07.1996; GP; Outdoor: Clay; Draw: 48

Round	Opponent	Ranking	Score
R64	Bye	N/A	W
R32	Marc-Kevin Goellner (GER)	111	L 0-6, 6-7(5)

This Event Points: 1, South African Airways ATP Ranking: 11, Prize Money: $6,300

Gstaad, Switzerland; 08.07.1996; GP; Outdoor: Clay; Draw: 32

Round	Opponent	Ranking	Score
R32	Jiri Novak (CZE)	46	L 6-7(3), 6-3, 2-6

This Event Points: 1, South African Airways ATP Ranking: 11, Prize Money: $5,250

Roland Garros, France; 27.05.1996; GS; Outdoor: Clay; Draw: 128

Round	Opponent	Ranking	Score
R128	Michael Joyce (USA)	69	W 7-6(4), 6-1, 6-4
R64	Jason Stoltenberg (AUS)	40	W 6-4, 6-3, 6-3
R32	Petr Korda (CZE)	36	W 6-3, 6-3, 6-2
R16	Cedric Pioline (FRA)	19	L 4-6, 1-6, 2-6

This Event Points: 138, South African Airways ATP Ranking: 10, Prize Money: $46,583

St. Poelten, Austria; 20.05.1996; GP; Outdoor: Clay; Draw: 32

Round	Opponent	Ranking	Score
R32	Thomas Johansson (SWE)	103	W 6-4, 7-6(4)
R16	Marcelo Filippini (URU)	77	W 6-2, 6-2
Q	Francisco Clavet (ESP)	44	W 6-2, 1-6, 6-3

S	Slava Dosedel (CZE)	46	W 7-6(4), 6-3
W	Felix Mantilla (ESP)	62	W 6-2, 6-4

This Event Points: 195, South African Airways ATP Ranking: 10, Prize Money: $57,000

ATP Masters Series Rome, Italy; 13.05.1996; SU; Outdoor: Clay; Draw: 64

Round	Opponent	Ranking	Score
R64	Alex Corretja (ESP)	32	W 7-6(5), 3-6, 6-2
R32	Daniel Vacek (CZE)	37	W 6-3, 6-3
R16	Marc Rosset (SUI) 14		W 7-6(5), 6-4
Q	Thomas Muster (AUT)	2	L 3-6, 2-6

This Event Points: 128, South African Airways ATP Ranking: 10, Prize Money: $45,000

ATP Masters Series Hamburg, Germany; 06.05.1996; SU; Outdoor: Clay; Draw: 56

Round	Opponent	Ranking	Score
R64	Bye	N/A	W
R32	Adrian Voinea (ROU)	42	W 6-2, 6-1
R16	Slava Dosedel (CZE)	48	W 6-3, 6-4
Q	Wayne Ferreira (RSA)	10	W 3-6, 6-4, 6-4
S	Alex Corretja (ESP)	66	L 4-6, 4-6

This Event Points: 220, South African Airways ATP Ranking: 11, Prize Money: $89,000

ATP Masters Series Monte Carlo, Monaco; 22.04.1996; SU; Outdoor: Clay; Draw: 56

Round	Opponent	Ranking	Score
R64	Francisco Clavet (ESP)	42	W 6-4, 5-7, 6-4
R32	Jiri Novak (CZE) 32		W 6-3, 2-6, 6-2
R16	Boris Becker (GER)	5	W 6-4, 6-3
Q	Magnus Gustafsson (SWE) 45		W 6-3, 6-4
S	Albert Costa (ESP)	26	L 3-6, 6-4, 3-6

This Event Points: 241, South African Airways ATP Ranking: 13, Prize Money: $89,000

Barcelona, Spain; 15.04.1996; GP; Outdoor: Clay; Draw: 56

Round	Opponent	Ranking	Score

R64	Bye	N/A	W
R32	Galo Blanco (ESP)	141	W 6-4, 6-3
R16	Ignacio Truyol (ESP)	193	W 1-6, 6-1, 6-4
Q	Magnus Larsson (SWE)	86	W 2-6, 6-1, 6-2
S	Jim Courier (USA)	9	W 7-6(5), 4-6, 7-6(5)
F	Thomas Muster (AUT)	2	L 3-6, 6-4, 4-6, 1-6

This Event Points: 232, South African Airways ATP Ranking: 16, Prize Money: $70,000

CHI V CAN AZPO, Canada; 05.04.1996; DC; Indoor: Carpet; Draw: 5

| Round | Opponent | Ranking | Score |
| RR | Daniel Nestor (CAN) | N/A | W 6-4, 7-6, 6-7, 3-6, 14-12 |

This Event Points: , South African Airways ATP Ranking: , Prize Money: $

ATP Masters Series Miami, FL, U.S.A.; 18.03.1996; SU; Outdoor: Hard; Draw: 96

Round	Opponent	Ranking	Score
R128	Bye	N/A	W
R64	Karol Kucera (SVK)	75	W 6-4, 6-2
R32	Petr Korda (CZE)	50	L 4-6, 7-6(4), 4-6

This Event Points: 26, South African Airways ATP Ranking: 15, Prize Money: $13,640

ATP Masters Series Indian Wells, CA, U.S.A.; 11.03.1996; SU; Outdoor: Hard; Draw: 56

Round	Opponent	Ranking	Score
R64	Mark Knowles (BAH)	99	W 7-6(4), 6-3
R32	Jonathan Stark (USA)	167	W 7-6(3), 6-1
R16	Adrian Voinea (ROU)	40	W 6-3, 4-1 RET
Q	Wayne Ferreira (RSA)	10	W 7-5, 7-5
S	Michael Chang (USA)	5	L 6-7(6), 3-6

This Event Points: 212, South African Airways ATP Ranking: 20, Prize Money: $89,000

Scottsdale, AZ, U.S.A.; 04.03.1996; GP; Outdoor: Hard; Draw: 32

| Round | Opponent | Ranking | Score |
| R32 | Andrei Chesnokov (RUS) | 85 | W 6-1, 6-4 |

R16	Daniel Nestor (CAN)	181	W 7-6(6), 4-6, 7-6(7)
Q	Albert Costa (ESP)	16	W 7-6(6), 6-1
S	Sandon Stolle (AUS)	125	W 6-4, 7-5
F	Wayne Ferreira (RSA)	10	L 6-2, 3-6, 3-6

This Event Points: 138, South African Airways ATP Ranking: 20, Prize Money: $25,300

Philadelphia, PA, U.S.A.; 26.02.1996; GP; Indoor: Carpet; Draw: 32

Round	Opponent	Ranking	Score
R32	David Wheaton (USA)	64	W 6-4, 6-3
R16	Grant Stafford (RSA)	242	W 4-6, 6-4, 6-4
Q	Chris Woodruff (USA)	112	L 6-1, 4-6, 1-6

This Event Points: 56, South African Airways ATP Ranking: 22, Prize Money: $16,000

Memphis, TN, U.S.A.; 19.02.1996; GP; Indoor: Hard; Draw: 48

Round	Opponent	Ranking	Score
R64	Bye	N/A	W
R32	Jason Stoltenberg (AUS)	81	W 6-3, 6-3
R16	Mark Woodforde (AUS)	25	L 2-6, 4-6

This Event Points: 30, South African Airways ATP Ranking: 23, Prize Money: $9,000

BZL V CHI AZ1, Chile; 09.02.1996; DC; Outdoor: Clay; Draw: 4

Round	Opponent	Ranking	Score
RR	Jaime Oncins (BRA)	N/A	W 6-3, 6-2, 7-5
RR	Fernando Meligeni (BRA)	N/A	W 6-2, 7-6, 6-3

This Event Points: , South African Airways ATP Ranking: , Prize Money: $

Australian Open, Australia; 15.01.1996; GS; Outdoor: Hard; Draw: 128

Round	Opponent	Ranking	Score
R128	Patrick Rafter (AUS)	70	L 3-6, 4-6, 3-6

This Event Points: 1, South African Airways ATP Ranking: 23, Prize Money: $6,205

Sydney Outdoor, Australia; 08.01.1996; GP; Outdoor: Hard; Draw: 32

Round	Opponent	Ranking	Score

R32   Renzo Furlan (ITA)   31   L 1-6, 6-7(4)
This Event Points: 1, South African Airways ATP Ranking: 24, Prize
Money: $3,000

1997
Santiago, Chile; 03.11.1997; GP; Outdoor: Clay; Draw: 32
Round   Opponent   Ranking Score
R32   Davide Sanguinetti (ITA)   91   W 6-2, 7-5
R16   Sebastian Prieto (ARG)   176   W 5-7, 6-1, 6-4
Q   Fernando Meligeni (BRA)   70   W 1-6, 7-6(5), 6-1
S   Marcelo Filippini (URU)   47   W 6-1, 6-4
F   Julian Alonso (ESP)   45   L 2-6, 1-6
This Event Points: 130, South African Airways ATP Ranking: 12,
Prize Money: $25,300

ATP Masters Series Paris, France; 27.10.1997; SU; Indoor: Carpet;
Draw: 48
Round   Opponent   Ranking Score
R64   Bye   N/A   W
R32   Guillaume Raoux (FRA)   63   L 6-7(4), 6-3, 5-7
This Event Points: 1, South African Airways ATP Ranking: 13, Prize
Money: $15,880

ATP Masters Series Stuttgart, Germany; 20.10.1997; SU; Indoor:
Carpet; Draw: 48
Round   Opponent   Ranking Score
R64   Bye   N/A   W
R32   Karol Kucera (SVK)   26   W 6-7(7), 6-4, 6-4
R16   Yevgeny Kafelnikov (RUS)   6   W 7-6(6), 6-3
Q   Petr Korda (CZE)   17   L 3-6, 4-6
This Event Points: 134, South African Airways ATP Ranking: 10,
Prize Money: $51,100

Singapore, Singapore; 06.10.1997; GP; Indoor: Carpet; Draw: 32
Round   Opponent   Ranking Score
R32   Justin Gimelstob (USA)   82   W 6-2, 6-4
R16   Byron Black (ZIM)   61   W 6-2, 6-7(3), 7-6(3)
Q   Nicolas Kiefer (GER)   48   L 1-6, 5-7

This Event Points: 59, South African Airways ATP Ranking: 8, Prize Money: $14,900

Grand Slam Cup, Germany; 23.09.1997; GC; Indoor: Carpet; Draw: 16

Round	Opponent	Ranking	Score
R16	Mark Woodforde (AUS)	N/A	W 6-7, 6-3, 6-1
Q	Patrick Rafter (AUS)	N/A	L 1-6, 6-7

This Event Points: , South African Airways ATP Ranking: , Prize Money: $250,000

CHI V IND WGPO, India; 19.09.1997; DC; Outdoor: Grass; Draw: 4

Round	Opponent	Ranking	Score
RR	Mahesh Bhupathi (IND)	N/A	W 6-2, 3-6, 6-3, 6-4
RR	Leander Paes (IND)	N/A	W 6-7, 6-4, 6-0, 7-6

This Event Points: , South African Airways ATP Ranking: , Prize Money: $

US Open, NY, U.S.A.; 25.08.1997; GS; Outdoor: Hard; Draw: 128

Round	Opponent	Ranking	Score
R128	Luke Smith (AUS)	464	W 6-1, 6-1, 6-4 Stats
R64	Kenneth Carlsen (DEN)	92	W 6-4, 5-7, 3-6, 6-1, 7-6(3)
R32	Tommy Haas (USA)	78	W 6-4, 3-6, 6-3, 1-6, 6-1
R16	Sergi Bruguera (ESP)	8	W 7-5, 6-2, 6-4
Q	Michael Chang (USA)	2	L 5-7, 2-6, 6-4, 6-4, 3-6

This Event Points: 247, South African Airways ATP Ranking: 10, Prize Money: $90,000

Boston, MA, U.S.A.; 18.08.1997; GP; Outdoor: Hard; Draw: 32

Round	Opponent	Ranking	Score
R32	Jonathan Stark (USA)	65	W 6-7(1), 6-2, 7-6(1)
R16	Renzo Furlan (ITA)	86	W 6-4, 6-4
Q	Hernan Gumy (ARG)	73	W 6-4, 6-3
S	Jeff Tarango (USA)	60	W 6-4, 6-3
F	Sjeng Schalken (NED)	79	L 5-7, 3-6

This Event Points: 129, South African Airways ATP Ranking: 10, Prize Money: $25,300

Indianapolis, IN, U.S.A.; 11.08.1997; GP; Outdoor: Hard; Draw: 56

Round	Opponent	Ranking	Score
R64	Bye	N/A	W
R32	Thierry Champion (FRA)	175	W 3-6, 6-2, 6-3
R16	Mark Woodforde (AUS)	55	L 6-7(6), 4-6

This Event Points: 30, South African Airways ATP Ranking: 10, Prize Money: $11,500

ATP Masters Series Cincinnati, OH, U.S.A.; 04.08.1997; SU; Outdoor: Hard; Draw: 56

Round	Opponent	Ranking	Score
R64	Jonas Bjorkman (SWE)	25	W 6-3, 7-5
R32	Thomas Johansson (SWE)	37	W 6-3, 6-2
R16	Yevgeny Kafelnikov (RUS)	6	L 5-7, 2-6

This Event Points: 70, South African Airways ATP Ranking: 11, Prize Money: $25,700

Stuttgart Outdoor, Germany; 14.07.1997; GP; Outdoor: Clay; Draw: 48

Round	Opponent	Ranking	Score
R64	Bye	N/A	W
R32	Javier Sanchez (ESP)	41	W 6-2, 6-3
R16	Karol Kucera (SVK)	45	L 4-6, 4-6

This Event Points: 41, South African Airways ATP Ranking: 8, Prize Money: $12,000

Gstaad, Switzerland; 07.07.1997; GP; Outdoor: Clay; Draw: 32

Round	Opponent	Ranking	Score
R32	Jaime Oncins (BRA)	125	W 6-4, 6-2
R16	Juan Albert Viloca-Puig (ESP)	67	L 3-6, 6-7(3)

This Event Points: 22, South African Airways ATP Ranking: 9, Prize Money: $8,710

Wimbledon, England; 23.06.1997; GS; Outdoor: Grass; Draw: 128

Round	Opponent	Ranking	Score
R128	Mahesh Bhupathi (IND)	276	W 6-4, 6-4, 6-3
R64	Dennis van Scheppingen (NED)	97	W 6-2, 6-3, 6-7(1), 7-6(7)

| R32 | John van Lottum (NED) | 366 | W 7-6(4), 6-3, 6-7(5), 6-4 |
| R16 | Boris Becker (GER) | 18 | L 2-6, 2-6, 6-7(5) |

This Event Points: 88, South African Airways ATP Ranking: 10, Prize Money: $49,173

Nottingham, England; 16.06.1997; GP; Outdoor: Grass; Draw: 32

Round	Opponent	Ranking	Score
R32	Kenneth Carlsen (DEN)	93	L 4-6, 2-6

This Event Points: 1, South African Airways ATP Ranking: 10, Prize Money: $3,000

Roland Garros, France; 26.05.1997; GS; Outdoor: Clay; Draw: 128

Round	Opponent	Ranking	Score
R128	Wayne Black (ZIM)	249	W 6-4, 5-7, 4-6, 6-2, 6-1
R64	Byron Black (ZIM)	67	W 6-7(3), 6-7, 6-4, 7-6(4), 6-0
R32	Arnaud Boetsch (FRA)	45	W 7-6(6), 6-3, 6-4
R16	Hicham Arazi (MAR)	55	L 2-6, 1-6, 7-5, 6-7(4)

This Event Points: 118, South African Airways ATP Ranking: 10, Prize Money: $45,474

St. Poelten, Austria; 19.05.1997; GP; Outdoor: Clay; Draw: 32

Round	Opponent	Ranking	Score
R32	Andrea Gaudenzi (ITA)	125	W 6-4, 4-6, 6-4
R16	Tomas Nydahl (SWE)	185	L 4-6, 2-6

This Event Points: 20, South African Airways ATP Ranking: 7, Prize Money: $6,700

ATP Masters Series Rome, Italy; 12.05.1997; SU; Outdoor: Clay; Draw: 64

Round	Opponent	Ranking	Score
R64	Omar Camporese (ITA)	160	W 6-3, 7-5
R32	Fabrice Santoro (FRA)	56	W 6-2, 6-2
R16	Magnus Larsson (SWE)	41	W 4-6, 7-5, 6-4
Q	Jim Courier (USA)	24	W 6-3, 3-6, 7-6(4)
S	Alberto Berasategui (ESP)	16	W 6-3, 3-6, 6-1
F	Alex Corretja (ESP)	15	L 5-7, 5-7, 3-6

This Event Points: 326, South African Airways ATP Ranking: 9, Prize Money: $171,500

ATP Masters Series Hamburg, Germany; 05.05.1997; SU; Outdoor: Clay; Draw: 56

Round	Opponent	Ranking	Score
R64	Bye	N/A	W
R32	Christian Ruud (NOR)	45	W 6-1, 7-5
R16	Alberto Berasategui (ESP)	19	L 4-6, 1-6

This Event Points: 52, South African Airways ATP Ranking: 7, Prize Money: $25,700

Prague, Czech Republic; 28.04.1997; GP; Outdoor: Clay; Draw: 32

Round	Opponent	Ranking	Score
R32	Orlin Stanoytchev (BUL)	115	W 6-4, 6-3
R16	Stephane Simian (FRA)	127	W 6-4, 6-2
Q	Fabrice Santoro (FRA)	69	L 6-4, 3-6, 0-6

This Event Points: 37, South African Airways ATP Ranking: 8, Prize Money: $9,800

ATP Masters Series Monte Carlo, Monaco; 21.04.1997; SU; Outdoor: Clay; Draw: 56

Round	Opponent	Ranking	Score
R64	Bye	N/A	W
R32	Andrea Gaudenzi (ITA)	112	W 6-2, 6-2
R16	Albert Costa (ESP)	9	W 7-6(3), 6-4
Q	Magnus Larsson (SWE)	43	W 6-2, 6-1
S	Carlos Moya (ESP)	8	W 6-4, 7-6(5)
W	Alex Corretja (ESP)	18	W 6-4, 6-3, 6-3

This Event Points: 504, South African Airways ATP Ranking: 10, Prize Money: $377,000

Barcelona, Spain; 14.04.1997; GP; Outdoor: Clay; Draw: 56

Round	Opponent	Ranking	Score
R64	Bye	N/A	W
R32	Albert Portas (ESP)	133	L 5-7, 6-7(3)

This Event Points: 1, South African Airways ATP Ranking: 9, Prize Money: $5,450

ARG V CHI AZ1, Chile; 04.04.1997; DC; Outdoor: Clay; Draw: 4

Round	Opponent	Ranking	Score
RR	Javier Frana (ARG)	N/A	W 6-1, 6-4, 7-6
RR	Hernan Gumy (ARG)	N/A	W 6-4, 7-5, 6-4

This Event Points: , South African Airways ATP Ranking: , Prize Money: $

ATP Masters Series Miami, FL, U.S.A.; 17.03.1997; SU; Outdoor: Hard; Draw: 96

Round	Opponent	Ranking	Score
R128	Bye	N/A	W
R64	Jeff Tarango (USA)	72	W 7-5, 6-2
R32	Jonas Bjorkman (SWE)	29	L 3-6, 6-3, 1-6

This Event Points: 26, South African Airways ATP Ranking: 9, Prize Money: $14,500

ATP Masters Series Indian Wells, CA, U.S.A.; 10.03.1997; SU; Outdoor: Hard; Draw: 56

Round	Opponent	Ranking	Score
R64	Bye	N/A	W
R32	Magnus Larsson (SWE)	49	L 3-6, 7-5, 6-7(2)

This Event Points: 1, South African Airways ATP Ranking: 7, Prize Money: $13,600

Scottsdale, AZ, U.S.A.; 03.03.1997; GP; Outdoor: Hard; Draw: 32

Round	Opponent	Ranking	Score
R32	Byron Black (ZIM)	53	L 1-6, 6-4, 6-7(5)

This Event Points: 1, South African Airways ATP Ranking: 6, Prize Money: $3,000

Antwerp, Belgium; 17.02.1997; GP; Indoor: Hard; Draw: 32

Round	Opponent	Ranking	Score
R32	Adrian Voinea (ROU)	50	W 6-1, 6-4
R16	Martin Damm (CZE)	48	L 6-4, 5-7, 6-7(3)

This Event Points: 41, South African Airways ATP Ranking: 6, Prize Money: $12,500

Marseille, France; 10.02.1997; GP; Indoor: Hard; Draw: 32

Round	Opponent	Ranking	Score

R32	Juan Albert Viloca-Puig (ESP)	83	W 7-6(4), 6-4
R16	Johan Van Herck (BEL)	86	W 6-2, 6-4
Q	Magnus Larsson (SWE)	46	W 3-6, 7-5, 6-4
S	Sergi Bruguera (ESP)	53	W 6-3, 6-7(3), 6-4
F	Thomas Enqvist (SWE)	10	L 4-6, 0-1 RET

This Event Points: 147, South African Airways ATP Ranking: 7, Prize Money: $42,500

ECU V CHI AZ1, Chile; 07.02.1997; DC; Outdoor: Clay; Draw: 4

Round	Opponent	Ranking	Score
RR	Luis Adrian Morejon (ECU)	N/A	W 6-1, 6-3, 3-6, 6-2
RR	Nicolas Lapentti (ECU)	N/A	W 7-5, 6-7, 6-3, 6-7, 8-6

This Event Points: , South African Airways ATP Ranking: , Prize Money: $

Australian Open, Australia; 13.01.1997; GS; Outdoor: Hard; Draw: 128

Round	Opponent	Ranking	Score
R128	Petr Korda (CZE)	34	W 7-6(4), 6-3, 6-3
R64	Michael Joyce (USA)	99	W 6-0, 6-4, 6-2
R32	Gilbert Schaller (AUT)	96	W 4-6, 7-6(2), 6-1, 6-1
R16	Thomas Enqvist (SWE)	9	W 4-6, 6-4, 7-6(4), 6-7(5), 6-3
Q	Michael Chang (USA)	2	L 5-7, 1-6, 4-6

This Event Points: 271, South African Airways ATP Ranking: 11, Prize Money: $58,613

Auckland, New Zealand; 06.01.1997; GP; Outdoor: Hard; Draw: 32

Round	Opponent	Ranking	Score
R32	Karim Alami (MAR)	61	W 6-2, 6-3
R16	Jeff Tarango (USA)	92	W 6-2, 6-4
Q	Marcos Ondruska (RSA)	102	L 6-0, 3-6, 3-6

This Event Points: 42, South African Airways ATP Ranking: 11, Prize Money: $8,800

1998

ATP Tour World Championship, Germany; 23.11.1998; WC; Indoor: Hard; Draw: 64

Round	Opponent	Ranking	Score
RR	Tim Henman (GBR)	9	L 5-7, 1-6

This Event Points: , South African Airways ATP Ranking: 2, Prize Money: $40,000

Santiago, Chile; 09.11.1998; WS; Outdoor: Clay; Draw: 32

Round	Opponent	Ranking	Score
R32	Marcio Carlsson (BRA)	119	W 6-2, 1-6, 6-3
R16	Martin Rodriguez (ARG)	89	W 6-2, 6-2
Q	Juan Antonio Marin (CRC)	88	L 4-6, 7-6(5), 5-7

This Event Points: 38, South African Airways ATP Ranking: 2, Prize Money: $9,100

ATP Masters Series Paris, France; 02.11.1998; SU; Indoor: Carpet; Draw: 48

Round	Opponent	Ranking	Score
R64	Bye	N/A	W
R32	Todd Woodbridge (AUS)	71	W 6-0, 6-4
R16	Vincent Spadea (USA)	47	W 7-5, 6-4
Q	Yevgeny Kafelnikov (RUS)	8	L 3-6, 2-6

This Event Points: 98, South African Airways ATP Ranking: 2, Prize Money: $57,400

ATP Masters Series Stuttgart, Germany; 26.10.1998; SU; Indoor: Hard; Draw: 48

Round	Opponent	Ranking	Score
R64	Bye	N/A	W
R32	Tommy Haas (USA)	37	W 6-3, 7-5
R16	Jan Siemerink (NED)	15	W 6-2 RET
Q	Yevgeny Kafelnikov (RUS)	8	L W/O

This Event Points: 116, South African Airways ATP Ranking: 2, Prize Money: $55,000

Lyon, France; 19.10.1998; WS; Indoor: Carpet; Draw: 32

Round	Opponent	Ranking	Score

R32	Jeff Tarango (USA)	71	W 6-3, 6-3
R16	Nicolas Escude (FRA)	31	W 6-2, 6-3
Q	Arnaud Di Pasquale (FRA)	95	W 6-4, 6-0
S	Tommy Haas (USA)	53	L 2-6, 0-1 RET

This Event Points: 111, South African Airways ATP Ranking: 2, Prize Money: $35,300

Singapore, Singapore; 12.10.1998; CS; Indoor: Carpet; Draw: 32

Round	Opponent	Ranking	Score
R32	Sebastien Lareau (CAN)	86	W 6-2, 6-0
R16	Andrei Pavel (ROU)	73	W 6-2, 6-4
Q	Lleyton Hewitt (AUS)	137	W 5-7, 6-3, 6-4
S	Jim Courier (USA)	117	W 6-2, 6-1
W	Mark Woodforde (AUS)	91	W 6-4, 6-2

This Event Points: 266, South African Airways ATP Ranking: 3, Prize Money: $107,000

Grand Slam Cup, Germany; 28.09.1998; GC; Indoor: Hard; Draw: 16

Round	Opponent	Ranking	Score
R16	Bye	N/A	W
Q	Felix Mantilla (ESP)	21	W 7-6, 7-5
S	Mark Philippoussis (AUS)	15	W 7-6, 6-3, 6-4
W	Andre Agassi (USA)	8	W 6-4, 2-6, 7-6, 5-7, 6-3

This Event Points: , South African Airways ATP Ranking: 3, Prize Money: $1,300,000

US Open, NY, U.S.A.; 31.08.1998; GS; Outdoor: Hard; Draw: 128

Round	Opponent	Ranking	Score
R128	Daniel Vacek (CZE)	43	W 6-4, 6-2, 6-3
R64	Giorgio Galimberti (ITA)	320	W 6-2, 6-7(4), 6-2, 6-2
R32	Magnus Larsson (SWE)	34	L 1-6, 7-6(3), 6-2, 3-6, 2-6

This Event Points: 65, South African Airways ATP Ranking: 2, Prize Money: $30,000

Long Island, NY, U.S.A.; 24.08.1998; WS; Outdoor: Hard; Draw: 32

Round	Opponent	Ranking	Score
R32	Gustavo Kuerten (BRA)	27	L 3-6, 6-7(4)

This Event Points: 1, South African Airways ATP Ranking: 2, Prize Money: $3,150

Indianapolis, IN, U.S.A.; 17.08.1998; CS; Outdoor: Hard; Draw: 56

Round	Opponent	Ranking	Score
R64	Bye	N/A	W
R32	Bob Bryan (USA)	476	W 6-4, 6-4
R16	Byron Black (ZIM)	35	L 7-5, 1-6, 5-7

This Event Points: 27, South African Airways ATP Ranking: 1, Prize Money: $9,400

ATP Masters Series Cincinnati, OH, U.S.A.; 10.08.1998; SU; Outdoor: Hard; Draw: 56

Round	Opponent	Ranking	Score
R64	Bye	N/A	W
R32	Daniel Vacek (CZE)	53	L 3-6, 2-6

This Event Points: 1, South African Airways ATP Ranking: 1, Prize Money: $14,500

Stuttgart Outdoor, Germany; 20.07.1998; CS; Outdoor: Clay; Draw: 48

Round	Opponent	Ranking	Score
R64	Bye	N/A	W
R32	Jens Knippschild (GER)	121	W 7-6(5), 6-2
R16	Hendrik Dreekmann (GER)	97	W 6-3, 6-4
Q	Boris Becker (GER)	81	W 6-2, 6-0
S	Karol Kucera (SVK)	16	L 1-6, 7-6(8), 4-6

This Event Points: 123, South African Airways ATP Ranking: 2, Prize Money: $43,170

CHI V COL AZPO, Chile; 17.07.1998; DC; Outdoor: Carpet; Draw: 0

Round	Opponent	Ranking	Score
RR	Philippe Moggio (COL)	N/A	W 6-3, 6-0, 6-2
RR	Miguel Tobon (COL)	N/A	W 6-2, 6-2

This Event Points: , South African Airways ATP Ranking: , Prize Money: $

Gstaad, Switzerland; 06.07.1998; WS; Outdoor: Clay; Draw: 32

Round	Opponent	Ranking	Score

R32	Marc Rosset (SUI) 36		W 6-3, 6-3
R16	Lucas Arnold Ker (ARG)	88	W 6-4, 6-1
Q	Francisco Clavet (ESP)	29	W 6-3, 7-5
S	Boris Becker (GER)	119	L 4-6, 6-7(4)

This Event Points: 113, South African Airways ATP Ranking: 2, Prize Money: $25,500

Wimbledon, England; 22.06.1998; GS; Outdoor: Grass; Draw: 128

Round	Opponent	Ranking	Score
R128	Francisco Clavet (ESP)	36	L 3-6, 6-3, 5-7, 6-3, 3-6

This Event Points: 1, South African Airways ATP Ranking: 2, Prize Money: $10,916

Nottingham, England; 15.06.1998; WS; Outdoor: Grass; Draw: 32

Round	Opponent	Ranking	Score
R32	Gianluca Pozzi (ITA)	59	L 6-3, 4-6, 0-6

This Event Points: 1, South African Airways ATP Ranking: 2, Prize Money: $3,150

Roland Garros, France; 25.05.1998; GS; Outdoor: Clay; Draw: 128

Round	Opponent	Ranking	Score
R128	Brett Steven (NZL)	46	W 7-5, 6-2, 3-6, 6-3
R64	Emilio Benfele Alvarez (ESP)	144	W 6-4, 6-2, 6-2
R32	Wayne Ferreira (RSA)	30	W 6-1, 3-3 RET
R16	Albert Costa (ESP)	13	W 4-6, 6-4, 6-3, 6-3
Q	Carlos Moya (ESP)	12	L 1-6, 6-2, 2-6, 4-6

This Event Points: 275, South African Airways ATP Ranking: 3, Prize Money: $85,567

St. Poelten, Austria; 18.05.1998; WS; Outdoor: Clay; Draw: 32

Round	Opponent	Ranking	Score
R32	Scott Draper (AUS)	120	W 6-1, 6-3
R16	Marc-Kevin Goellner (GER)	86	W 6-4, 6-3
Q	Galo Blanco (ESP)	42	W 6-2, 6-2
S	Andrea Gaudenzi (ITA)	35	W 6-4, 6-3
W	Vincent Spadea (USA)	62	W 6-2, 6-0

This Event Points: 195, South African Airways ATP Ranking: 3, Prize Money: $57,000

ATP Masters Series Rome, Italy; 11.05.1998; SU; Outdoor: Clay; Draw: 64

Round	Opponent	Ranking	Score
R64	Marzio Martelli (ITA)	140	W 6-3, 6-0
R32	Tim Henman (GBR)	17	W 6-3, 6-1
R16	Thomas Muster (AUT)	24	W 6-3, 6-1
Q	Richard Krajicek (NED)	11	W 7-6(9), 6-3
S	Gustavo Kuerten (BRA)	9	W 6-0, 7-5
W	Albert Costa (ESP)	20	W W/O

This Event Points: 474, South African Airways ATP Ranking: 3, Prize Money: $350,000

ATP Masters Series Hamburg, Germany; 04.05.1998; SU; Outdoor: Clay; Draw: 56

Round	Opponent	Ranking	Score
R64	Bye	N/A	W
R32	Wayne Ferreira (RSA)	32	L 6-4, 4-6, 3-6

This Event Points: 1, South African Airways ATP Ranking: 3, Prize Money: $14,500

CHI V ARG AZI, Argentina; 03.04.1998; DC; Outdoor: Clay; Draw: 5

Round	Opponent	Ranking	Score
RR	Hernan Gumy (ARG)	N/A	W 6-4, 3-6, 6-3, 7-5

This Event Points: , South African Airways ATP Ranking: , Prize Money: $

ATP Masters Series Miami, FL, U.S.A.; 16.03.1998; SU; Outdoor: Hard; Draw: 96

Round	Opponent	Ranking	Score
R128	Bye	N/A	W
R64	Hendrik Dreekmann (GER)	94	W 6-3, 6-4
R32	Tommy Haas (USA)	34	W 6-4, 6-3
R16	Goran Ivanisevic (CRO)	22	W 6-2, 6-3
Q	Thomas Enqvist (SWE)	24	W 6-3, 2-0 RET
S	Tim Henman (GBR)	20	W 6-2, 4-6, 6-0
W	Andre Agassi (USA)	31	W 7-5, 6-3, 6-4

This Event Points: 469, South African Airways ATP Ranking: 3, Prize Money: $360,000

ATP Masters Series Indian Wells, CA, U.S.A.; 09.03.1998; SU; Outdoor: Hard; Draw: 56

Round	Opponent	Ranking	Score
R64	Bye N/A		W
R32	Hendrik Dreekmann (GER)	92	W 6-4, 7-6(4)
R16	Nicolas Kiefer (GER)	27	W 6-4, 6-3
Q	Petr Korda (CZE)	2	W 6-4, 6-2
S	Jan-Michael Gambill (USA)	126	W 7-6(3), 6-3
W	Greg Rusedski (GBR)	6	W 6-3, 6-7(15), 7-6(4), 6-4

This Event Points: 510, South African Airways ATP Ranking: 7, Prize Money: $361,000

Memphis, TN, U.S.A.; 16.02.1998; CS; Indoor: Hard; Draw: 48

Round	Opponent	Ranking	Score
R64	Bye N/A		W
R32	Steve Campbell (USA)	117	W 6-2, 6-4
R16	Vincent Spadea (USA)	69	W 6-2, 6-3
Q	Grant Stafford (RSA)	79	W 6-2, 6-3
S	Mark Philippoussis (AUS)	16	L 4-6, 6-7(5)

This Event Points: 116, South African Airways ATP Ranking: 7, Prize Money: $33,100

Dubai, U.A.E.; 09.02.1998; WS; Outdoor: Hard; Draw: 32

Round	Opponent	Ranking	Score
R32	Brett Steven (NZL)	50	L 3-6, 3-6

This Event Points: 1, South African Airways ATP Ranking: 5, Prize Money: $10,080

Australian Open, Australia; 19.01.1998; GS; Outdoor: Hard; Draw: 128

Round	Opponent	Ranking	Score
R128	Grant Stafford (RSA)	77	W 6-1, 6-3, 6-3
R64	Thomas Enqvist (SWE)	26	W 6-4, 7-6(4), 4-6, 6-4
R32	Andrew Ilie (AUS)	282	W 6-2, 6-3, 6-2
R16	Lionel Roux (FRA)	62	W 6-2, 4-6, 6-2, 6-4
Q	Alberto Berasategui (ESP)	25	W 6-7(6), 6-4, 6-4, 6-0
S	Nicolas Escude (FRA)	81	W 6-1, 6-3, 6-2
F	Petr Korda (CZE)	7	L 2-6, 2-6, 2-6

This Event Points: 633, South African Airways ATP Ranking: 8, Prize Money: $203,688

Auckland, New Zealand; 12.01.1998; WS; Outdoor: Hard; Draw: 32

Round	Opponent	Ranking	Score
R32	Nicolas Lapentti (ECU)	63	W 6-3, 6-3
R16	Mark Nielsen (NZL)	317	W 7-5, 6-1
Q	Kenneth Carlsen (DEN)	96	W 5-7, 6-4, 6-1
S	Byron Black (ZIM)	75	W 6-1, 6-3
W	Richard Fromberg (AUS)	73	W 4-6, 6-4, 7-6(3)

This Event Points: 171, South African Airways ATP Ranking: 10, Prize Money: $45,000

1999

ATP Masters Series Paris, France; 01.11.1999; SU; Indoor: Carpet; Draw: 48

Round	Opponent	Ranking	Score
R64	Bye	N/A	W
R32	Michael Chang (USA)	72	L 5-7, 2-6

This Event Points: 1, South African Airways ATP Ranking: 8, Prize Money: $15,880

ATP Masters Series Stuttgart, Germany; 25.10.1999; SU; Indoor: Hard; Draw: 48

Round	Opponent	Ranking	Score
R64	Bye	N/A	W
R32	Sebastien Grosjean (FRA)	26	W 6-3, 6-4
R16	Nicolas Lapentti (ECU)	11	W 6-4, 6-3
Q	Thomas Enqvist (SWE)	18	L 4-6, 2-6

This Event Points: 98, South African Airways ATP Ranking: 9, Prize Money: $55,000

Singapore, Singapore; 11.10.1999; CS; Indoor: Hard; Draw: 32

Round	Opponent	Ranking	Score
R32	Fredrik Jonsson (SWE)	125	W 6-4, 6-2
R16	Daniel Nestor (CAN)	70	W 6-4, 6-1
Q	Jan-Michael Gambill (USA)	58	W 6-4, 6-4

S	Lleyton Hewitt (AUS)	31	W 7-5, 6-3
W	Mikael Tillstrom (SWE)	142	W 6-2, 7-6(5)

This Event Points: 222, South African Airways ATP Ranking: 6, Prize Money: $111,500

Shanghai, China; 04.10.1999; WS; Outdoor: Hard; Draw: 32

Round	Opponent	Ranking	Score
R32	Laurence Tieleman (ITA)	90	W 6-2, 6-1
R16	Ivan Ljubicic (CRO)	99	W 6-3, 6-2
Q	Todd Woodbridge (AUS)	153	W 6-3, 6-3
S	Jonas Bjorkman (SWE)	63	W 6-4, 6-1
F	Magnus Norman (SWE)	23	L 6-2, 3-6, 5-7

This Event Points: 97, South African Airways ATP Ranking: 7, Prize Money: $27,000

ZIM v CHI, WGPO, Harare, Zimbabwe; 24.09.1999; DC; Indoor: Hard; Draw: 6

Round	Opponent	Ranking	Score
RR	Wayne Black (ZIM)	N/A	L 5-7, 7-5, 6-7(3), 6-7(4)
RR	Byron Black (ZIM)	N/A	L 6-7(3), 6-3, 2-6, 6-7(6)

This Event Points: , South African Airways ATP Ranking: , Prize Money: $

US Open, NY, U.S.A.; 30.08.1999; GS; Outdoor: Hard; Draw: 128

Round	Opponent	Ranking	Score
R128	Martin Damm (CZE)	97	W 6-4, 7-6(5), 3-6, 5-7, 6-1
R64	George Bastl (SUI)	175	W 4-6, 6-3, 6-2, 6-3
R32	Jan Kroslak (SVK)	58	W 6-3, 6-4, 6-4
R16	Nicolas Escude (FRA)	136	L 2-6, 3-6, 5-7

This Event Points: 83, South African Airways ATP Ranking: 10, Prize Money: $55,000

Boston, MA, U.S.A.; 23.08.1999; WS; Outdoor: Hard; Draw: 32

Round	Opponent	Ranking	Score
R32	James Blake (USA)	329	W 6-3, 7-6(4)
R16	Daniel Nestor (CAN)	58	W 6-7(6), 6-2, 6-4

Q   Sjeng Schalken (NED)   51   L 5-7, 0-6
This Event Points: 31, South African Airways ATP Ranking: 10, Prize Money: $9,350

Indianapolis, IN, U.S.A.; 16.08.1999; CS; Outdoor: Hard; Draw: 56

Round	Opponent	Ranking	Score
R64	Bye	N/A	W
R32	Harel Levy (ISR)	165	W 6-2, 7-6(5)
R16	Sebastien Grosjean (FRA)	32	L 4-6, 2-6

This Event Points: 22, South African Airways ATP Ranking: 11, Prize Money: $9,400

Stuttgart Outdoor, Germany; 19.07.1999; CS; Outdoor: Clay; Draw: 48

Round	Opponent	Ranking	Score
R64	Bye	N/A	W
R32	Hernan Gumy (ARG)	103	W 6-7(2), 7-6(6), 6-0
R16	Jens Knippschild (GER)	91	W 6-4, 6-4
Q	Jiri Novak (CZE)	59	L 2-6, 2-6

This Event Points: 50, South African Airways ATP Ranking: 11, Prize Money: $23,000

Gstaad, Switzerland; 05.07.1999; WS; Outdoor: Clay; Draw: 32

Round	Opponent	Ranking	Score
R32	Bohdan Ulihrach (CZE)	38	W 6-2, 6-7(7), 7-6(1)
R16	Younes El Aynaoui (MAR)	33	L 6-7(5), 6-7(5)

This Event Points: 26, South African Airways ATP Ranking: 9, Prize Money: $8,710

Roland Garros, France; 24.05.1999; GS; Outdoor: Clay; Draw: 128

Round	Opponent	Ranking	Score
R128	Axel Pretzsch (GER)	127	W 6-3, 6-2, 7-5
R64	Arnaud Boetsch (FRA)	660	W 6-2, 6-3, 7-5
R32	Albert Costa (ESP)	25	W 7-5, 6-4, 7-5
R16	Alberto Berasategui (ESP)	97	W 3-6, 3-6, 6-3, 6-4, 6-3
Q	Dominik Hrbaty (SVK)	30	L 6-7(4), 2-6, 7-6(6), 3-6

This Event Points: 171, South African Airways ATP Ranking: 9, Prize Money: $88,132

St. Poelten, Austria; 17.05.1999; WS; Outdoor: Clay; Draw: 32

Round	Opponent	Ranking	Score
R32	Davide Sanguinetti (ITA)	75	W 7-6(4), 5-7, 6-3
R16	Alberto Berasategui (ESP)	101	W 7-6(4), 6-2
Q	Stefan Koubek (AUT)	69	W 6-4, 6-0
S	Younes El Aynaoui (MAR)	36	W 6-1, 6-3
W	Mariano Zabaleta (ARG)	26	W 4-4 RET

This Event Points: 163, South African Airways ATP Ranking: 9, Prize Money: $57,000

ATP Masters Series Rome, Italy; 10.05.1999; SU; Outdoor: Clay; Draw: 64

Round	Opponent	Ranking	Score
R64	David Prinosil (GER)	80	L 2-6, 7-5, 3-6

This Event Points: 1, South African Airways ATP Ranking: 6, Prize Money: $7,400

ATP Masters Series Hamburg, Germany; 03.05.1999; SU; Outdoor: Clay; Draw: 56

Round	Opponent	Ranking	Score
R64	Bye	N/A	W
R32	Oliver Gross (GER)	101	W 7-6(6), 7-5
R16	Wayne Ferreira (RSA)	24	W 6-1, 3-6, 6-2
Q	Tommy Haas (USA)	20	W 6-4, 6-4
S	Carlos Moya (ESP)	6	W 6-4, 7-6(4)
W	Mariano Zabaleta (ARG)	48	W 6-7(5), 7-5, 5-7, 7-6(5), 6-2

This Event Points: 380, South African Airways ATP Ranking: 8, Prize Money: $361,000

ATP Masters Series Monte Carlo, Monaco; 19.04.1999; SU; Outdoor: Clay; Draw: 56

Round	Opponent	Ranking	Score
R64	Bye	N/A	W
R32	Andrei Pavel (ROU)	75	W 0-6, 6-4, 7-6(6)
R16	Hicham Arazi (MAR)	37	W 6-3, 6-3

Q	Mark Philippoussis (AUS)	8	W 6-2, 6-7(2), 6-4
S	Jerome Golmard (FRA)	25	W 6-4, 3-6, 6-2
F	Gustavo Kuerten (BRA)	19	L 4-6, 1-2 RET

This Event Points: 270, South African Airways ATP Ranking: 13, Prize Money: $190,000

Barcelona, Spain; 12.04.1999; CS; Outdoor: Clay; Draw: 56

Round	Opponent	Ranking	Score
R64	Bye	N/A	W
R32	Andrei Pavel (ROU)	47	W 3-6, 6-3, 6-2
R16	Albert Costa (ESP)	14	L 4-6, 1-6

This Event Points: 32, South African Airways ATP Ranking: 13, Prize Money: $10,430

Estoril, Portugal; 05.04.1999; WS; Outdoor: Clay; Draw: 32

Round	Opponent	Ranking	Score
R32	Adrian Voinea (ROU)	76	W 3-6, 6-4, 6-2
R16	Albert Portas (ESP)	91	W 6-3, 6-3
Q	Gustavo Kuerten (BRA)	18	W 6-4, 6-3
S	Todd Martin (USA)	8	L 3-6, 6-7(3)

This Event Points: 92, South African Airways ATP Ranking: 13, Prize Money: $29,200

CHI V COL AZI, Bogota, Columbia; 02.04.1999; DC; Outdoor: Clay; Draw: 6

Round	Opponent	Ranking	Score
RR	Miguel Tobon (COL)	N/A	W 6-1, 7-6(4), 6-1
RR	Eduardo Rincon (COL)	N/A	W 6-1, 7-6(1)

This Event Points: , South African Airways ATP Ranking: , Prize Money: $

ATP Masters Series Miami, FL, U.S.A; 15.03.1999; SU; Outdoor: Hard; Draw: 96

Round	Opponent	Ranking	Score
R128	Bye	N/A	W
R64	Scott Draper (AUS)	47	W 7-6(6), 6-3
R32	Byron Black (ZIM)	28	W 6-3, 6-4
R16	Dominik Hrbaty (SVK)	40	L 2-6, 0-6

This Event Points: 56, South African Airways ATP Ranking: 8, Prize Money: $27,600

ATP Masters Series Indian Wells, CA, U.S.A.; 08.03.1999; SU; Outdoor: Hard; Draw: 56

Round	Opponent	Ranking	Score
R64	Bye	N/A	W
R32	Cedric Pioline (FRA)	19	W 7-6(3), 6-1
R16	Todd Martin (USA)	11	L 6-4, 2-6, 2-6

This Event Points: 51, South African Airways ATP Ranking: 6, Prize Money: $28,000

Auckland, New Zealand; 11.01.1999; WS; Outdoor: Hard; Draw: 32

Round	Opponent	Ranking	Score
R32	Andrei Pavel (ROU)	64	L 7-5, 0-2 RET

This Event Points: 1, South African Airways ATP Ranking: 2, Prize Money: $3,250

2000

Basel, Switzerland; 23.10.2000; WS; Indoor: Carpet; Draw: 32

Round	Opponent	Ranking	Score
R32	Nicolas Lapentti (ECU)	17	L 6-3, 4-6, 4-6

This Event Points: 5, South African Airways ATP Ranking: 30, Prize Money: $9,800

Toulouse, France; 16.10.2000; WS; Indoor: Hard; Draw: 32

Round	Opponent	Ranking	Score
R32	Fernando Vicente (ESP)	43	W 6-4, 3-6, 6-1
R16	Karim Alami (MAR)	39	W 6-7(4), 6-3, 6-4
Q	Juan Albert Viloca-Puig (ESP)	220	W 6-4, 6-4
S	Alex Corretja (ESP)	9	L 6-7(6), 3-6

This Event Points: 75, South African Airways ATP Ranking: 33, Prize Money: $18,400

Hong Kong, China; 02.10.2000; WS; Outdoor: Hard; Draw: 32

Round	Opponent	Ranking	Score
R32	David Prinosil (GER)	61	W 6-3, 6-1
R16	Sergi Bruguera (ESP)	97	L 6-2, 6-7(2), 4-6

This Event Points: 15, South African Airways ATP Ranking: 17, Prize Money: $5,900

Sydney Olympics, Sydney, Australia; 18.09.2000; OL; Outdoor: Hard; Draw: 64

Round	Opponent	Ranking	Score
R64	Mariano Zabaleta (ARG)	55	L 7-6(8), 4-6, 5-7

This Event Points: 5, South African Airways ATP Ranking: 17, Prize Money: $

US Open, NY, U.S.A.; 28.08.2000; GS; Outdoor: Hard; Draw: 128

Round	Opponent	Ranking	Score
R128	Nicolas Massu (CHI)	64	W 6-3, 7-5, 1-6, 7-6(6)
R64	Jens Knippschild (GER)	126	W 4-6, 6-4, 6-4, 7-5
R32	Thomas Enqvist (SWE)	5	L 5-7, 5-7, 3-6

This Event Points: 75, South African Airways ATP Ranking: 19, Prize Money: $35,000

Indianapolis, IN, U.S.A.; 14.08.2000; CS; Outdoor: Hard; Draw: 56

Round	Opponent	Ranking	Score
R64	Bye	N/A	W
R32	Xavier Malisse (BEL)	172	L 4-6 RET

This Event Points: 5, South African Airways ATP Ranking: 19, Prize Money: $4,650

ATP Masters Series Cincinnati, OH, U.S.A.; 07.08.2000; SU; Outdoor: Hard; Draw: 64

Round	Opponent	Ranking	Score
R64	Marc Rosset (SUI)	29	W 6-4, 6-4
R32	Mark Philippoussis (AUS)	18	L 7-6(3), 4-6, 6-7(4)

This Event Points: 35, South African Airways ATP Ranking: 20, Prize Money: $16,250

ATP Masters Series Canada, Toronto, Canada; 31.07.2000; SU; Outdoor: Hard; Draw: 64

Round	Opponent	Ranking	Score
R64	Tim Henman (GBR)	17	W 6-4, 3-6, 6-3
R32	Arnaud Clement (FRA)	50	W 6-4, 7-6(5)
R16	Jerome Golmard (FRA)	61	L 6-2, 5-7, 5-7

This Event Points: 75, South African Airways ATP Ranking: 22, Prize Money: $30,800

Los Angeles, CA, U.S.A.; 24.07.2000; WS; Outdoor: Hard; Draw: 32

Round	Opponent	Ranking	Score
R32	Gouichi Motomura (JPN)	176	L 3-5 DEF

This Event Points: 5, South African Airways ATP Ranking: 22, Prize Money: $3,500

Umag, Croatia; 17.07.2000; WS; Outdoor: Clay; Draw: 32

Round	Opponent	Ranking	Score
R32	Jan Kroslak (SVK)	137	W 6-3, 6-1
R16	German Puentes (ESP)	128	W 6-3, 6-2
Q	David Sanchez (ESP)	104	W 7-6(6), 6-2
S	Carlos Moya (ESP)	54	W 6-2, 7-5
W	Mariano Puerta (ARG)	21	W 7-6(1), 4-6, 6-3

This Event Points: 175, South African Airways ATP Ranking: 23, Prize Money: $54,000

Gstaad, Switzerland; 10.07.2000; WS; Outdoor: Clay; Draw: 32

Round	Opponent	Ranking	Score
R32	Slava Dosedel (CZE)	56	W 7-5, 6-7(2), 6-2
R16	George Bastl (SUI)	75	W 6-3, 7-5
Q	Alex Corretja (ESP)	10	L 7-6(6), 1-6, 3-6

This Event Points: 50, South African Airways ATP Ranking: 24, Prize Money: $16,455

Roland Garros, France; 29.05.2000; GS; Outdoor: Clay; Draw: 128

Round	Opponent	Ranking	Score
R128	Tommy Haas (USA)	21	L 3-6, 2-6 RET

This Event Points: 5, South African Airways ATP Ranking: 19, Prize Money: $8,781

World Team Cup, Dusseldorf, Germany; 21.05.2000; WT; Outdoor: Clay; Draw: 64

Round	Opponent	Ranking	Score
RR	Yevgeny Kafelnikov (RUS)	N/A	L 3-6, 5-7
RR	Lleyton Hewitt (AUS)	N/A	L 0-5 RET
RR	Felix Mantilla (ESP)	N/A	L 4-6, 1-6

This Event Points: , South African Airways ATP Ranking: , Prize Money: $43,200

ATP Masters Series Hamburg, Germany; 15.05.2000; SU; Outdoor: Clay; Draw: 64

Round	Opponent	Ranking	Score
R64	Nicolas Escude (FRA)	21	W 6-4, 6-1
R32	Michael Kohlmann (GER)	179	W 6-1, 6-0
R16	Mariano Puerta (ARG)	30	W 7-6(4), 6-0
Q	Francisco Clavet (ESP)	55	W 6-4, 6-3
S	Marat Safin (RUS)	14	L 6-7(8), 2-6

This Event Points: 225, South African Airways ATP Ranking: 20, Prize Money: $111,200

ATP Masters Series Rome, Italy; 08.05.2000; SU; Outdoor: Clay; Draw: 64

Round	Opponent	Ranking	Score
R64	Marat Safin (RUS)	14	L 1-6, 4-6

This Event Points: 5, South African Airways ATP Ranking: 20, Prize Money: $8,550

Mallorca, Spain; 01.05.2000; WS; Outdoor: Clay; Draw: 32

Round	Opponent	Ranking	Score
R32	Juan Balcells (ESP)	155	W 7-6(3), 7-6(3)
R16	Albert Portas (ESP)	73	L 6-2, 6-7(4), 4-6

This Event Points: 15, South African Airways ATP Ranking: 13, Prize Money: $8,000

Barcelona, Spain; 24.04.2000; CS; Outdoor: Clay; Draw: 56

Round	Opponent	Ranking	Score
R64	Bye	N/A	W
R32	Andrei Pavel (ROU)	68	W 6-3, 4-6, 7-6(1)
R16	Andreas Vinciguerra (SWE)	53	W 7-6(3), 7-5
Q	Juan Carlos Ferrero (ESP)	25	L 3-6, 4-6

This Event Points: 75, South African Airways ATP Ranking: 13, Prize Money: $21,550

ATP Masters Series Monte Carlo, Monaco; 17.04.2000; SU; Outdoor: Clay; Draw: 64

Round   Opponent   Ranking Score
R64   Felix Mantilla (ESP)   47   L 4-6, 6-0, 2-6
This Event Points: 5, South African Airways ATP Ranking: 8, Prize Money: $8,550

CHI V ARG AZI, Chile, Santiago; 07.04.2000; DC; Indoor: Hard; Draw: 5

Round   Opponent   Ranking Score
RR   Hernan Gumy (ARG)   N/A   W 6-4, 6-3, 4-6, 6-1
This Event Points: , South African Airways ATP Ranking: , Prize Money: $

ATP Masters Series Miami, FL, U.S.A.; 20.03.2000; SU; Outdoor: Hard; Draw: 96

Round   Opponent   Ranking Score
R128   Bye   N/A   W
R64   Michael Chang (USA)   37   W 6-4, 6-4
R32   Nicolas Escude (FRA)   28   W 6-2, 3-6, 6-1
R16   Tim Henman (GBR)   10   L 1-6, 6-1, 6-7(4)
This Event Points: 75, South African Airways ATP Ranking: 8, Prize Money: $31,400

ATP Masters Series Indian Wells, CA, U.S.A.; 13.03.2000; SU; Outdoor: Hard; Draw: 64

Round   Opponent   Ranking Score
R64   Daniel Vacek (CZE)   44   W 7-6(5), 6-1
R32   Mariano Zabaleta (ARG)   28   L 6-7(4), 3-6
This Event Points: 35, South African Airways ATP Ranking: 7, Prize Money: $16,250

Scottsdale, AZ, U.S.A.; 06.03.2000; WS; Outdoor: Hard; Draw: 32
Round   Opponent   Ranking Score
R32   Vincent Spadea (USA)   29   W 6-4, 6-4
R16   Alberto Martin (ESP)   60   W 7-6(7), 7-6(3)
Q   Lleyton Hewitt (AUS)   18   L 6-7(5), 2-4 RET
This Event Points: 40, South African Airways ATP Ranking: 7, Prize Money: $10,100

Santiago, Chile; 28.02.2000; WS; Outdoor: Clay; Draw: 32

Round   Opponent   Ranking Score
R32   Bohdan Ulihrach (CZE)   151   L 4-6, 6-7(3)
This Event Points: 5, South African Airways ATP Ranking: 7, Prize
Money: $3,500

2001

Santiago, Chile; 29.10.2001; CH; Outdoor: Clay; Draw: 32
Round   Opponent   Ranking Score
R32   Fernando Gonzalez (CHI)   159   W 4-6, 6-4, 7-5
R16   Adrian Garcia (CHI)   372   W 6-3, 6-1
Q   Alexandre Simoni (BRA)   100   W 6-0, 6-4
S   Agustin Calleri (ARG)   92   W 6-4, 7-5
W   Edgardo Massa (ARG)   149   W 6-4, 6-2
This Event Points: 60, South African Airways ATP Ranking: 45, Prize
Money: $10,800

Stockholm, Sweden; 22.10.2001; WS; Indoor: Hard; Draw: 32
Round   Opponent   Ranking Score
R32   Michael Russell (USA)   92   W 6-2, 3-6, 6-4
R16   Sebastien Grosjean (FRA)   8   W 6-3, 6-4
Q   Thomas Enqvist (SWE)   20   L 4-6, 7-6(7), 5-7
This Event Points: 55, South African Airways ATP Ranking: 44, Prize
Money: $22,200

ATP Masters Series Stuttgart, Germany; 15.10.2001; SU; Indoor:
Hard; Draw: 48
Round   Opponent   Ranking Score
R64   Fabrice Santoro (FRA)   19   W 4-6, 6-1, 6-2
R32   Marat Safin (RUS) 7   W 7-6(4), 6-3
R16   Pete Sampras (USA)   10   L 6-4, 6-7(3), 4-6
This Event Points: 75, South African Airways ATP Ranking: 46, Prize
Money: $33,250

Vienna, Austria; 08.10.2001; CS; Indoor: Hard; Draw: 32
Round   Opponent   Ranking Score
R32   Tommy Robredo (ESP)   31   L 6-7(4), 6-1, 2-6

This Event Points: 5, South African Airways ATP Ranking: 44, Prize Money: $5,240

Tokyo, Japan; 01.10.2001; CS; Outdoor: Hard; Draw: 56

Round	Opponent	Ranking	Score
R64	Bye	N/A	W
R32	Byron Black (ZIM)	141	W 6-2, 7-5
R16	Danai Udomchoke (THA)	314	W 6-3, 6-2
Q	James Blake (USA)	109	L 6-4, 4-6, 1-6

This Event Points: 60, South African Airways ATP Ranking: 45, Prize Money: $16,750

Hong Kong, China; 24.09.2001; WS; Outdoor: Hard; Draw: 32

Round	Opponent	Ranking	Score
R32	Daniel Vacek (CZE)	560	W 6-2, 6-1
R16	Kenneth Carlsen (DEN)	182	W 7-5, 6-3
Q	Sebastien Grosjean (FRA)	9	W 6-2, 6-3
S	Andrew Ilie (AUS)	80	W 6-4, 6-2
W	Rainer Schuettler (GER)	44	W 7-6(3), 6-2

This Event Points: 175, South African Airways ATP Ranking: 58, Prize Money: $54,000

CHI v SVK WGPO, Presov; 21.09.2001; DC; Indoor: Carpet; Draw: 6

Round	Opponent	Ranking	Score
RR	Karol Kucera (SVK)	N/A	W 6-3, 6-2, 6-3
RR	Dominik Hrbaty (SVK)	N/A	L 6-2, 6-4, 2-6, 4-6, 2-6

This Event Points: , South African Airways ATP Ranking: , Prize Money: $

US Open, NY, U.S.A.; 27.08.2001; GS; Outdoor: Hard; Draw: 128

Round	Opponent	Ranking	Score
R128	Markus Hipfl (AUT)	73	W 3-6, 7-5, 6-2, 6-0
R64	Andrei Pavel (ROU)	21	W 7-5, 6-4, 6-0
R32	Thomas Johansson (SWE)	14	L 4-6, 6-2, 3-6, 2-6

This Event Points: 75, South African Airways ATP Ranking: 56, Prize Money: $35,000

Washington, DC, U.S.A.; 13.08.2001; CS; Outdoor: Hard; Draw: 56

Round	Opponent	Ranking	Score

R64	Hyung-Taik Lee (KOR)	60	W 6-4, 7-5
R32	Michael Joyce (USA)	258	W 6-2, 6-2
R16	Alex Corretja (ESP)	10	W 7-6(2), 6-3
Q	Andy Roddick (USA)	30	L 3-6, 4-6

This Event Points: 60, South African Airways ATP Ranking: 64, Prize Money: $16,750

Roland Garros, France; 28.05.2001; GS; Outdoor: Clay; Draw: 128

Round	Opponent	Ranking	Score
R128	Wayne Ferreira (RSA)	19	W 3-6, 6-4, 3-6, 6-4, 6-1
R64	Nicolas Coutelot (FRA)	184	L 3-6, 4-6, 4-6

This Event Points: 35, South African Airways ATP Ranking: 39, Prize Money: $14,741

St. Poelten, Austria; 21.05.2001; WS; Outdoor: Clay; Draw: 32

Round	Opponent	Ranking	Score
R32	Andrea Gaudenzi (ITA)	120	L 7-5, 1-6, 4-6

This Event Points: 5, South African Airways ATP Ranking: 40, Prize Money: $4,000

ATP Masters Series Hamburg, Germany; 14.05.2001; SU; Outdoor: Clay; Draw: 64

Round	Opponent	Ranking	Score
R64	Carlos Moya (ESP)	24	W 6-4, 6-4
R32	Jan-Michael Gambill (USA)	15	L 3-6, 4-6

This Event Points: 35, South African Airways ATP Ranking: 26, Prize Money: $16,250

ATP Masters Series Rome, Italy; 07.05.2001; SU; Outdoor: Clay; Draw: 64

Round	Opponent	Ranking	Score
R64	Davide Sanguinetti (ITA)	56	W 4-6, 6-3, 6-4
R32	Juan Carlos Ferrero (ESP)	9	L 1-6, 3-6

This Event Points: 35, South African Airways ATP Ranking: 27, Prize Money: $16,250

Munich, Germany; 30.04.2001; WS; Outdoor: Clay; Draw: 32

Round	Opponent	Ranking	Score

| R32 | Sargis Sargsian (ARM) | 108 | W 6-2, 6-4 |
| R16 | Flavio Saretta (BRA) | 239 | L 3-6, 2-6 |

This Event Points: 15, South African Airways ATP Ranking: 26, Prize Money: $6,250

ATP Masters Series Monte Carlo, Monaco; 16.04.2001; SU; Outdoor: Clay; Draw: 64

Round	Opponent	Ranking	Score
R64	Karol Kucera (SVK)	74	W 6-4, 6-4
R32	Albert Costa (ESP)	36	L W/O

This Event Points: 35, South African Airways ATP Ranking: 28, Prize Money: $16,250

CHI v BAH AGI Rd 2, Nassau, Bahamas; 06.04.2001; DC; Outdoor: Hard; Draw: 4

Round	Opponent	Ranking	Score
RR	Mark Merklein (BAH)	N/A	W 6-0, 6-2, 7-5
RR	Mark Knowles (BAH)	N/A	W 6-3, 6-4, 6-4

This Event Points: , South African Airways ATP Ranking: , Prize Money: $

ATP Masters Series Miami, FL, U.S.A.; 19.03.2001; SU; Outdoor: Hard; Draw: 96

Round	Opponent	Ranking	Score
R128	Bye	N/A	W
R64	Andy Roddick (USA)	119	L 4-6, 1-6

This Event Points: 5, South African Airways ATP Ranking: 26, Prize Money: $9,400

ATP Masters Series Indian Wells, California, USA; 12.03.2001; SU; Outdoor: Hard; Draw: 64

Round	Opponent	Ranking	Score
R64	Yevgeny Kafelnikov (RUS)	6	L 4-6, 5-7

This Event Points: 5, South African Airways ATP Ranking: 25, Prize Money: $8,550

Scottsdale, AZ, U.S.A.; 05.03.2001; WS; Outdoor: Hard; Draw: 32

Round	Opponent	Ranking	Score
R32	Adrian Voinea (ROU)	146	W 7-6(4), 6-2
R16	Rainer Schuettler (GER)	53	W 3-6, 6-3, 6-2

Q Lleyton Hewitt (AUS) 6 L 5-7, 2-6
This Event Points: 40, South African Airways ATP Ranking: 25, Prize Money: $10,800

Buenos Aires, Argentina; 19.02.2001; WS; Outdoor: Clay; Draw: 32
Round Opponent Ranking Score
R32 Markus Hipfl (AUT) 123 L 3-6, 1-6
This Event Points: 5, South African Airways ATP Ranking: 22, Prize Money: $6,000

Vina del Mar, Chile; 12.02.2001; WS; Outdoor: Clay; Draw: 32
Round Opponent Ranking Score
R32 Karim Alami (MAR) 72 L 6-7(1), 2-6
This Event Points: 5, South African Airways ATP Ranking: 22, Prize Money: $3,500

Australian Open, Australia; 15.01.2001; GS; Outdoor: Hard; Draw: 128
Round Opponent Ranking Score
R128 Carlos Moya (ESP) 42 L 3-6, 3-6, 2-6
This Event Points: 5, South African Airways ATP Ranking: 23, Prize Money: $7,129

Auckland, New Zealand; 08.01.2001; WS; Outdoor: Hard; Draw: 32
Round Opponent Ranking Score
R32 Arnaud Di Pasquale (FRA) 61 L 6-3, 1-6, 6-7(2)
This Event Points: 5, South African Airways ATP Ranking: 23, Prize Money: $3,500

Doha, Qatar; 01.01.2001; WS; Outdoor: Hard; Draw: 32

Round	Opponent	Ranking	Score
R32	Nenad Zimonjic (SRB)	N/A	W 6-4, 3-6, 6-1
R16	Gianluca Pozzi (ITA)	N/A	W 6-2, 6-2
Q	Fernando Vicente (ESP)	N/A	W 7-6(4), 7-5
S	Vladimir Voltchkov (BLR)	N/A	W 6-1, 6-3
W	Bohdan Ulihrach (CZE)	N/A	W 6-3, 2-6, 6-3

This Event Points: 250, South African Airways ATP Ranking: , Prize Money: $137,000

2002

ATP Masters Series Paris, France; 28.10.2002; SU; Indoor: Carpet;
Draw: 48

Round	Opponent	Ranking	Score
R64	Olivier Rochus (BEL)	62	L 5-7, 0-1 RET

This Event Points: 5, South African Airways ATP Ranking: 25, Prize
Money: $8,550

Stockholm, Sweden; 21.10.2002; WS; Indoor: Hard; Draw: 32

Round	Opponent	Ranking	Score
R32	Wayne Arthurs (AUS)	50	W 6-4, 6-7(5), 6-1
R16	Jan-Michael Gambill (USA)	45	W 6-2 RET
Q	Andreas Vinciguerra (SWE)	121	W 6-3, 7-6(3)
S	Hicham Arazi (MAR)	84	W 6-3, 7-5
F	Paradorn Srichaphan (THA)	24	L 7-6(2), 0-6, 3-6, 2-6

This Event Points: 140, South African Airways ATP Ranking: 26,
Prize Money: $50,200

ATP Masters Series Madrid, Madrid, Spain; 14.10.2002; SU; Indoor:
Hard; Draw: 48

Round	Opponent	Ranking	Score
R64	Gaston Gaudio (ARG)	22	W 6-2, 6-2
R32	Roger Federer (SUI)	7	L 4-6, 2-6

This Event Points: 35, South African Airways ATP Ranking: 25, Prize
Money: $16,200

Moscow, Russia; 30.09.2002; WS; Indoor: Carpet; Draw: 32

Round	Opponent	Ranking	Score
R32	Jarkko Nieminen (FIN)	35	L 6-7(5), 6-3, 6-7(4)

This Event Points: 5, South African Airways ATP Ranking: 25, Prize
Money: $9,400

Palermo, Italy; 23.09.2002; WS; Outdoor: Clay; Draw: 32

Round	Opponent	Ranking	Score
R32	Ruben Ramirez Hidalgo (ESP)	165	W 6-2, 6-4
R16	Attila Savolt (HUN)	89	W 6-1, 6-2
Q	David Sanchez (ESP)	58	W 7-5, 4-6, 7-6(7)

S   Jose Acasuso (ARG)   46   L 4-6, 4-6
This Event Points: 75, South African Airways ATP Ranking: 22, Prize Money: $16,900

US Open, NY, U.S.A.; 26.08.2002; GS; Outdoor: Hard; Draw: 128

Round	Opponent	Ranking	Score
R128	Jonas Bjorkman (SWE)	50	W 1-6, 6-2, 6-4, 6-1
R64	Robin Soderling (SWE)	227	W 6-4, 3-6, 6-3, 6-3
R32	Jiri Novak (CZE)	14	L 3-6, 3-6 RET

This Event Points: 75, South African Airways ATP Ranking: 22, Prize Money: $36,500

Washington, DC, U.S.A.; 12.08.2002; CS; Outdoor: Hard; Draw: 56

Round	Opponent	Ranking	Score
R64	Bye	N/A	W
R32	Bob Bryan (USA)	249	W 7-6(7), 3-6, 6-2
R16	Jerome Golmard (FRA)	91	W 6-3, 6-1
Q	Fernando Meligeni (BRA)	61	W 3-6, 6-4, 7-5
S	Paradorn Srichaphan (THA)	54	L 6-3, 2-6, 2-6

This Event Points: 110, South African Airways ATP Ranking: 23, Prize Money: $31,000

ATP Masters Series Cincinnati, Ohio, USA; 05.08.2002; SU; Outdoor: Hard; Draw: 64

Round	Opponent	Ranking	Score
R64	Gaston Gaudio (ARG)	21	W 6-3, 6-2
R32	Taylor Dent (USA)	67	L 2-6, 3-6

This Event Points: 35, South African Airways ATP Ranking: 24, Prize Money: $15,800

ATP Masters Series Canada, Toronto, Canada; 29.07.2002; SU; Outdoor: Hard; Draw: 64

Round	Opponent	Ranking	Score
R64	Kenneth Carlsen (DEN)	109	W 7-6(5), 7-6(6)
R32	Carlos Moya (ESP)	16	W 7-5, 7-5
R16	Marat Safin (RUS)	2	L 6-3, 3-6, 6-7(3)

This Event Points: 75, South African Airways ATP Ranking: 27, Prize Money: $30,000

Kitzbuhel, Austria; 22.07.2002; CS; Outdoor: Clay; Draw: 48
Round   Opponent   Ranking Score
R64   Bye   N/A   W
R32   Jean-Rene Lisnard (MON)   127   L 5-7, 4-6
This Event Points: 5, South African Airways ATP Ranking: 27, Prize Money: $5,720

Umag, Croatia; 15.07.2002; WS; Outdoor: Clay; Draw: 32
Round   Opponent   Ranking Score
R32   Victor Hanescu (ROU)   185   L 0-6, 4-6
This Event Points: 5, South African Airways ATP Ranking: 27, Prize Money: $3,440

MEX v. CHI AG 2nd RD PO, Queretaro, Mexico; 12.07.2002; DC; Indoor: Carpet; Draw: 0
Round   Opponent   Ranking Score
RR   Marcelo Amador (MEX)   N/A   W 7-5, 6-7(3), 6-3, 6-2
RR   Alejandro Hernandez (MEX)   N/A   L 6-7(5), 6-3, 6-2, 0-6, 2-6
This Event Points: , South African Airways ATP Ranking: , Prize Money: $

ATP Masters Series Monte Carlo, Monaco; 15.04.2002; SU; Outdoor: Clay; Draw: 64
Round   Opponent   Ranking Score
R64   Fabrice Santoro (FRA)   22   W 6-3, 6-2
R32   Younes El Aynaoui (MAR)   18   W 1-6, 6-3, 6-4
R16   Juan Carlos Ferrero (ESP)   4   L 0-6, 0-2 RET
This Event Points: 75, South African Airways ATP Ranking: 23, Prize Money: $28,500

CAN v CHI AGI Rd 2, Calgary; 05.04.2002; DC; Indoor: Carpet; Draw: 4
Round   Opponent   Ranking Score
RR   Daniel Nestor (CAN)   N/A   L 6-7(1), 7-6(2), 3-6, 6-1, 5-7
This Event Points: , South African Airways ATP Ranking: , Prize Money: $

ATP Masters Series Miami, FL, U.S.A.; 18.03.2002; SU; Outdoor: Hard; Draw: 96

Round	Opponent	Ranking	Score
R128	Bye	N/A	W
R64	Mardy Fish (USA)	150	W 6-2, 6-4
R32	Yevgeny Kafelnikov (RUS)	4	W 6-4, 7-6(4)
R16	Alex Corretja (ESP)	18	W 6-2, 6-2
Q	Juan Ignacio Chela (ARG)	37	W 7-6, 6-2
S	Andre Agassi (USA)	10	L 7-6(7), 4-6 RET

This Event Points: 225, South African Airways ATP Ranking: 33, Prize Money: $126,050

ATP Masters Series Indian Wells, California, USA; 11.03.2002; SU; Outdoor: Hard; Draw: 64

Round	Opponent	Ranking	Score
R64	Ivan Ljubicic (CRO)	29	W 7-6(5), 7-5
R32	Michel Kratochvil (SUI)	44	W 6-4, 6-2
R16	Rainer Schuettler (GER)	37	L 2-6, 2-6

This Event Points: 75, South African Airways ATP Ranking: 35, Prize Money: $30,000

Buenos Aires, Argentina; 18.02.2002; WS; Outdoor: Clay; Draw: 32

Round	Opponent	Ranking	Score
R32	Edgardo Massa (ARG)	140	W 4-6, 6-4, 7-5
R16	Mariano Zabaleta (ARG)	78	L 6-7(4), 6-1, 3-6

This Event Points: 15, South African Airways ATP Ranking: 36, Prize Money: $6,600

Vina del Mar, Chile; 11.02.2002; WS; Outdoor: Clay; Draw: 32

Round	Opponent	Ranking	Score
R32	Mariano Zabaleta (ARG)	65	L 4-6, 6-7(6)

This Event Points: 5, South African Airways ATP Ranking: 38, Prize Money: $3,440

Australian Open, Australia; 14.01.2002; GS; Outdoor: Hard; Draw: 128

Round	Opponent	Ranking	Score
R128	Jaymon Crabb (AUS)	248	W 6-2, 6-0, 5-7, 6-4
R64	Karol Kucera (SVK)	81	W 7-6(5), 7-5, 6-2

R32	Alberto Martin (ESP)	39	W 6-4, 6-3, 7-6(3)
R16	Nicolas Lapentti (ECU)	27	W 7-5, 6-1, 6-4
Q	Tommy Haas (USA)	9	L 6-7(2), 4-6, 7-6(2), 6-7(5)

This Event Points: 250, South African Airways ATP Ranking: 48, Prize Money: $65,000

Sydney, Australia; 07.01.2002; WS; Outdoor: Hard; Draw: 32

Round	Opponent	Ranking	Score
R32	Ivan Ljubicic (CRO)	38	W 6-7(5), 6-3, 7-6(1)
R16	Andrei Pavel (ROU)	27	W 6-1, 6-4
Q	Roger Federer (SUI)	13	L 7-6(2), 6-7(4), 3-6

This Event Points: 40, South African Airways ATP Ranking: 47, Prize Money: $9,940

Adelaide, Australia; 31.12.2001; WS; Outdoor: Hard; Draw: 32

Round	Opponent	Ranking	Score
R32	Thomas Enqvist (SWE)	N/A	L 0-6, 3-6

This Event Points: 5, South African Airways ATP Ranking: , Prize Money: $3,200

2003

VEN v CHI AG1 2nd RD PO, Caracas, Venezuela; 11.07.2003; DC; Outdoor: Hard; Draw: 4

Round	Opponent	Ranking	Score
RR	Jose De Armas (VEN)	N/A	L 5-7, 2-6, 6-3, 6-3, 6-8
RR	Kepler Orellana (VEN)	N/A	L 6-7(4) RET

This Event Points: , South African Airways ATP Ranking: , Prize Money: $

Roland Garros, France; 26.05.2003; GS; Outdoor: Clay; Draw: 128

Round	Opponent	Ranking	Score
R128	Mario Ancic (CRO)	74	L 1-6, 0-1 RET

This Event Points: 5, South African Airways ATP Ranking: 42, Prize Money: $14,790

World Team Championship, Dusseldorf, Germany; 19.05.2003; WT; Outdoor: Clay; Draw: 64

Round	Opponent	Ranking	Score
RR	Tomas Behrend (GER)	102	L 6-3, 5-7, 6-7(2)
RR	Gaston Gaudio (ARG)	22	W 6-3, 6-3
F	Radek Stepanek (CZE)	47	L 3-6, 6-7(5)

This Event Points: , South African Airways ATP Ranking: 42, Prize Money: $176,000

ATP Masters Series Miami, FL, U.S.A.; 17.03.2003; SU; Outdoor: Hard; Draw: 96

Round	Opponent	Ranking	Score
R128	Bye N/A		W
R64	Taylor Dent (USA)	41	W 6-1, 6-1
R32	Juan Carlos Ferrero (ESP)	3	W 6-3, 7-6(2)
R16	Paradorn Srichaphan (THA)	13	L W/O

This Event Points: 75, South African Airways ATP Ranking: 31, Prize Money: $35,050

ATP Masters Series Indian Wells, California, USA; 10.03.2003; SU; Outdoor: Hard; Draw: 64

Round	Opponent	Ranking	Score
R64	Gaston Gaudio (ARG)	20	W 4-0 RET
R32	Max Mirnyi (BLR)	36	L 3-6, 3-6

This Event Points: 35, South African Airways ATP Ranking: 29, Prize Money: $15,000

Delray Beach, FL, U.S.A.; 03.03.2003; WS; Outdoor: Hard; Draw: 32

Round	Opponent	Ranking	Score
R32	Jeff Morrison (USA)	111	W 6-3, 6-3
R16	Martin Verkerk (NED)	67	W 2-6, 6-4, 7-5
Q	Hyung-Taik Lee (KOR)	63	W 6-3, 6-4
S	Mardy Fish (USA)	66	L 3-6, 4-6

This Event Points: 75, South African Airways ATP Ranking: 30, Prize Money: $18,000

Acapulco, Mexico; 24.02.2003; CS; Outdoor: Clay; Draw: 32

Round	Opponent	Ranking	Score
R32	Franco Squillari (ARG)	85	W 2-6, 6-0, 6-4
R16	Juan Antonio Marin (CRC)	154	W 6-3, 6-1
Q	Agustin Calleri (ARG)	61	L 3-6, 5-7

This Event Points: 60, South African Airways ATP Ranking: 32, Prize Money: $18,600

Vina del Mar, Chile; 10.02.2003; WS; Outdoor: Clay; Draw: 32

Round	Opponent	Ranking	Score
R32	Adrian Garcia (CHI)	424	W 6-3, 6-2
R16	Albert Portas (ESP)	94	W 6-4, 7-6(3)
Q	Agustin Calleri (ARG)	46	W 6-4, 7-6(2)
S	Gaston Gaudio (ARG)	22	W 6-3, 6-2
F	David Sanchez (ESP)	57	L 6-1, 3-6, 3-6

This Event Points: 120, South African Airways ATP Ranking: 37, Prize Money: $27,500

ECU v. CHI AG1, Quito, Ecuador; 07.02.2003; DC; Outdoor: Clay; Draw: 4

Round	Opponent	Ranking	Score
RR	Giovanni Lapentti (ECU)	N/A	L 3-6, 6-7(5), 3-6
RR	Nicolas Lapentti (ECU)	N/A	W 3-6, 6-4, 7-6, 7-6(5)

This Event Points: , South African Airways ATP Ranking: , Prize Money: $

2004

San Luis Potosi, Mexico; 05.04.2004; CH; Outdoor: Clay; Draw: 32

Round	Opponent	Ranking	Score
R32	Florent Serra (FRA)	213	W 7-5, 6-3
R16	Mariano Delfino (ARG)	224	L 7-5, 3-6 RET

This Event Points: 6, South African Airways ATP Ranking: 862, Prize Money: $860

Salinas, Ecuador; 29.03.2004; CH; Outdoor: Hard; Draw: 32

Round	Opponent	Ranking	Score
R32	David Gonzalez (ECU)	N/A	W 6-0, 6-0
R16	Juan-Pablo Guzman (ARG)	N/A	L 4-6, 3-6

This Event Points: 5, South African Airways ATP Ranking: , Prize Money: $430

Marcelo Rios ATP Results - doubles

1993

Vina Del Mar, Chile; 22.02.1993; CH; Outdoor: Clay; Draw: 32 ;
Partner: Silberstein, Gabriel (CHI)
Round   Opponent   Ranking Score
R16   Sergio Cortes (CHI) / Felipe Rivera (CHI)   242 / 1,018
W 7-5, 3-6, 6-4
Q   Marcelo Rebolledo (CHI) / Martin Rodriguez (ARG)   313
/ 403   L 5-7, 7-5, 5-7
This Event Points: 13, South African Airways ATP Ranking: 631,
Prize Money: $160

1994
Santiago, Chile; 24.10.1994; GP; Outdoor: Clay; Draw: 32 ; Partner:
Silberstein, Gabriel (CHI)
Round   Opponent   Ranking Score
R16   Alberto Berasategui (ESP) / Sergio Cortes (CHI)   422
/ 243   L 6-7, 6-3, 3-6
This Event Points: 1, South African Airways ATP Ranking: 1,173,
Prize Money: $685

Scheveningen, The Netherlands; 18.07.1994; CH; Outdoor: Clay;
Draw: 32 ; Partner: Cortes, Sergio (CHI)
Round   Opponent   Ranking Score
R16   Martijn Bok (NED) / Sjeng Schalken (NED)   367 / 475
L 6-2, 3-6, 4-6
This Event Points: 1, South African Airways ATP Ranking: 1,127,
Prize Money: $275

Gstaad, Switzerland; 04.07.1994; GP; Outdoor: Clay; Draw: 32 ;
Partner: Manta, Lorenzo (SUI)
Round   Opponent   Ranking Score
R16   Mike Bauer (USA) / Francisco Montana (USA)   47
/ 48   L 2-6, 5-7

This Event Points: 1, South African Airways ATP Ranking: , Prize Money: $1,635

1995

Buenos Aires, Argentina; 06.11.1995; GP; Outdoor: Clay; Draw: 32 ; Partner: Schalken, Sjeng (NED)
Round   Opponent   Ranking Score
R16   Luis Lobo (ARG) / Javier Sanchez (ESP)   28 / 26 L
3-6, 7-6, 4-6
This Event Points: 1, South African Airways ATP Ranking: 186, Prize Money: $550

Santiago, Chile; 23.10.1995; GP; Outdoor: Clay; Draw: 32 ; Partner: Schalken, Sjeng (NED)
Round   Opponent   Ranking Score
R16   Nicolas Pereira (VEN) / Fabrice Santoro (FRA)   83
/ 155   L 1-6, 7-6, 3-6
This Event Points: 1, South African Airways ATP Ranking: 185, Prize Money: $550

Bogota, Colombia; 11.09.1995; GP; Outdoor: Clay; Draw: 32 ; Partner: Pereira, Nicolas (VEN)
Round   Opponent   Ranking Score
R16   Sergio Casal (ESP) / Emilio Sanchez (ESP)   32 / 33 W
4-6, 6-3, 6-3
Q   Bryan Shelton (USA) / Roger Smith (BAH)   139 / 236
W 4-6, 7-6, 7-5
S   Jiri Novak (CZE) / David Rikl (CZE)   122 / 56   L
1-6, 6-4, 6-7
This Event Points: 78, South African Airways ATP Ranking: 231, Prize Money: $3,750

Aruba, Aruba; 04.09.1995; CH; Outdoor: Hard; Draw: 32 ; Partner: Meligeni, Fernando (BRA)
Round   Opponent   Ranking Score
R16   Jim Pugh (USA) / Derrick Rostagno (USA)   N/A / N/A
L 4-6, 1-1 DEF

This Event Points: 1, South African Airways ATP Ranking: , Prize Money: $450

Amsterdam, The Netherlands; 24.07.1995; GP; Outdoor: Clay; Draw: 32 ; Partner: Schalken, Sjeng (NED)

Round	Opponent	Ranking Score
R16	Jacco Eltingh (NED) / Paul Haarhuis (NED)	1 / 1 W
W/O		
Q	Libor Pimek (BEL) / Byron Talbot (RSA)	72 / 97 W
2-6, 6-2, 6-4		
S	Tom Kempers (NED) / Piet Norval (RSA)	103 / 51
W 3-6, 6-3, 6-4		
W	Wayne Arthurs (AUS) / Neil Broad (GBR)	57 / 61 W
7-6, 6-2		

This Event Points: 182, South African Airways ATP Ranking: 599, Prize Money: $17,500

Gstaad, Switzerland; 10.07.1995; GP; Outdoor: Clay; Draw: 32 ; Partner: Schalken, Sjeng (NED)

Round	Opponent	Ranking Score
R16	Luis Lobo (ARG) / Javier Sanchez (ESP)	49 / 45 L
4-6, 6-1, 6-7		

This Event Points: 1, South African Airways ATP Ranking: 668, Prize Money: $550

Nottingham, England; 19.06.1995; GP; Outdoor: Grass; Draw: 32 ; Partner: Carlsen, Kenneth (DEN)

Round	Opponent	Ranking Score
R16	Thomas Enqvist (SWE) / Lionel Roux (FRA)	239 / 809
L 5-7, 4-6		

This Event Points: 1, South African Airways ATP Ranking: 660, Prize Money: $550

Bologna, Italy; 22.05.1995; GP; Outdoor: Clay; Draw: 32 ; Partner: Cane, Paolo (ITA)

Round	Opponent	Ranking Score
R16	Danie Visser (RSA) / Ellis Ferreira (RSA)	117 / 79
W 6-7, 7-6, 6-4		

Q   Byron Black (ZIM) / Jonathan Stark (USA)   8 / 7   L
3-6, 6-7
This Event Points: 36, South African Airways ATP Ranking: 1,109,
Prize Money: $2,155

1996

Santiago, Chile; 04.11.1996; GP; Outdoor: Clay; Draw: 32 ; Partner:
Pereira, Nicolas (VEN)
Round   Opponent   Ranking Score
R16   Rikard Bergh (SWE) / Greg Van Emburgh (USA)   98
/ 84   L 4-6, 6-2, 2-6
This Event Points: 1, South African Airways ATP Ranking: 484, Prize
Money: $550

PER V CHI AZG1, Chile; 20.09.1996; DC; Outdoor: Clay; Draw: 4 ;
Partner: Bustos, Oscar (CHI)
Round   Opponent   Ranking Score
RR   Luis Horna (PER) / Americo Tupi Venero (PER)   N/A
/N/A W 6-4, 6-3, 6-7, 3-6, 8-6
This Event Points: , South African Airways ATP Ranking: , Prize
Money: $

New Haven, CT, U.S.A.; 12.08.1996; GP; Outdoor: Hard; Draw: 56 ;
Partner: Joyce, Michael (USA)
Round   Opponent   Ranking Score
R32   Wayne Black (ZIM) / Kevin Ullyett (ZIM)   141 / 222
W 3-6, 7-6, 6-1
R16   Yevgeny Kafelnikov (RUS) / Daniel Vacek (CZE)   11
/ 8   L 3-6, 5-7
This Event Points: 30, South African Airways ATP Ranking: 345,
Prize Money: $2,350

Amsterdam, The Netherlands; 29.07.1996; GP; Outdoor: Clay;
Draw: 32 ; Partner: Burillo, Jordi (ESP)
Round   Opponent   Ranking Score
R16   Shelby Cannon (USA) / Greg Van Emburgh (USA)   N/A
/ N/A   W 6-4, 6-2

Q   David Rikl (CZE) / Pavel Vizner (CZE)   47 / N/A
L W/O
This Event Points: 44, South African Airways ATP Ranking: 432,
Prize Money: $3,550

Kitzbuhel, Austria; 22.07.1996; GP; Outdoor: Clay; Draw: 48 ;
Partner: Dosedel, Slava (CZE)
Round   Opponent   Ranking Score
R32   Rikard Bergh (SWE) / Jack Waite (USA)   N/A / 82
L 7-6, 4-6, 4-6
This Event Points: 1, South African Airways ATP Ranking: 209, Prize
Money: $550

Gstaad, Switzerland; 08.07.1996; GP; Outdoor: Clay; Draw: 32 ;
Partner: Sanchez, Emilio (ESP)
Round   Opponent   Ranking Score
R16   Cedric Pioline (FRA) / Marc Rosset (SUI)   254 / 141
L 4-6, 6-7
This Event Points: 1, South African Airways ATP Ranking: 205, Prize
Money: $550

St. Poelten, Austria; 20.05.1996; GP; Outdoor: Clay; Draw: 32 ;
Partner: Lundgren, Peter (SWE)
Round   Opponent   Ranking Score
R16   Ken Flach (USA) / David Wheaton (USA)   85 / 76 L
3-6, 7-5, 4-6
This Event Points: 1, South African Airways ATP Ranking: 188, Prize
Money: $550

ATP Masters Series Rome, Italy; 13.05.1996; SU; Outdoor: Clay;
Draw: 64 ; Partner: Washington, MaliVai (USA)
Round   Opponent   Ranking Score
R32   Marius Barnard (RSA) / Greg Van Emburgh (USA)   68
/ N/A   L 4-6, 4-6
This Event Points: 1, South African Airways ATP Ranking: 188, Prize
Money: $1,000

CHI V CAN AZPO, Canada; 05.04.1996; DC; Indoor: Carpet; Draw: 5
; Partner: Bustos, Oscar (CHI)

Round   Opponent   Ranking Score
RR   Grant Connell (CAN) / Sebastien Lareau (CAN)   N/A
/ N/A   L 3-6, 4-6, 5-7
This Event Points: , South African Airways ATP Ranking: , Prize
Money: $

BZL V CHI AZ1, Chile; 09.02.1996; DC; Outdoor: Clay; Draw: 4 ;
Partner: Rebolledo, Marcelo (CHI)
Round   Opponent   Ranking Score
RR   Gustavo Kuerten (BRA) / Jaime Oncins (BRA)   N/A
/ N/A   L 5-7, 3-6, 6-4, 2-6
This Event Points: , South African Airways ATP Ranking: , Prize
Money: $

1997

Santiago, Chile; 03.11.1997; GP; Outdoor: Clay; Draw: 32 ; Partner:
Massu, Nicolas (CHI)
Round   Opponent   Ranking Score
R16   Martin Rodriguez (ARG) / Andre Sa (BRA)   178 / 148
W 6-3, 6-2
Q   Lucas Arnold Ker (ARG) / Daniel Orsanic (ARG)   54
/ 32   L 6-4, 3-6, 4-6
This Event Points: 34, South African Airways ATP Ranking: 293,
Prize Money: $2,155

Singapore, Singapore; 06.10.1997; GP; Indoor: Carpet; Draw: 32 ;
Partner: Johansson, Thomas (SWE)
Round   Opponent   Ranking Score
R16   Bill Behrens (USA) / Patrick McEnroe (USA)   137 / 234
W 6-4, 6-4
Q   Rick Leach (USA) / Jonathan Stark (USA)   11 / 20 L
3-6, 4-6
This Event Points: 51, South African Airways ATP Ranking: 366,
Prize Money: $3,255

CHI V IND WGPO, India; 19.09.1997; DC; Outdoor: Grass; Draw: 4 ;
Partner: Massu, Nicolas (CHI)

Round   Opponent   Ranking Score
RR   Mahesh Bhupathi (IND) / Leander Paes (IND)   N/A
/ N/A   L 6-3, 3-6, 4-6, 7-6, 3-6
This Event Points: , South African Airways ATP Ranking: , Prize
Money: $

Indianapolis, IN, U.S.A.; 11.08.1997; GP; Outdoor: Hard; Draw: 56 ;
Partner: Groen, Sander (NED)
Round   Opponent   Ranking Score
R32   Marcos Ondruska (RSA) / Grant Stafford (RSA)   60
/ 72   L 2-6, 3-6
This Event Points: 1, South African Airways ATP Ranking: 336, Prize
Money: $1,000

ATP Masters Series Cincinnati, OH, U.S.A.; 04.08.1997; SU; Outdoor:
Hard; Draw: 56 ; Partner: Haas, Tommy (USA)
Round   Opponent   Ranking Score
R32   Sander Groen (NED) / Gustavo Kuerten (BRA)   72
/ 49   W 6-4, 4-6, 6-3
R16   Daniel Nestor (CAN) / Cyril Suk (CZE)   9 / 17   L
2-6, 5-7
This Event Points: 46, South African Airways ATP Ranking: 420,
Prize Money: $5,600

Gstaad, Switzerland; 07.07.1997; GP; Outdoor: Clay; Draw: 32 ;
Partner: Kiefer, Nicolas (GER)
Round   Opponent   Ranking Score
R16   Sander Groen (NED) / Sasa Hirszon (CRO)   74 / 92 L
6-4, 4-6, 2-6
This Event Points: 1, South African Airways ATP Ranking: 324, Prize
Money: $550

ATP Masters Series Rome, Italy; 12.05.1997; SU; Outdoor: Clay;
Draw: 64 ; Partner: Medvedev, Andrei (UKR)
Round   Opponent   Ranking Score
R32   Jacco Eltingh (NED) / Paul Haarhuis (NED)   4 / 3   L
6-7, 1-6
This Event Points: 1, South African Airways ATP Ranking: 315, Prize
Money: $1,000

Prague, Czech Republic; 28.04.1997; GP; Outdoor: Clay; Draw: 32 ; Partner: Ulihrach, Bohdan (CZE)

Round	Opponent	Ranking	Score
R16	David Rikl (CZE) / Pavel Vizner (CZE)	68 / 32	W 7-6, 6-3
Q	Mahesh Bhupathi (IND) / Leander Paes (IND)	67 / 64	L 1-6, 4-6

This Event Points: 45, South African Airways ATP Ranking: 400, Prize Money: $2,450

Barcelona, Spain; 14.04.1997; GP; Outdoor: Clay; Draw: 56 ; Partner: Medvedev, Andrei (UKR)

Round	Opponent	Ranking	Score
R32	Karim Alami (MAR) / Sjeng Schalken (NED)	173 / 51	W 6-3, 6-4
R16	Tomas Carbonell (ESP) / Francisco Roig (ESP)	43 / 44	L 0-6, 3-6

This Event Points: 30, South African Airways ATP Ranking: 486, Prize Money: $2,085

ARG V CHI AZ1, Chile; 04.04.1997; DC; Outdoor: Clay; Draw: 4 ; Partner: Silberstein, Gabriel (CHI)

Round	Opponent	Ranking	Score
RR	Javier Frana (ARG) / Luis Lobo (ARG)	N/A / N/A	W 3-6, 7-6, 4-6, 6-3, 6-2

This Event Points: , South African Airways ATP Ranking: , Prize Money: $

Scottsdale, AZ, U.S.A.; 03.03.1997; GP; Outdoor: Hard; Draw: 32 ; Partner: Cash, Pat (AUS)

Round	Opponent	Ranking	Score
R16	Luis Lobo (ARG) / Javier Sanchez (ESP)	23 / 25	L 2-6, 2-6

This Event Points: 1, South African Airways ATP Ranking: 487, Prize Money: $550

Marseille, France; 10.02.1997; GP; Indoor: Hard; Draw: 32 ; Partner: Rosset, Marc (SUI)

Round	Opponent	Ranking	Score

R16   Thomas Enqvist (SWE) / Magnus Larsson (SWE)   363
/ 439   L 2-6, 6-2, 1-6
This Event Points: 1, South African Airways ATP Ranking: 489, Prize
Money: $550

ECU V CHI AZ1, Chile; 07.02.1997; DC; Outdoor: Clay; Draw: 4 ;
Partner: Bustos, Oscar (CHI)
Round   Opponent   Ranking Score
RR   Pablo Campana (ECU) / N. Lapentti (ECU) N/A / N/A L
6-4, 4-6, 0-6, 3-6
This Event Points: , South African Airways ATP Ranking: , Prize
Money: $

Auckland, New Zealand; 06.01.1997; GP; Outdoor: Hard; Draw: 32
; Partner: Rusedski, Greg (GBR)
Round   Opponent   Ranking Score
R16   Alistair Hunt (NZL) / Brett Steven (NZL)   250 / 166
L 2-6, 6-4, 5-7
This Event Points: 1, South African Airways ATP Ranking: 489, Prize
Money: $550

1998

Santiago, Chile; 09.11.1998; WS; Outdoor: Clay; Draw: 32 ; Partner:
Lobo, Luis (ARG)
Round   Opponent   Ranking Score
R16   Brandon Coupe (USA) / Paul Rosner (RSA)   75 / 73 W
6-2, 6-7, 6-1
Q   Massimo Bertolini (ITA) / Devin Bowen (USA)   92
/ 87   L W/O
This Event Points: 39, South African Airways ATP Ranking: 243,
Prize Money: $1,850

ATP Masters Series Cincinnati, OH, U.S.A.; 10.08.1998; SU; Outdoor:
Hard; Draw: 56 ; Partner: Korda, Petr (CZE)
Round   Opponent   Ranking Score

R32   David Adams (RSA) / Fernon Wibier (NED)   33 / 74 W
1-6, 6-3, 6-2
R16   Yevgeny Kafelnikov (RUS) / Daniel Vacek (CZE)   13
/ 14   L W/O
This Event Points: 46, South African Airways ATP Ranking: 216,
Prize Money: $5,300

Gstaad, Switzerland; 06.07.1998; WS; Outdoor: Clay; Draw: 32 ;
Partner: Costa, Albert (ESP)
Round Opponent   Ranking Score
R16   Juan Balcells (ESP) / Alberto Berasategui (ESP)   186
/ 105   L 6-7, 6-7
This Event Points: 1, South African Airways ATP Ranking: 196, Prize
Money: $750

Nottingham, England; 15.06.1998; WS; Outdoor: Grass; Draw: 32 ;
Partner: Lapentti, Nicolas (ECU)
Round Opponent   Ranking Score
R16   Marius Barnard (RSA) / David Prinosil (GER) 128 / 56
L 2-6, 1-6
This Event Points: 1, South African Airways ATP Ranking: 188, Prize
Money: $750

ATP Masters Series Rome, Italy; 11.05.1998; SU; Outdoor: Clay;
Draw: 64 ; Partner: Enqvist, Thomas (SWE)
Round Opponent   Ranking Score
R32   Marc-Kevin Goellner (GER) / Jeff Tarango (USA)   45
/ 74   W 6-4, 7-6
R16   Jonas Bjorkman (SWE) / Patrick Rafter (AUS)   9 /
16   L 3-6, 6-7
This Event Points: 46, South African Airways ATP Ranking: 209,
Prize Money: $5,000

ATP Masters Series Hamburg, Germany; 04.05.1998; SU; Outdoor:
Clay; Draw: 56 ; Partner: Henman, Tim (GBR)
Round Opponent   Ranking Score
R32   Tom Kempers (NED) / Menno Oosting (NED)   49
/ 47   W 6-2, 6-3

R16   Joshua Eagle (AUS) / Andrew Florent (AUS) 22 / 32 L
4-6, 4-6
This Event Points: 52, South African Airways ATP Ranking: 249,
Prize Money: $5,300

CHI V ARG AZI, Argentina; 03.04.1998; DC; Outdoor: Clay; Draw: 5 ;
Partner: Massu, Nicolas (CHI)
Round   Opponent   Ranking Score
RR   Lucas Arnold Ker (ARG) / Luis Lobo (ARG)   N/A / N/A
L 5-7, 3-6, 3-6
This Event Points: , South African Airways ATP Ranking: , Prize
Money: $

Memphis, TN, U.S.A.; 16.02.1998; CS; Indoor: Hard; Draw: 48 ;
Partner: Enqvist, Thomas (SWE)
Round   Opponent   Ranking Score
R32   Grant Stafford (RSA) / Michael Tebbutt (AUS)   90
/ 95   W 7-6, 7-6
R16   Jacco Eltingh (NED) / Paul Haarhuis (NED)   3 / 6   W
7-5, 7-6
Q   Ellis Ferreira (RSA) / David Roditi (MEX)   11 / 82 L
4-6, 3-6
This Event Points: 101, South African Airways ATP Ranking: 273,
Prize Money: $3,500

Dubai, U.A.E.; 09.02.1998; WS; Outdoor: Hard; Draw: 32 ; Partner:
Kiefer, Nicolas (GER)
Round   Opponent   Ranking Score
R16   Donald Johnson (USA) / Francisco Montana (USA)   22
/ 24   L 2-6, 1-6
This Event Points: 1, South African Airways ATP Ranking: 274, Prize
Money: $750

1999

Shanghai, China; 04.10.1999; WS; Outdoor: Hard; Draw: 32 ;
Partner: Lobo, Luis (ARG)
Round   Opponent   Ranking Score

R16   Sebastien Lareau (CAN) / Daniel Nestor (CAN)   5 /
33   L 4-6, 1-6
This Event Points: 1, South African Airways ATP Ranking: 329, Prize Money: $750

Graz, Austria; 12.07.1999; CH; Outdoor: Clay; Draw: 32 ; Partner: Lobo, Luis (ARG)
Round   Opponent   Ranking Score
R16   Diego Del Rio (ARG) / Martin Rodriguez (ARG)   70
/ 96   L 6-7(1), 1-6
This Event Points: 1, South African Airways ATP Ranking: 280, Prize Money: $365

Gstaad, Switzerland; 05.07.1999; WS; Outdoor: Clay; Draw: 32 ; Partner: Lobo, Luis (ARG)
Round   Opponent   Ranking Score
R16   Daniel Orsanic (ARG) / Mariano Puerta (ARG)   43
/ 82   W 6-2, 6-4
Q   Martin Damm (CZE) / Daniel Vacek (CZE)   37 / 11 L
3-6, 7-6(5), 6-7(6)
This Event Points: 37, South African Airways ATP Ranking: 339, Prize Money: $3,560

ATP Masters Series Monte Carlo, Monaco; 19.04.1999; SU; Outdoor: Clay; Draw: 56 ; Partner: Lobo, Luis (ARG)
Round   Opponent   Ranking Score
R32   Joshua Eagle (AUS) / Andrew Florent (AUS) 28 / 29 W
2-6, 6-2, 6-1
R16   Andrea Gaudenzi (ITA) / Diego Nargiso (ITA)   333
/ 277   L W/O
This Event Points: 46, South African Airways ATP Ranking: 290, Prize Money: $5,300

Estoril, Portugal; 05.04.1999; WS; Outdoor: Clay; Draw: 32 ; Partner: Lobo, Luis (ARG)
Round   Opponent   Ranking Score
R16   Chris Haggard (RSA) / Francisco Montana (USA)   41
/ 28   L 3-6, 1-6

This Event Points: 1, South African Airways ATP Ranking: 296, Prize Money: $750

CHI V COL AZI, Bogota, Columbia; 02.04.1999; DC; Outdoor: Clay; Draw: 6 ; Partner: Gamonal, Hermes (CHI)

Round	Opponent	Ranking Score
RR	Mauricio Hadad (COL) / Miguel Tobon (COL)	N/A / N/A

W 6-4, 6-4, 2-6, 1-6, 6-4

This Event Points: , South African Airways ATP Ranking: , Prize Money: $

2000

Hong Kong, China; 02.10.2000; WS; Outdoor: Hard; Draw: 32 ; Partner: Massu, Nicolas (CHI)

Round	Opponent	Ranking Score
R16	Michael Hill (AUS) / Jeff Tarango (USA)	67 / 59 L

6-7(5), 6-7(2)

This Event Points: 5, South African Airways ATP Ranking: 170, Prize Money: $750

Sydney Olympics, Sydney, Australia; 18.09.2000; OL; Outdoor: Hard; Draw: 64 ; Partner: Massu, Nicolas (CHI)

Round	Opponent	Ranking Score
R32	Hyung-Taik Lee (KOR) / Yong-Il Yoon (KOR)	218 / 250

L 3-6, 4-6

This Event Points: , South African Airways ATP Ranking: 170, Prize Money: $

Umag, Croatia; 17.07.2000; WS; Outdoor: Clay; Draw: 32 ; Partner: Puerta, Mariano (ARG)

Round	Opponent	Ranking Score
R16	Roberto Carretero (ESP) / Carlos Moya (ESP)	744 / 371
	W 7-6(4), 6-3	
Q	Massimo Bertolini (ITA) / Cristian Brandi (ITA)	53 / 54
	W 6-3, 7-5	
S	Ivan Ljubicic (CRO) / Lovro Zovko (CRO)	256 / 237
	L W/O	

This Event Points: 75, South African Airways ATP Ranking: 204, Prize Money: $4,580

Gstaad, Switzerland; 10.07.2000; WS; Outdoor: Clay; Draw: 32 ; Partner: Puerta, Mariano (ARG)

Round	Opponent	Ranking	Score
R16	Petr Pala (CZE) / Pavel Vizner (CZE)	84 / 85	L 5-7, 2-6

This Event Points: 5, South African Airways ATP Ranking: 203, Prize Money: $750

ATP Masters Series Rome, Italy; 08.05.2000; SU; Outdoor: Clay; Draw: 64 ; Partner: Lapentti, Nicolas (ECU)

Round	Opponent	Ranking	Score
R32	David Adams (RSA) / John-Laffnie de Jager (RSA)	11 / 14	W 6-4, 6-4
R16	Tomas Carbonell (ESP) / Donald Johnson (USA)	49 / 29	W 7-6(3), 6-7(4), 6-4
Q	Paul Haarhuis (NED) / Sandon Stolle (AUS)	9 / 10	W 6-4, 6-0
S	Martin Damm (CZE) / Dominik Hrbaty (SVK)	34 / 59	L 6-3, 5-7, 3-6

This Event Points: 225, South African Airways ATP Ranking: 617, Prize Money: $21,150

Scottsdale, AZ, U.S.A.; 06.03.2000; WS; Outdoor: Hard; Draw: 32 ; Partner: Corretja, Alex (ESP)

Round	Opponent	Ranking	Score
R16	Wayne Ferreira (RSA) / Scott Humphries (USA)	40 / 34	L 6-4, 3-6, 4-6

This Event Points: 5, South African Airways ATP Ranking: 421, Prize Money: $750

2001

Long Island, New York, USA; 20.08.2001; WS; Outdoor: Hard; Draw: 32 ; Partner: Vacek, Daniel (CZE)

Round   Opponent   Ranking Score

R16   Jaime Oncins (BRA) / Daniel Orsanic (ARG)   61 / 54 W
6-4, 7-6(4)
Q   Leos Friedl (CZE) / Radek Stepanek (CZE)   50 / 74 L
4-6, 3-6
This Event Points: 40, South African Airways ATP Ranking: 297,
Prize Money: $2,350

Munich, Germany; 30.04.2001; WS; Outdoor: Clay; Draw: 32 ;
Partner: Lapentti, Nicolas (ECU)

Round	Opponent	Ranking	Score
R16	Petr Pala (CZE) / Pavel Vizner (CZE)	46 / 51	L 3-6, 6-3, 4-6

This Event Points: 5, South African Airways ATP Ranking: 146, Prize
Money: $750

Scottsdale, AZ, U.S.A.; 05.03.2001; WS; Outdoor: Hard; Draw: 32 ;
Partner: Schalken, Sjeng (NED)

Round	Opponent	Ranking	Score
R16	Simon Aspelin (SWE) / Johan Landsberg (SWE)	64 / 66	W 2-6, 7-6(5), 7-5
Q	James Blake (USA) / Mardy Fish (USA)	176 / 316	W 3-6, 7-6(2), 6-3
S	John-Laffnie de Jager (RSA) / Ellis Ferreira (RSA)	44 / 14	W 6-4, 6-3
F	Donald Johnson (USA) / Jared Palmer (USA)	18 / 10	L 6-7(3), 2-6

This Event Points: 120, South African Airways ATP Ranking: 174,
Prize Money: $7,815

Buenos Aires, Argentina; 19.02.2001; WS; Outdoor: Clay; Draw: 32
; Partner: Lobo, Luis (ARG)

Round	Opponent	Ranking	Score
R16	Antonio Prieto (BRA) / Eyal Ran (ISR)	126 / 74	L 4-6, 6-3, 6-7(6)

This Event Points: 5, South African Airways ATP Ranking: 178, Prize
Money: $750

Vina del Mar, Chile; 12.02.2001; WS; Outdoor: Clay; Draw: 32 ;
Partner: Alami, Karim (MAR)
Round   Opponent   Ranking Score

R16   Mariano Hood (ARG) / Sebastian Prieto (ARG)   91
/ 102   L 3-6, 6-7(1)
This Event Points: 5, South African Airways ATP Ranking: 185, Prize
Money: $750

2002

Stockholm, Sweden; 21.10.2002; WS; Indoor: Hard; Draw: 32 ;
Partner: Chela, Juan Ignacio (ARG)
Round   Opponent   Ranking Score
R16   Wayne Black (ZIM) / Kevin Ullyett (ZIM)   13 / 11 L
6-4, 1-6, 4-6
This Event Points: 5, South African Airways ATP Ranking: 438, Prize
Money: $1,250

Washington, DC, U.S.A.; 12.08.2002; CS; Outdoor: Hard; Draw: 56 ;
Partner: Gonzalez, Fernando (CHI)
Round   Opponent   Ranking Score
R32   Christophe Rochus (BEL) / Olivier Rochus (BEL)   291
/ 308   W 6-3, 6-2
R16   Justin Gimelstob (USA) / Michael Hill (AUS) 93 / 37 L
W/O
This Event Points: 25, South African Airways ATP Ranking: 412,
Prize Money: $1,640

MEX v. CHI AG 2nd RD PO, Queretaro, Mexico; 12.07.2002; DC;
Indoor: Carpet; Draw: 0 ; Partner: Massu, Nicolas (CHI)
Round   Opponent   Ranking Score
RR   Bruno Echagaray (MEX) / Santiago Gonzalez (MEX)   N/A
/ N/A L 3-6, 6-3, 3-6, 2-6
This Event Points: , South African Airways ATP Ranking: , Prize
Money: $

ATP Masters Series Monte Carlo, Monaco; 15.04.2002; SU; Outdoor:
Clay; Draw: 64 ; Partner: Lapentti, Nicolas (ECU)
Round   Opponent   Ranking Score
R32   Lucas Arnold Ker (ARG) / Gaston Etlis (ARG) 32 / 41 L
1-6, 2-6

This Event Points: 5, South African Airways ATP Ranking: 417, Prize Money: $2,000

ATP Masters Series Miami, FL, U.S.A.; 18.03.2002; SU; Outdoor: Hard; Draw: 96 ; Partner: Lapentti, Nicolas (ECU)

Round	Opponent	Ranking Score
R64	Gaston Etlis (ARG) / Martin Rodriguez (ARG) / 61	43
	L 6-3, 6-7(1), 3-6	

This Event Points: 5, South African Airways ATP Ranking: 426, Prize Money: $1,750

Vina del Mar, Chile; 11.02.2002; WS; Outdoor: Clay; Draw: 32 ; Partner: Massu, Nicolas (CHI)

Round	Opponent	Ranking Score
R16	Enzo Artoni (ITA) / Daniel Melo (BRA)	75 / 80 L
	1-6, 6-4, 7-10	

This Event Points: 5, South African Airways ATP Ranking: 240, Prize Money: $1,000

Adelaide, Australia; 31.12.2001; WS; Outdoor: Hard; Draw: 32 ; Partner: Enqvist, Thomas (SWE)

Round	Opponent	Ranking Score
R16	Julien Boutter (FRA) / Wayne Ferreira (RSA)	N/A / N/A
	W 7-6(6), 7-6(5)	
Q	Joshua Eagle (AUS) / Sandon Stolle (AUS)	N/A / N/A
	L 2-6, 3-6	

This Event Points: 40, South African Airways ATP Ranking: , Prize Money: $2,080

2003

Delray Beach, FL, U.S.A.; 03.03.2003; WS; Outdoor: Hard; Draw: 32 ; Partner: Lobo, Luis (ARG)

Round	Opponent	Ranking Score
R16	Mariano Hood (ARG) / Andrew Kratzmann (AUS) / 50	49
	W 6-2, 6-4	
Q	Jan-Michael Gambill (USA) / Graydon Oliver (USA) / 44	30
	L 6-7(9), 2-6	

This Event Points: 40, South African Airways ATP Ranking: 444, Prize Money: $1,700

Vina del Mar, Chile; 10.02.2003; WS; Outdoor: Clay; Draw: 32 ; Partner: Massu, Nicolas (CHI)

Round	Opponent	Ranking Score
R16	Alberto Martin (ESP) / David Sanchez (ESP)	157 / 284 W W/O
Q	Agustin Calleri (ARG) / Mariano Hood (ARG)	216 / 77 L W/O

This Event Points: 40, South African Airways ATP Ranking: 634, Prize Money: $1,500

2004

Salinas, Ecuador; 29.03.2004; CH; Outdoor: Hard; Draw: 32 ; Partner: Garcia, Adrian (CHI)

Round	Opponent	Ranking Score
R16	Gilles Muller (LUX) / Janko Tipsarevic (SRB)	N/A / N/A W 6-2, 6-2
Q	Federico Browne (ARG) / Aisam-Ul-Haq Qureshi (PAK)	N/A / N/A L 1-6, 2-6

This Event Points: 12, South African Airways ATP Ranking: , Prize Money: $160

Source: ATP Tour

Chapter 11
"He'd look at you like Mozart, Picasso..."

"To be the best in the world at anything, you need to get blood on your hands."
- Philip H. Anselmo

Alberto Berasategui (ATP Player): "When Rios was healthy, he had an unbelievable facility to play tennis. He made you run around the court all the time, like so easily. And he was hard to find in his court any weakness against him. Maybe his mental thing was maybe his weakness. Or he didn't like to run too much after the ball. And every time I play against him I just try to do that. To make him run. And every time I played him I knew he was going to be a tough match, a very hard match. That was the only thing I could find against him."

Question: Did you enjoy playing him?

Berasategui: "Obviously, yeah. Play him, he make tennis so easy. To watch him was fun. He was a different kind of player. He was very pleasurable to watch. One of the better players I have played against on a tennis court."

Question: How did you get along with him?

Berasategui: "I got along much better after he quit tennis or when he was at the end of his career. At the beginning he was shy. He was introverted. He didn't like to talk to many people. Because he was shy. But he was a nice guy. You have to know him. Because if you didn't, you could think of him as an arrogant person. He wasn't like that. He was a nice person. He was too shy and he didn't let his emotions out."

Question: How did you finally get to know him and break the ice later on?

Berasategui: "Playing on the circuit, you spend a lot of time with the players. Chino was one of them. To play against him a few times, he beat me, obviously more times. To beat him and run him on the court - I guess it made us friends and we got along, even though he was younger than me."

Question: Lasting memory of Rios?

Berasategui: "I think the last time I played him was at the Australian Open quarterfinal. Once in French Open. Both of them I lost. At French Open I was two sets up against him, round of 16 I think it was. And I started cramping after the third set. Because, like I told you before, he made you run so much around the court. I finished the match but I was cramping up in the third set. So that was a really tough match for me. And also in quarterfinal in Australian Open, I had such a tough road until I played him. I knew I could play a good match against him and I knew I could win but he was playing unbelievable. I won the first set but after that my physical went down. And he was like a machine on the court. He went to the finals that year. It's those matches I remember the most."

Question: Was Rios the best you ever played, talent-wise?

Berasategui: "I don't know 'the best.' I think most talented for sure. But to be most talented doesn't mean you are the best on the court. Maybe him or Agassi or Pete Sampras but I didn't get to play Pete Sampras. But I think Rios was one of the better players that I found on a tennis court."

Alex Bancila (Former ATP Player): "I first saw Rios in Santiago in 1991 – we were both playing the COSAT (South American ITF Tour). We are the same age but I was playing in the 18s and he was playing in the 16s. Santiago was the seventh of the ten tournaments of the tour but the first one where the 16s and 18s overlapped (played at the same venues). He was playing in the 16s final against a Brazilian named Marcelo Cesana, the two of them were dominating the 16s tour and between the two had won every single tournament. Rios actually lost that match 3-6, 6-3, 6-4 despite playing at home. It's weird but I can remember the score of every match that I have played or seen. Cesana simply outlasted Rios – he was a tricky player, a great counterpuncher who never missed yet could also make shots, a combination of Murray, Coria, and Mecir if you like. Rios on the other hand was an amazing ball striker, his timing, sense of the court, of his opponent, and of where the ball was going to were spectacular."

"I saw him again during the ensuing Italian and European tour a few months after that and again the next year at the Italian Open, Roland Garros, etc. I thought he was even more impressive despite his small size. By 1993 he was already ranked #1 in the world under 18. In Caracas (the first tourney of the COSAT tour, which has/had an "A" rating, similar to the majors or the Orange Bowl, 128 draw) I lost in the quarters while he lost in the final against a countryman of mine, Razvan Sabau who went on to win junior Wimbledon later that year despite being only 16."

"A couple of months later, I played Rios in Santa Croce, Italy, the tournament preceding the Italian Open in Bonfiglio. Believe it or not, I beat him 3 and 4. We had a similar game, I am also a lefty, I was/am significantly taller, and my serve was better than his. I roomed with him and two other Argentineans for two nights. I do not recall why exactly – I seem to recall some sort of mishap with the tournament's hotel rooms. Rios and I knew each other but other than hello, how did you do in your match, etc. we never really talked. I don't think he talked to anyone actually, not even with his fellow South Americans, whom you probably know usually stay close together at tournaments. At least not meaningful stuff. He usually was around his coach - do not remember who he was - and I don't ever recall him being involved in a conversation with anyone. He had this look about him like he wasn't interested in anyone or anything. His nickname back then was 'Chino' or 'Chinudo', which stands for Chinese and Chinese-like, respectively. He looks a little Asian despite having blue eyes actually."

"I stopped playing on the ITF/ATP Tour in '94 and I have not seen him since, other than on TV, but his subsequent success did not surprise me at all. I remember back when I first saw him in Santiago, I told my dad that, 'This guy will be #1 in the world some day.' He wasn't my favorite person but then again he never did anything to annoy me. To this day, he is the best ball striker I have ever seen, better than Agassi because he was more fluid than Agassi and hit with less effort. He also had great touch and hands, something that Agassi didn't. Agassi had a different type of hands – quick hands, his hands were great in hitting through the ball but he did not have good touch, definitely not in the classic sense anyway. For me, Rios is the biggest underachiever of anyone that I have seen – he should have had at least four majors and should have won them all except Wimbledon."

Isaiah Morales (US Open Locker Room Attendant): "I see when they talk about Rios on The Tennis Channel. They say he was mean. I don't remember him as mean. I remember he was nice. I remember when he wanted his locker unlocked, he'd yell, 'Locker! Locker!' But it wasn't in a mean way, he was kind of joking around. Most of the other players will nod or signal with their hand that they want their locker unlocked, they won't say anything. Roger (Federer) does that too, hell say, 'Locker!'"

Jan Michael Gambill (ATP Player): "My first memory of Marcelo Rios is him staring me down across the room in the player's lounge. He used to do that to guys. Marcelo would sit in the corner of a room and stare people down from across the room. And I'm a tough guy to intimidate. So I stared him back down. And what's really funny is, I was actually one of the few guys that got along just fine with Marcelo. I had no problems with him. I stared him back down and he cracked a smile. And from then on - we were never friends - but we competed a few times against each other. We only played twice. He beat me in Indian Wells one year and I beat him in Hamburg. It should have been the opposite. I don't know how I beat him on clay. But I actually got along just fine with him. He was out there to compete and I respected that."

Question: Did you talk much with him? Or was it more a non-verbal?

Gambill: "We talked a few times. There wasn't a whole lot to say. You don't need to be friends with everybody on the Tour - I learned that pretty early - but certainly not enemies. We practiced quite a few times. Some guys didn't want to practice with him. I don't know why. I wanted to get every chance to play him that I could. The guy was a genius on the court."

Question: How did you beat him on the clay in Hamburg? What do you remember from that match?

Gambill: "[Laughs] I remember the one in Indian Wells more. Because it was a huge point for my career. And that was like my kinda come-out tournament. Semifinals - he beat me there. Close match and I had the set point in the first set. The clay court was kinda me playing one of my best matches ever on clay. I didn't play well on clay. The only clay I could actually play on was Hamburg because it was really wet. Most people thought I wouldn't be good on it because it was slower - that was actually fine with me - what was hard was I couldn't really move on the dry clay. Because I take little steps. I don't know how to slide. So being that I'm the big, funky American, I just didn't have the sure-footed ability to slide. On that clay in Hamburg, I could actually push off. So it was kind of a fair match. At the time I was top 20 and so was he, or higher. I played great."

Question: A lasting memory of Rios?

Gambill: "I think watching him play was always a pleasure. I watched his matches quite often. The guy, frankly, was brilliant. A lot of players don't live up to their potential but I think he could have done so much more. I think if he had a little better serve, he could have been #1 for a long time. Because his ground strokes, his ability to create angles from seemingly nothing was incredible."

Question: You played him at his very best, in the midst of his Indian Wells-Miami streak.

Gambill: "We were both playing very good tennis. He won 6 and 4, one break in the second set. At the time, I didn't feel like anybody could beat me from the baseline. He beat me from the baseline. I had just beaten Andre the match before that, and Courier before that. Those guys were good ground strokers. And what do you say to that? He took me out on the court, just running me off the court. Using angles where other guys weren't doing that to me."

Question: You played all the best - Sampras, Agassi, Courier - where does Rios at his best stack up with them?

Gambill: "Well, for me, at his best, Andre was the toughest for me. He simply did - except for serve - I served a little bigger than him - but he returned it like he didn't care. Andre did everything that I did a little bit better. I played Andre 13 times and I only played Rios twice. So my catalogue of memories has a lot more memories of Andre and how many times he beat me - 11 of those 13. Rios is right up there. He won't get the credit because he didn't win the Slams. It's that simple. It's the end-all, you just don't get the credit if you don't win Slams. It's just bizarre. Because I feel I had a damn good career that was ended by injuries. Not as good as Rios' was but it was still good. You just kind of fade away if you don't win any Slams. That's just the way it is."

Question: But talent-wise, Rios was right there?

Gambill: "Oh, absolutely. His talent may have been the top of all time. Right there. Sometimes he had a bad attitude, frankly, which didn't help him."

Harel Levy (ATP Player): "I played and lost to him in Indianapolis. I remember a funny thing. The chair umpire asked us to sit for a minute - because of TV coverage [laughs]. The first changeover, Rios just puts the racquets down, takes a drink of water, and goes to the other side. And the chair umpire said, 'No, no, no!' Rios said, 'I'm ready. I'm ready to play.' I practiced with him a couple of times. We always had a good relationship. With me he was always nice. We talked a lot, basically about tennis. What could we talk about? Racquets, whatever. He changed from the long body to the short body. He told me, 'How can you play with the long?' He told me whenever he doesn't have confidence, he goes back to the short. Which was interesting."

Manny Sequeira (Tennis Fan): "Marcelo Rios was playing James Blake in an exhibition match in Longwood in '99 or 2000. It was a close first set. I remember the score - 76 61 Rios. But during one time, late in the first set - Blake was the hometown kid, he played at Harvard - someone yelled out from the crowd, 'Come on James, this is YOUR house!' And Rios turned around and glared at him. Like for two or three seconds. It was a long time. Then when he won that game, he glared at him some more, like to say: How do you like that?!"

Luke Jensen (Former ATP Player): "I remember Rios when he was in juniors and just coming out, playing some of the top guys, getting some wildcards into some events. Right away you could see he had a mastery of the game. He saw the court in different ways. He wasn't just a banger but he wasn't just a retriever. He kind of took a little of Agassi, taking the ball early. And he looked a lot like McEnroe because he could do different things. I always just saw thought in his play. Not just before the point but as the point was being developed. And so it's really hard as a youngster to guage because everybody's a little shy and it's a whole new environment and everything. But he looked like he belonged. The great players have an aura. They have some kind of halo - you know there's something special there. And you wonder will it be realized and everything. And then as he began to win and get comfortable out there, you could just see him start to find even more game and having the right leadership with Larry Stefanki really put him in the direction to get that talent kind of realized. It's just unfortunate he didn't get more looks at Slams. But I truly feel he found the game interesting, almost like an Agassi did, because it was so complex and a challenge to him. And sometimes it was too easy. It really wasn't beating the other guy - it was how HE played the game. And it was just so much fun to watch him create works of art all the time as he played."

Question: You mentioned how you respected how Rios entered the ATP as a rebel type outlaw and never changed. He always stayed true to himself. Could you elaborate on that?

Luke Jensen: "I love that. Because it's so easy to sell out to the dollar. Sell out to the economy and all these things. He never did. The guy that came in as the shy kid from South America really just reinvented the game - if you saw it. And if you didn't see it, you were never gonna see it. But you really had to see the genius that was out there and the person that created this, like, beautiful kind of game of tennis. That we really hadn't seen - a little bit of McEnroe, a little bit of Agassi, a little bit of rock 'n roll, a little bit of more soul and what was really inside him. It was almost like he'd play and you try to ask him questions and try to understand it - and he looked at you like Mozart, Picasso whatever: You can't really understand. So what's the point? I always got that. You can't really understand really what I do. And that was to other players that were higher ranked than him. And it wasn't disrespect. What's the point of trying to explain to you what I do? When you can't understand the verbiage anyway? You're in elementary school with your game. I'm a doctorate. I can do this, that...and it was an incredible kind of frustration for him because it was always: Why can't you conform? Why don't you just realize it would be so much easier for you and just get along in the locker room? And it wasn't about that. It was about going out there and trying to play a very difficult game, the way he played and the way he had to play. Guys were throwing bullets at him - Ivanisevic, Becker, and all the big hitters, and Sampras and Agassi - he was right in thick of all of that. And he just kind of, like, leapfrogged, he didn't go right through it. He thought his way through the situation. And it was just kind of like flippin' off the establishment. And I'm lovin' that. I mean, I was all about that. And it was just fun to watch him do it, whether it was to the corporate world, to the ATP, and all that stuff. They were just trying to get him to conform. And the more you pushed up against him, the more he resisted. And it was just interesting to watch his career, where it went. But it was never really about the tennis, to me. For him, it was the beauty of the game, all the different things he could do with a tennis ball against the best players in the world."

Question: How were your relations with Rios?

Luke Jensen: "I got along with him really well. We were really different. At one time, we were both with adidas. In those years we did a lot of events together. And so it was fun because I always felt we were on the same side, going up against the wave of the establishment. It was more about the movement. It wasn't a revolution. We weren't trying to change the game but we were trying to move the game to a different level which was more fan-friendly. He wasn't really 'Mr. Kids' and everything like that - we did that. But, boy, I'll tell you, if you like someone who is going out and playing a different game than everybody else, instead of powering through the game - he manipulated the game, he changed the game, he was a Rubik's Cube of the game. He'd just sit there and fire away and just keep going with that. He was more part of the movement, there wasn't a revolution for him. It was like, Boy, this game is so much more interesting. I feel it so much more than these brutal hit and miss, hit big, hard...he could counterpunch, he could attack, and he kind of lived his life like that. Just leave him alone and let me do my thing. But people just kept trying to say you need to be X,Y and Z and he wasn't that. He wasn't even close to that."

Question: What is a lasting image of Rios you have?

Luke Jensen: "The biggest thing that will always jump out to me was, you know, he gets to #1 in the world and he tells Stefanki: I just don't like the direction I'm going in [laughs]. That will always stick in my mind. Just because, again, it wasn't about #1. It wasn't about beating everybody. It was kind of about playing the game. I truly believe, if you believe in people from another planet and stuff like that, one day we'll unmask Rios as a person from another planet. His game was that way. He acted that way. He just wasn't about our kind. He had his own kind. His own way. And just let him do his thing. A love for everything that he brought to the game. Don't try to resist it or box it up and everything like that. Just keep his game. And everything that he brought was truly from a universe far away. Because we haven't seen anything like it. You can see specks of it. But it's just like the thing with Roger Federer - nobody plays that way. Every once in a while it jumps up. The game evolves. And if you're not here to see it, not at the Grand Slams and personally in the front row watching it, from the media, from the fans, or the other players, you can't see it on TV. And that's what he did. He just made that massive jump. He played a game that we really haven't seen yet. We've seen glimpses of it. But he was just that - I keep on saying genius. But that's truly what he was. Just a misunderstood genius that was more of a movement/revolution. He wasn't a jerk. You may not have liked the way he treated you. But there's one spot out there - one person is gonna win, one person is gonna lose. That's a tough business to be in. And it's a very difficult locker room. Not everybody is gonna play nice."

Question: Why do you think he fell short of winning a major?

Luke Jensen: "It's when you make certain decisions at certain times, we all do, they have lasting impacts. When you get to #1, all the sudden, you're the hunted. Not the hunter. And I think that was a different dynamic. Now, instead of hangin' in the weeds a little bit - being this talented guy that could do something. Now he's THE GUY. And everybody's going for him. Everywhere he goes - there's Rios. Let's watch him practice. It's a different place in the game. And I think, in the end, it wasn't about that. It was about the Rubik's Cube. Let's figure this thing out. Give me another challenge, give me another challenge. I think that's why he did not last as long. He had injuries and everything. But week after week, the relentless pressure of the road just hammered you. He can't keep up the pace. It's tough."

Question: Did you ever see Rios out of character from his typical persona?

Luke Jensen: "No. It was always the same [laughs]. He was who he was. I never saw him outside of - what you saw is what you got. Whether it was to the people in his camp, before matches, after matches, getting the transportation, everything. I just think people just wanted him to be somebody that he wasn't capable of, or didn't want to be. When you go into this tennis thing, you don't know you're supposed to sign off and be a certain way. And when you get up against that establishment, they want you to fit in...he just wasn't that guy. And he'll never be that guy."

Question: They completely failed to conform him?

Luke Jensen: "It sure did seem that way. Everybody go to their mandatory meeting and vote on this, let's put this board up, let's be this Tour and let's be all this other stuff...Let's JUST PLAY. I don't care if it's just a parking lot of the stadium, let's just play tennis. Let's just get out there and do our thing. And sometimes he practiced hard, sometimes he didn't. I don't think they could ever get to the point to get a grade, pass or fail, to conform him. Don't think they could understand him. We don't understand him. As a personality, I think he would have been perfect. We didn't try to understand Lendl. We just hated him. We didn't try to understand McEnroe. We just hated and loved that guy. Connors. Somehow in the 90's, we tried to - Sampras was the nice, cookie cutter thing. Agassi was off on his own thing, shooting off in his orbit. And I just think we could have really maximized Rios' persona, the brilliance of what he brought to the game, and his attitude. I could just see him coming into the locker room - he was just so polarizing. You like him or you hate him. There's no middle ground, even today. That, to me, I think is what attracts the interest still for this comet that you see once every million years, going through your galaxy. And he's out there somewhere, he's doing something. He's got a kid that's playing now. You see him bumpin' around a little bit. It's fun to even think about what could have been, if he could have kept in going. But again, he keeps bouncing off, that comet keeps racing somewhere."

• • •

"If thou wouldst be an artist, foresake all sadness and care, save for thy art. Let thy soul be as a mirror, which reflects all objects, all movements and colors, remaining itself unmoved and clear."
- Leonardo Da Vinci

After their 1998 Key Biscayne final match, Andre Agassi discussed Marcelo Rios...

Q. Do you think it's going to take you a few times playing a guy like him? Seemed like you were having trouble reading his shot. Was it your game being off or, This guy is good, I'm going to have to play him a few times?

ANDRE AGASSI: I definitely had trouble reading some of his forehands. When I would hit my backhand crosscourt, I had trouble having a sense for when to cut it off and take it up the line. Sometimes he was flicking it up the line. A little trouble reading his serve, his forehand, wasn't quite pulling the trigger on my own shots. He's the kind of guy that you can't wait for him to miss; you've got to be able to take it to him. I didn't quite do it. I mean, I was hitting the ball okay, but I wasn't stepping in and really getting good wood on it.

Q. Andre, how much did it hurt you not to have played a couple big finals, be on a regular roll when you come to this stage?

ANDRE AGASSI: Honestly, I felt like it had more to do with Marcelo than that particular situation. You know, you have to address him like a big player. I was going out there and playing him like he's five-foot-eight. I thought I could back him into the paint. The bottom line is, you know, he doesn't play his size. He has good stick, he moves well, serves better than you expect. You know, he puts you in a position to have to do something early in the point. That's to his credit.

Q. A match like this, long rallies, two guys who weren't six-foot-four hitting 180 miles an hour serves, how good is this for tennis in the United States?

ANDRE AGASSI: It's nice. You know, I never thought we'd see a player as good as Marcelo again after Chang. He plays well. Brings another dimension to tennis. It's nice for me as a competitor to get out there and play that kind of tennis. It really forces you to think, forces you to move, forces you to execute. I think it's good for the game. There's no question about it, especially in America where, you know, people tend to be a bit -- have more options for big-time sports, they don't want to tune into tennis if they're watching a big serve here, a big serve there. This is good for tennis all-around, especially here.

31641502R00200

Made in the USA
Lexington, KY
19 April 2014